DEPARTMENT OF THE NAVY
OFFICE OF THE SECRETARY
1000 NAVY PENTAGON
WASHINGTON, DC 20350-1000

SECNAVINST 1650.1H
NDBDM

AUG 2 2 2008

SECNAV INSTRUCTION 1650.1H

From: Assistant Secretary of the Navy (Manpower and Reserve Affairs)

Subj: NAVY AND MARINE CORPS AWARDS MANUAL

1. Purpose. To provide guidance and regulations concerning awards available for recognizing individuals and units in the Naval Service.

2. Cancellation. SECNAVINST 1650.1G.

3. Award Websites

    a. Navy: https://awards.navy.mil.

    b. Marine Corps: http://awards.manpower.usmc.mil.

4. Summary of Changes. This instruction has been updated and administratively revised and should be reviewed in its entirety. The following specific changes have been incorporated:

    a. Establishment of the Afghanistan Campaign Medal, Iraq Campaign Medal, Global War on Terrorism Expeditionary Medal, Global War on Terrorism Service Medal, Korea Defense Service Medal, and Ceremonial Guard Ribbon.

    b. Addition of a Prior Service and Veteran Awards Chapter.

    c. Revision of the Combat Action Ribbon eligibility criteria to include Improvised Explosive Devices (IEDs).

    d. Change in award concurrence requirements for Naval personnel temporarily assigned to other U.S. Armed Services.

    e. Establishment of gold 5/16-inch Arabic numerals as the attachment to denote award(s) of an Individual Air Medal.

    f. Revision of Navy and Marine Corps Overseas Service Ribbon eligibility criteria for Reserve personnel.

g. Notice of the Fleet Marine Force (FMF) Officer and Enlisted Warfare Qualification Badges as superseding the FMF Ribbon.

h. Separation of Foreign Awards and Foreign Gifts into two chapters.

i. Clarification of premature disclosure policy.

j. Revisions to Delegated Awarding Authority.

k. Revision of policy regarding the wear of foreign military decorations and U.S. non-military decorations.

l. Delineation of specific instructions regarding processing awards for entry into the Navy Department Awards Web Service (NDAWS).

m. Inclusion of updated listings of operations approved for various campaign and service medals.

n. Administrative changes in citation formatting, including clarification of required and optional language, and the addition of an acknowledgement of years of service in awards for retiring personnel.

5. Forms and Reports

a. OPNAV 1650/3 Personal Award Recommendation and OPNAV 1650/14 Unit Award Recommendation may be downloaded from the Navy Awards website at https://awards.navy.mil.

b. The reporting requirements contained in Chapter 9 are assigned symbol 0216-DOS-AN(1650) and are approved per SECNAV M-5214.1.

William A. Navas, Jr.
Assistant Secretary of the Navy
(Manpower and Reserve Affairs)

Distribution:
Electronic only, via Navy Directives Website
http://neds.daps.dla.mil

TABLE OF CONTENTS

Chapter 1 - General Information

Chapter 3 - Unit Awards

Chapter 4 - Campaign and Service Awards

Chapter 5 - U.S. Non-Military Decorations

Chapter 6 - U.S. Awards to Foreign Military Personnel

Chapter 7 - Foreign Awards and Service Decorations to U.S. Personnel

Chapter 8 - Prior Service and Veteran Awards

CHAPTER 1 - GENERAL INFORMATION

SECTION 1 - GENERAL

110. PURPOSE OF THE NAVY AND MARINE CORPS AWARDS MANUAL

1. To provide guidance and regulations concerning awards available for recognizing individuals and units in the Naval Service.

2. Other directives govern Department of Defense (DoD) awards and other Services' awards. The Manual of Military Decorations & Awards (DoD 1348.33-M), hereinafter referred to as the DoD Awards Manual, provides guidance for Defense and Joint awards.

3. Commands publishing specific award instructions must comply with the guidance established herein.

111. AUTHORITY TO ESTABLISH AWARDS. Awards may be established through laws passed by Congress, by Executive Order, or by directives issued by the Secretary of Defense (SECDEF) or the Secretary of the Navy (SECNAV). All Department of the Navy (DON) recommendations for the establishment of a new award must be addressed via the chain of command to SECNAV and contain full justification for the new award, proposed criteria, and eligible personnel. All new awards require coordination and concurrence from the Institute of Heraldry, who provides heraldic services to DoD. Coordination with the Institute ensures all decorations, medals, and service ribbons are developed in accordance with existing regulations and do not duplicate any previously authorized designs. The Institute may be contacted via mail at 9325 Gunston Road, Fort Belvoir, VA 22060-5579 or via their website at www.tioh.hqda.pentagon.mil.

112. AUTHORITY TO APPROVE AWARDS. In general SECNAV retains awarding authority for all awards under his purview. However, he has delegated authority to approve the Legion of Merit and below, in certain situations. Appendix A to this chapter provides a listing of those delegations. Delegation of authority not specified requires direction in writing from SECNAV, CNO, or CMC, as appropriate. In addition, awarding authority for the Combat Distinguishing Device must be

specifically delegated by SECNAV, CNO, or CMC; e.g., commanding officers with Navy and Marine Corps Commendation Medal and/or Navy and Marine Corps Achievement Medal authority may not award these medals with the Combat Distinguishing Device unless this authority has been specifically delegated to them.

1. The Medal of Honor is approved and awarded by the President, in the name of Congress.

2. The Navy Cross, Distinguished Service Medal, and Silver Star Medal are approved and awarded by SECNAV, in the name of the President.

3. The Legion of Merit, Distinguished Flying Cross, Navy and Marine Corps Medal, Bronze Star Medal, Purple Heart Medal, Meritorious Service Medal, and Air Medal may be approved and awarded by SECNAV, CNO, CMC, and their designees, under delegated awarding authority from SECNAV, in the name of the President.

4. The Joint Service Commendation Medal and Joint Service Achievement Medal may be approved and awarded by SECNAV in the name of SECDEF, when SECNAV is the Executive Agent for the Joint function.

5. The Navy and Marine Corps Commendation Medal and Navy and Marine Corps Achievement Medal may be approved and awarded by numerous commands, in the name of SECNAV.

6. The Combat Action Ribbon may be approved and awarded by CNO, CMC, and their designees, under delegated awarding authority from SECNAV, in the name of SECNAV.

113. POLICY CONSIDERATIONS

1. Public Recognition

a. Awards are important symbols of public recognition for rewarding heroism or valor, exceptionally meritorious service, or outstanding achievement and other acts or services which are above and beyond what is normally expected, and which distinguish an individual or unit among those performing similar acts or services.

b. Awards are intended to recognize Sailors and Marines who demonstrate exceptional valor, heroism, or meritorious service. An award should only be recommended in cases where the circumstances clearly merit special recognition of the actions or service.

2. Duplication of Awards. Only one award will be made for the same act, achievement, or period of meritorious service for any individual or unit. However, an award for individual valor, heroism, or specific achievement within a longer period of meritorious service will not be considered duplication, provided the Summary of Action and citation for the meritorious service award do not cite any of the actions for which the heroic or specific achievement award was given. A copy of the heroic or specific achievement award citation must be included in the submission package for the meritorious service award. In addition, the fact that a unit receives a unit award in no way limits the awarding of personal decorations to deserving individuals of that unit for the same period.

3. Classified Awards. Every effort should be made to forward unclassified personal and unit award recommendations. Only those recommendations involving the most sensitive operations should be forwarded as classified documents. Classified awards slow the process considerably and, in most cases, valid documentation can be drafted without classification. A classified award recommendation must include an unclassified proposed citation. All Navy, CNO-level classified awards must be mailed to the SECNAV Special Awards Board, at the address below, for processing; specific arrangements should be made with the Special Awards Board. For Marine Corps, CMC-level classified awards, the highest level of classification that may be processed is SECRET. In the rare instance in which information classified higher than SECRET is essential for proper adjudication, coordinate with CMC (MMMA) and submit the recommendation directly to:

Secretary of the Navy
Special Awards Board
1000 Navy Pentagon, Room 5E541
Washington, DC 20350-1000

114. PERSONNEL ELIGIBLE. The terms "Naval Service" and "serving in any capacity with the U.S. Navy," as used in this instruction include service in the U.S. Navy, U.S. Marine Corps,

all Reserve components thereof, and the U.S. Coast Guard, when the Coast Guard, or units thereof, operate under the control of the Navy.

1. <u>Midshipmen Eligibility</u>

    a. U.S. Naval Academy midshipmen are eligible for those awards for which they may qualify.

    b. Naval Reserve Officer Training Corps (NROTC) midshipmen are eligible for awards for which they may qualify <u>when serving under orders on active duty</u>, but not for periods spent as full-time college students.

2. <u>Awards to DON Personnel from Other U.S. Armed Services</u>

    a. Naval Personnel <u>Permanently</u> Assigned to Other Service Commands

        (1) Permanently assigned personnel may accept, retain, and wear personal non-combat awards, Meritorious Service Medal and below, tendered by the other Service.

        (2) Award of the Legion of Merit and above, and all combat awards, must be processed through DON for concurrence. Concurrence may be given by SECNAV, the Assistant Secretary of the Navy (Manpower and Reserve Affairs) (ASN(M&RA)), CNO, CMC, or their designees, as appropriate (see paragraph c. below).

    b. Naval Personnel <u>Temporarily</u> Assigned to Other Service Commands. For the purpose of other Service combat awards, a temporary assignment is generally considered six months or more. However, assignments of shorter duration may be considered on a case-by-case basis.

        (1) Combat Area Service. Naval personnel temporarily assigned to another Service in support of combat operations (e.g., member is in receipt of Imminent Danger Pay) may be considered to receive another Service's awards. Naval personnel may accept, retain, and wear Commendation and Achievement Medals directly from the other Service to which assigned, without DON concurrence. However, this does <u>not</u> include awards with the Combat Distinguishing Device (Combat "V"). Awards with the Combat "V" and all awards of the

Meritorious Service Medal and above require DON concurrence before they may be accepted, retained, or worn. Recommendations for Silver Star Medals and above must be forwarded via CNO or CMC to SECNAV for final concurrence. Concurrence may be requested for other combat awards from ASN(M&RA), CNO, CMC, or their designees, as appropriate (see paragraph c. below).

(2) Non-combat Area Service. Naval personnel temporarily assigned to another Service in a non-combat area are not authorized to accept, retain, or wear another Service's award. A recommendation should be submitted to the member's parent command for a special achievement award or inclusion in an end of tour award. In exceptional cases, a waiver may be requested from SECNAV, via CNO or CMC.

c. Concurrence authority is restricted and is always specifically delegated in writing. It is not commensurate with a commander's awarding authority. Concurrence will not be granted to accept awards from other Services for acts that have already been recognized by a DON award.

3. <u>DON Awards to Personnel of Other U.S. Armed Services (Army, Air Force, and Coast Guard)</u>

a. Other Service Personnel <u>Permanently</u> Assigned to DON Commands

(1) Permanently assigned personnel may receive personal non-combat awards, Meritorious Service Medal and below, tendered by DON. These awards may be approved by commanders commensurate with their delegated awarding authority.

(2) SECNAV, CNO, CMC, and their designees are the approval authorities for award of the Legion of Merit and above and all combat awards for other Service personnel permanently assigned to DON. In addition, these awards must be processed through the member's parent Service headquarters for concurrence.

b. Other Service Personnel <u>Temporarily</u> Assigned to DON Commands

(1) Combat Area Service. Other Service personnel temporarily assigned to DON in support of combat operations are eligible to receive DON awards. SECNAV, CNO, and CMC are the

approval authorities for these awards. The awards must be processed in accordance with the member's parent Service awards policy, as concurrence may be required.

   (2) Non-combat Area Service. Other Service personnel temporarily assigned to DON in a non-combat area may not receive DON awards. When a member's service is worthy of special recognition, a recommendation to that effect shall be submitted to the member's parent command for appropriate action.

   c. Limitations

   (1) Other U.S. Armed Services personnel are eligible to receive any of the military decorations listed herein from DON, except the Medal of Honor and the Combat Action Ribbon.

   (2) DON decorations shall not be awarded for service that has already been recognized by another Service.

4. Awards to U.S. Merchant Marine Personnel. Since the Department of Transportation has established its own awards program, from 1953 forward, U.S. Merchant Marine personnel are not eligible to receive DON awards for U.S. Merchant Marine service. However, U.S. Merchant Marine personnel may be eligible for DON awards based on appropriate service in the Navy Reserve on the same basis as all other Navy Reservists. See Chapter 8 for eligibility prior to 1953.

5. Military Awards to U.S. Public Health Service Officers

   a. Authorization. 42 U.S.C. §213(b).

   b. Policy. Effective 2 August 1990, commissioned officers of the U.S. Public Health Service (USPHS), assigned or attached for full-time duty to DoD or any of its components, are eligible for military awards and decorations on the same basis as officers of the military Services.

   c. No military ribbon, medal or decoration shall be awarded to an officer of the USPHS without approval of the Secretary of Health and Human Services (HHS) or a designee.

   d. SECNAV is the sole approval authority for Naval decorations to members of the USPHS. Recommendations shall be forwarded using OPNAV 1650/3 via the chain of command. DON shall secure HHS concurrence prior to final award approval.

6. <u>Awards from Non-military Federal Agencies</u>. See Chapter 5.

7. <u>U.S. Awards to Foreign Personnel</u>. See Chapter 6.

8. <u>Foreign Awards to U.S. Personnel</u>. See Chapter 7.

9. <u>Military Awards to Civilians</u>

a. Civilians are <u>not normally</u> awarded military decorations. In most cases, <u>non-military decorations</u> are available for specific services rendered by civilians, and they are considered more appropriate than military decorations. Liaison with the local civilian human resources director is recommended when considering civilian awards.

b. Laws, Executive Orders, and other directives state that certain decorations shall be awarded to any person, who, while serving in any capacity with the Naval service, qualifies for the award. By such criteria, the following are decorations for which civilians could be eligible: Navy Cross, Distinguished Service Medal, Silver Star Medal, Distinguished Flying Cross, Navy and Marine Corps Medal, Bronze Star Medal, Air Medal, and Navy and Marine Corps Commendation Medal.

c. Military awards to civilians are rare; should a case warrant a military award, the recommendation will be forwarded to SECNAV, Navy Department Board of Decorations and Medals (NDBDM) via CNO or CMC, as appropriate. <u>A military award should only be considered if a civilian award is clearly not appropriate.</u>

d. The Office of Personnel Management website at http://www.opm.gov/perform/honorawd.asp provides information regarding awards available to all federal government civilians. Many federal agencies also have additional awards for which their own employees may be eligible; agency specific policy regulations should be reviewed for further information. MCO 12451.2C, with Change 1-2, contains Marine Corps guidance regarding civilian awards.

SECTION 2 - ADMINISTRATIVE PROCEDURES

120. <u>PRECEDENCE OF AWARDS</u>. The precedence of U.S. military and non-military decorations, medals, and ribbons authorized for personnel of the Navy and Marine Corps is listed in Appendix B to this chapter.

121. <u>PROTECTION OF AWARDS</u>. 18 U.S.C. §704 prohibits, and imposes a suitable penalty for the unauthorized wear, manufacture, or sale of any decoration, medal, or ribbon which has been or may be authorized by the Armed Forces of the United States, except under regulations made under law.

122. <u>WEARING OF AWARDS</u>. Active duty, retired, and discharged personnel are authorized to wear awards as prescribed by the provisions of this instruction, and the applicable provisions of Navy Uniform Regulations or Marine Corps Uniform Regulations, as appropriate.

123. <u>APPURTENANCES WORN ON RIBBONS AND MEDALS</u>. The following appurtenances may be authorized for wear on more than one decoration. Additional attachments that have limited application are listed with the awards to which they apply.

   1. <u>Stars</u>. All stars will be worn with two points (rays) pointing down. The larger size (5/16 inch for Naval personal decorations, and 3/16 inch for unit, campaign, service, and engagement awards, with the exception of the Navy "E" Ribbon) is worn on the suspension ribbon of the large medal, and service ribbon or ribbon bar, to denote subsequent awards received. The smaller size (1/8 inch) is worn on miniature medals. For subsequent personal Naval decorations, gold stars are used for the 2nd through the 5th, 7th through 10th, 12th and so forth. Silver stars are worn in lieu of multiples of five gold stars; i.e., the 6th, 11th, etc. With the exception of the Navy "E" Ribbon, for unit, campaign, service, and engagement (or battle star) awards, bronze and silver stars are used similarly.

   2. <u>Letter Devices</u>

      a. Silver "E" (3/16 inch) is authorized for wear on the Navy "E" Ribbon for the first, second, and third awards.

For four or more awards, one wreathed "E" centered on the ribbon bar is authorized.

b. Silver "E" (1/4 inch block letter) is authorized for wear on the ribbon bar of the Navy Expert Rifleman and Expert Pistol Shot Medals.

c. Bronze "S" (1/4 inch block letter) is authorized for wear on the Navy Rifle and Pistol Marksmanship ribbon bars for personnel who qualify as Sharpshooters.

d. Bronze "V" is the Combat Distinguishing Device, which may only be worn if specifically authorized in the award citation. Eligibility for the Combat Distinguishing Device shall be based solely on acts or services by individuals who are exposed to personal hazard involving direct participation in combat operations and not upon the geographic area in which the acts or services are performed. The "V" may be authorized for wear on the following decorations:

(1) Prior to 4 April 1974, the "V" was authorized for wear on the Legion of Merit, Bronze Star Medal, Joint Service Commendation Medal, Navy Commendation Medal, and Navy Achievement Medal.

(2) From 4 April 1974 through 16 January 1991, the "V" was authorized for wear on the Distinguished Flying Cross, Bronze Star Medal, Air Medal (Individual Award), Joint Service Commendation Medal, and Navy Commendation Medal.

(3) Beginning 17 January 1991, the "V" was authorized for wear on the Legion of Merit, Distinguished Flying Cross, Bronze Star Medal, Air Medal (Individual Award), Navy and Marine Corps Commendation Medal, and Navy and Marine Corps Achievement Medal.

3. Miscellaneous Devices

a. Fleet Marine Force (FMF) Combat Operation Insignia

(1) The FMF Combat Operation Insignia is a miniature bronze Marine Corps emblem that may be authorized for wear by Navy personnel attached to and operating with units of the Marine Corps operating forces, or by Navy personnel attached to Navy units operating with units of the Marine Corps operating

forces, and under Marine Corps operational control. This is a restricted device; attachment to operations with a Marine Corps unit is not sufficient to establish eligibility. The Marine Corps unit and the individual must have been engaged in active combat action with an armed enemy during the period of the individual's service with the unit. Questions regarding eligibility for the FMF Combat Operation Insignia should be addressed via the Marine Corps chain of command; CMC (MMMA) is the final authority for eligibility.

(2) The insignia may be authorized for wear centered on the suspension ribbon and ribbon bar of World War II campaign medals, Korean Service Medal, Armed Forces Expeditionary Medal, Vietnam Service Medal, Southwest Asia Service Medal, Kosovo Campaign Medal, Afghanistan Campaign Medal, Iraq Campaign Medal, Global War on Terrorism Expeditionary Medal and, upon approval of CMC, on future medals so designated.

b. Oak-Leaf Cluster. The oak-leaf cluster, which is issued in two sizes and two colors, is worn on the service and suspension ribbon of all Defense, Army, and Air Force decorations and the Joint Meritorious Unit Award. The larger size (13/32 inch) is worn on the suspension ribbon of the medal and the smaller size (5/16 inch) on the service ribbon and suspension ribbon of the miniature medal. The bronze oak-leaf cluster is used for the 2nd through 5th, 7th through 10th awards, and so forth. A silver oak-leaf cluster is used for the 6th, 11th and so forth, entitlement or award in lieu of five bronze oak-leaf clusters.

124. MAINTENANCE OF RECORDS

1. CNO (DNS-35) and CMC (MMMA) maintain the master list of personal and unit military decorations awarded by all Navy and Marine Corps awarding authorities.

2. For Navy personnel:

a. Pertinent information from the OPNAV 1650/3 is entered into the Navy Department Awards Web Service (NDAWS) database, and transferred on a weekly basis into the Navy Personnel Command (NPC) Master Awards File. PERS 32 makes extractions from this file to complete the awards information section in the electronic Performance Summary Record (PSR). In most instances, only personal awards, Navy and Marine Corps Achievement Medal and above, are recorded in NDAWS. Unit and campaign/service awards are entered into NDAWS by command, not by individual names; consequently, these awards are not electronically documented in the PSR. Future system changes will allow other awards to be entered by name.

b. NDAWS Authorities are authorized to perform direct entry of approved awards into NDAWS. A list of NDAWS Authorities is available on the Navy Awards website at https://awards.navy.mil. All delegated awarding authorities shall forward copies of signed award citations, or certificates in the case of Navy and Marine Corps Commendation and Achievement Medals, to the appropriate NDAWS Authority (not to CNO) for entry into individual records. The member's Social Security Number (SSN) shall be entered in the upper right hand corner of the citation/certificate and, due to the member's name and SSN appearing on the document, these citations/certificates shall be marked "Privacy Sensitive." The NDAWS Authority shall submit these citations/certificates to PERS 312 for entry into the member's electronic service record.

c. Each delegated awarding authority shall maintain a permanent record of all awards processed, including the OPNAV 1650/3, a signed copy of the citation, supporting documents, and any related correspondence. Award documentation shall not be disposed of in accordance with the standards used for other types of correspondence and records.

3. For Marine Corps personnel:

a. The Headquarters Marine Corps Awards Processing System (APS) is an electronic awards system that fulfills all record-keeping requirements; paper documentation of awards approved by delegated Marine Corps awarding authorities is not required.

b. In the case of Marine Corps personnel awarded a personal decoration while assigned to a Navy command, forward a copy of the approved OPNAV 1650/3, including the Summary of Action, and signed award citation to CMC (MMMA) for recording and entry into the Marine's official military record.

4. Activities holding individual service records shall make appropriate entries regarding personal, unit, campaign, and service awards, or provide said information to their appropriate servicing command. Eligibility may be established by documentary evidence in service records, such as orders to officer personnel, Page Five service record entries for Navy enlisted personnel, and entries in the Marine Corps Total Force System for Marine Corps personnel. In cases where a determination cannot be made at the local level, requests for eligibility shall be submitted to PERS 312 for Navy personnel or CMC (MMMA) for Marine Corps personnel.

125. <u>PUBLIC DISPLAY OF MEDALS AND RIBBONS</u>

1. <u>Government Agencies</u>. Medals and ribbons for official display may be procured from Service sources or authorized commercial vendors for an attractive, dignified, and secure display. The Medal of Honor is strictly controlled; upon approval by CNO or CMC, one set may be furnished, on a no-cost basis, and will be engraved with the words "FOR DISPLAY ONLY."

2. <u>Non-government Agencies</u>. Except for the Medal of Honor, all medals and ribbons may be purchased from commercial sources. Civilian institutions that desire to obtain military decorations for display should coordinate directly with an authorized vendor.

3. <u>Medal of Honor Displays</u>. CNO and CMC enforce strict control of the issuance of the Medal of Honor and allow purchase of a display medal <u>only in exceptional cases</u> by museums, libraries, and national headquarters of historical and military societies, and institutions of such public nature as will assure an opportunity for the public to view the exhibits under circumstances beneficial to DON. Discontinued displays of the Medal of Honor shall be returned to CNO or CMC, as appropriate. All Medal of Honor displays must be placed in secure areas in locked cases. Requests for a display Medal of Honor shall be addressed to CNO (DNS-35) or CMC (MMMA), as appropriate, and include the following information:

a. Manner of display and description of the security measures in the display area.

b. Number of visitors per year.

c. Cost of admission, if any.

d. Any other pertinent information that describes the venue, reason for the display, and the benefit to DON.

126. LAPEL BUTTONS FOR NEXT OF KIN. Public Law 80-306 of 1 August 1947, as amended by 10 U.S.C. §1126 of 11 August 1966, established lapel buttons to provide an appropriate identification for next of kin of members of the Armed Forces of the United States who lost their lives while in active military service. Next of kin includes widow or widower, each parent, child, stepchild, child through adoption, brother, half brother, sister, and half sister. The term widow or widower includes those who have since remarried, and the term parent includes stepmother, stepfather, mother through adoption, father through adoption, and foster parents who stood in loco parentis. There are two types of lapel buttons, as listed below.

1. A lapel button with a gold star on a purple circular background, bordered in gold and surrounded by gold laurel leaves, will be presented to the next of kin of those personnel who lost their lives and were awarded the Purple Heart Medal while serving in the following: World War I, 6 April 1917 to 3 March 1921; World War II, 8 September 1939 through 25 July 1947; any subsequent period of armed hostilities in which the United States was engaged before 1 July 1958 (United Nations action in Korea, 27 June 1950 through 27 July 1954); or after 30 June 1958, while engaged in an action against an enemy of the United States; or while engaged in military operations involving conflict with an opposing foreign force; or while serving with friendly foreign forces in an armed conflict, against an opposing armed force, in which the United States was not a belligerent party.

2. A lapel button with a gold star within a circle surrounded by sprigs of oak will be presented to the next of kin of those personnel who lost their lives while not serving in an armed conflict and did not receive a Purple Heart Medal.

3. The Casualty Assistance Calls Officer (CACO) will deliver the appropriate lapel button with the Benefits Package provided by the Navy Personnel Command or the Marine Corps Casualty Branch.

127. <u>THE NAVY DEPARTMENT BOARD OF DECORATIONS AND MEDALS</u>. The Navy Department Board of Decorations and Medals (NDBDM) was established in 1919 by SECNAV to provide assistance in all matters of policy, procedure, and administration with regard to Navy decorations and medals. NDBDM, guided by law, executive order, and DoD and SECNAV policy, shall:

1. Review and recommend appropriate action on awards submitted to SECNAV for approval or concurrence.

2. Assist SECNAV in providing oversight and guidance for the Navy and Marine Corps Awards Program.

3. Recommend policy and procedures for awards and related subjects to SECNAV to maintain and preserve the high standards and integrity of the DON awards system.

4. Review correspondence and directives regarding awards prior to approval by SECNAV.

5. Maintain close liaison with the CNO, CMC, and other DON awarding authorities on all matters pertaining to awards.

6. Maintain liaison with the award branches of the other military Services, the Office of the Joint Chiefs of Staff, and the Office of the Secretary of Defense to exchange information on award policies and procedures.

7. Maintain the Navy and Marine Corps Awards Manual.

128. <u>CNO AND CMC AWARDS BRANCHES</u>. The CNO Awards Branch (DNS-35) and the CMC Awards Branch (MMMA) have the following responsibilities:

1. Provide advice and assistance to CNO and CMC in all matters of policy, procedure, and administration with regard to Navy decorations and medals.

2. Initiate and implement policies and regulations for a military awards program.

3. Maintain close liaison with NDBDM and the awards branches of the other Services.

4. Transmit all awards approved by CNO or CMC.

5.   Process recommendations for Navy and Marine Corps personal decorations to be awarded to foreign nationals.

6.   Obtain concurrence from other Services for their members to receive Navy awards.

7.   Control the Medal of Honor for display purposes.

8.   Prepare messages, notices, and instructions providing guidance to commands regarding personal awards, unit awards, and campaign and service medals.

9.   Provide technical guidance and assistance to delegated awarding authorities, including Navy Personnel Command (PERS-312) and the Retired Records Section in St. Louis, Missouri.

10.   Maintain the master lists of personal awards and ships and units that qualify for unit, campaign, and service awards.

11.   Process awards and gifts of more than minimal value from foreign governments to DON personnel and prepare the yearly report of such gifts to the Secretary of State.

DELEGATION OF AWARDING AUTHORITY

AUTHORITY RETAINED BY THE SECRETARY OF THE NAVY

1. All awards to O-10 Flag and General Officers

2. Silver Star Medal and above

3. Presidential Unit Citation and Navy Unit Commendation

4. All awards to foreign nationals, unless specifically delegated in writing

5. All determinations of Extraordinary Heroism

6. All awards for personnel serving with the Secretariat Staffs, including the staffs of the Assistant Secretaries of the Navy

AUTHORITY DELEGATED TO THE ASSISTANT SECRETARY OF THE NAVY (MANPOWER AND RESERVE AFFAIRS)

1. Combat awards below the Silver Star Medal to Flag and General Officers, O-9 and below

2. New operations for the Combat Action Ribbon

3. New areas and/or operations for the Strike/Flight Air Medal

4. Designation of areas and/or operations for inclusion of the Combat Distinguishing Device (Combat "V") on specific personal decorations

5. Legions of Merit and lesser personal decorations for personnel serving with commands and organizations not under the authority of CNO or CMC, including the organizations listed below. This authority includes the ability to sub-delegate the Meritorious Service Medal and below.

    a. Office of Naval Research

    b. Office of the General Counsel

c. Naval Criminal Investigative Service

d. Office of Program Appraisal

e. Office of Legislative Affairs

f. Office of the Judge Advocate General

g. Office of Information

h. Office of the Naval Inspector General

i. Personnel assigned to OSD and joint commands who are recommended for non-DoD and non-Joint awards

j. All other commands/offices not under the authority of CNO or CMC

AUTHORITY DELEGATED TO THE CHIEF OF NAVAL OPERATIONS AND THE COMMANDANT OF THE MARINE CORPS

1. All personal awards not specified above, including:

a. Non-combat awards, Legion of Merit and below, to all grades O-9 and below.

b. All combat and terrorist incident related awards, Legion of Merit and below, to all grades O-6 and below.

c. CNO and CMC may sub-delegate to Flag and General Officers in the grades of O-10 and O-9 the authority to approve both combat and non-combat Legions of Merit and below. CNO and CMC may sub-delegate to other grades the authority to approve the Meritorious Service Medal and below.

2. Meritorious Unit Commendation

AUTHORITY SUB-DELEGATED BY SERVICE CHIEFS

1. Further Sub-delegation. Further sub-delegation of awarding authority may be authorized by CNO and CMC. Such additional sub-delegation will be provided via separate correspondence in accordance with the policies contained in this Manual.

2. <u>Combat Action Ribbon</u>. Although the Combat Action Ribbon is lower in precedence than all other personal decorations, it is considered a combat award. Therefore, awarding authority for the Combat Action Ribbon is delegated specifically in writing and is <u>not</u> included in the sub-delegations below.

3. <u>Combat Distinguishing Device (Combat "V")</u>. Those officers with delegated awarding authority for the Navy and Marine Corps Commendation and Achievement Medals, as indicated below, may <u>not</u> award these decorations with the Combat Distinguishing Device unless specific, written authorization has been received.

4. <u>Concurrence for Other U.S. Armed Service Awards to DON Personnel</u>. Concurrence authority is restricted and is always specifically delegated in writing. It is <u>not</u> commensurate with a commander's awarding authority.

5. <u>Legion of Merit</u>

   a. <u>Navy</u>. Admirals (O-10) may approve the Legion of Merit for all Navy personnel in their chain of command, and for other U.S. Armed Forces personnel (Marine Corps, Army, Air Force, and Coast Guard), O-6 and below, in their chain of command. Vice Admirals (O-9) may approve the Legion of Merit as outlined above, with the exception of Flag Officer awards, which shall be approved by the next Admiral (O-10) in the chain of command.

   b. <u>Marine Corps</u>. The Commanders, Marine Forces Command Atlantic and Pacific, and the Commanding Generals, Marine Corps Combat Development Command and Marine Forces Reserve, may only approve the Legion of Merit specifically in cases of retirement.

6. <u>Meritorious Service Medal and Below</u>

   a. <u>Navy</u>. All Rear Admirals (Upper Half) (O-8) and above, and Rear Admirals (Lower Half) (O-7) in command, may approve the Meritorious Service Medal and below for all O-6 and below Navy and other U.S. Armed Forces personnel (Marine Corps, Army, Air Force, and Coast Guard) in their chain of command.

   b. <u>Marine Corps</u>. Commanders in the grade of brigadier general and above, including those frocked. Further sub-delegation is not authorized. Commanders may issue <u>written</u>

temporary authorization to an acting commander pursuant to the following:

(1) If the acting commander is a general officer, he or she may be granted authority to award the MM and below.

(2) If the acting commander is an O-6, he or she may be granted authority to award the NC and below.

(3) Such temporary authority may not be granted below the grade of O-6.

7. Navy and Marine Corps Commendation Medal and Below

    a. Navy

    (1) Rear Admirals (Lower Half) (O-7) and above may approve the Navy and Marine Corps Commendation Medal and below for all O-6 and below Navy and other U.S. Armed Forces personnel (Marine Corps, Army, Air Force, and Coast Guard) in their chain of command.

    (2) Captains (O-6) in command, eligible to wear the Command at Sea or Command Ashore device by virtue of their current billet, may approve the Navy and Marine Corps Commendation Medal and below for all O-5 and below Navy and other U.S. Armed Forces personnel (Marine Corps, Army, Air Force, and Coast Guard) in their chain of command.

    b. Marine Corps

    (1) Awarding authority is sub-delegated to commanders in the grade of colonel (O-6), listed on the colonel command slate, including those frocked. Further sub-delegation is not authorized. Commanders may issue written temporary authorization to an acting commander, pursuant to the following:

        (a) If the acting commander is an O-6, he or she may be granted authority to award the NC and below.

        (b) If the acting commander is an O-5, he or she may be granted authority to award the NA.

        (c) Such temporary authority may not be granted below the grade of O-5.

(2) Marine Corps limits the awarding authority to one Navy and Marine Corps Commendation Medal <u>for every 50 Marines and Sailors</u> on their T/O per calendar year.

8. <u>Navy and Marine Corps Achievement Medal</u>

a. <u>Navy</u>. Commanders or commanding officers eligible to wear the Command at Sea or Command Ashore device, by virtue of current billet, and prospective commanding officers of new construction.

b. <u>Marine Corps</u>. Battalion and squadron level commanders, battalion inspectors and instructors, and site officers in charge, or other command positions of battalion or squadron level command equivalency. Requests for exceptions to policy shall be directed, via the chain of command, to CMC (MMMA).

GENERAL ADMINISTRATIVE POLICY

1. <u>Routing for SECNAV or ASN(M&RA) Approval</u>. All awards submitted for SECNAV or ASN(M&RA) approval shall be routed through the Navy Department Board of Decorations and Medals (NDBDM) for review and recommendation.

2. <u>Quarterly Combat Awards Report to SECNAV</u>. CNO and CMC shall provide a quarterly report of combat decorations awarded. This report shall be routed via NDBDM and ASN(M&RA) to SECNAV.

3. <u>Awards for Members of a Flag or General Officer's Immediate Personal Staff</u>. Award recommendations for immediate staff (e.g., Executive Assistant, Aide, Flag Secretary, etc.) shall be forwarded to the next higher awarding authority in the chain of command for appropriate action.

4. <u>Dual Reporting Relationships</u>. When commands with dual reporting relationships to SECNAV and either CNO or CMC submit award recommendations for Secretariat level review, the recommendations shall be submitted via NDBDM. This includes award recommendations for members of a Flag or General Officer's immediate personal staff, or other personnel whose chain of command is a Secretariat function. When an award is for an individual whose chain of command is not a Secretariat function, CNO or CMC's delegated authority applies; i.e., Flag and General

Officers, in the grades of O-9 or O-10, are delegated authority to approve Legions of Merit and below. In such cases, NDBDM or Secretariat review is not required.

5. Delegation Outside DON. Authority to award Naval decorations will not be delegated to commands outside of the Department of the Navy.

PRECEDENCE OF AWARDS

The precedence of decorations authorized for personnel of the Navy and Marine Corps is listed below. Navy Uniform Regulations and Marine Corps Uniform Regulations contain further information regarding the precedence and appropriate wear of all personal, unit, and service awards.

a. U.S. Military Personal Decorations:
    (1) Medal of Honor
    (2) Navy Cross
    (3) Defense Distinguished Service Medal
    (4) Distinguished Service Medal
    (5) Silver Star Medal
    (6) Defense Superior Service Medal
    (7) Legion of Merit
    (8) Distinguished Flying Cross
    (9) Navy and Marine Corps Medal
    (10) Bronze Star Medal
    (11) Purple Heart Medal
    (12) Defense Meritorious Service Medal
    (13) Meritorious Service Medal
    (14) Air Medal
    (15) Joint Service Commendation Medal
    (16) Navy and Marine Corps Commendation Medal
    (17) Joint Service Achievement Medal
    (18) Navy and Marine Corps Achievement Medal
    (19) Combat Action Ribbon

b. U.S. Military Unit Awards (after U.S. personal decorations):
    (1) Presidential Unit Citation
    (2) Joint Meritorious Unit Award
    (3) Navy Unit Commendation
    (4) Meritorious Unit Commendation
    (5) Navy "E" Ribbon

c. U.S. Non-Military Decorations take precedence after all U.S. Military Unit Awards, in the order earned, except when more than one decoration is from the same agency, in which case the precedence is as established by the awarding agency.

d. U.S. Campaign and Service Awards:
    (1) Prisoner of War Medal
    (2) Good Conduct Medal (Navy and Marine Corps)
    (3) Naval Reserve Meritorious Service Medal
    (4) Selected Marine Corps Reserve Medal
    (5) Navy Fleet Marine Force Ribbon
    (6) Expeditionary Medal (Navy or Marine Corps)
    (7) China Service Medal
    (8) Navy Occupation Service Medal
    (9) National Defense Service Medal
    (10) Korean Service Medal
    (11) Antarctica Service Medal
    (12) Armed Forces Expeditionary Medal
    (13) Vietnam Service Medal
    (14) Southwest Asia Service Medal
    (15) Kosovo Campaign Medal
    (16) Afghanistan Campaign Medal
    (17) Iraq Campaign Medal
    (18) Global War on Terrorism Expeditionary Medal
    (19) Global War on Terrorism Service Medal
    (20) Korea Defense Service Medal
    (21) Armed Forces Service Medal
    (22) Humanitarian Service Medal
    (23) Military Outstanding Volunteer Service Medal
    (24) Sea Service Deployment Ribbon
    (25) Navy Arctic Service Ribbon
    (26) Naval Reserve Sea Service Ribbon
    (27) Navy and Marine Corps Overseas Service Ribbon
    (28) Navy Recruiting Service Ribbon
    (29) Marine Corps Recruiting Ribbon
    (30) Marine Corps Drill Instructor Ribbon
    (31) Marine Corps Security Guard Ribbon
    (32) Navy Recruit Training Service Ribbon
    (33) Navy Ceremonial Guard Ribbon
    (34) Coast Guard Special Operations Service Ribbon
    (35) Armed Forces Reserve Medal

e. U.S. Non-Military Service Awards:
    (1) Merchant Marine Gallant Ship Unit Citation
    (2) Merchant Marine Combat Bar
    (3) Merchant Marine Korean Service Bar
    (4) Merchant Marine Vietnam Service Bar
    (5) Merchant Marine Expeditionary Medal

f. When authorized for wear, foreign military personal decorations are worn in the order of receipt; if from the same country, the respective country's precedence is used.

g. Foreign Military Unit Awards:
    (1) Philippine Republic Presidential Unit Citation
    (2) Republic of Korea Presidential Unit Citation
    (3) Vietnam Presidential Unit Citation
    (4) Republic of Vietnam Meritorious Unit Citation
        (Gallantry Cross Color with Palm)
    (5) Republic of Vietnam Meritorious Unit Citation
        (Civil Actions First Class Color with Palm)

h. Multilateral Military Service Awards:
    (1) United Nations Service Medal
    (2) United Nations Medal
    (3) NATO Medal
    (4) Multinational Force and Observers Medal
    (5) Inter-American Defense Board Medal

i. Foreign Military Service Medals:
    (1) Republic of Vietnam Campaign Medal
    (2) Kuwait Liberation Medal (Saudi Arabia)
    (3) Kuwait Liberation Medal (Kuwait)
    (4) Republic of Korea War Service Medal

j. Marksmanship Awards (Navy and Marine Corps personnel are not authorized to wear other Services' marksmanship awards):
    (1) Competition Badges - consult individual service
        regulations
    (2) Rifle Qualification Award
    (3) Pistol Qualification Award

CHAPTER 2 - PERSONAL MILITARY DECORATIONS

SECTION 1 - GENERAL

210. <u>DEFINITION</u>. A military decoration is an award bestowed on an individual for a specific act or acts of gallantry or meritorious service.

211. <u>POLICY CONSIDERATIONS</u>

1. <u>Initiation of Recommendation</u>. A recommendation for a personal award may be submitted by any commissioned officer senior, in grade or billet, to the individual being recommended, who has knowledge of any act, achievement, or service that may warrant such award. A recommendation originated by other than the commanding officer of the individual concerned must be forwarded to the commanding officer for endorsement. If an officer is not assigned, the senior enlisted member may forward documentation to the first officer in the chain of command for consideration of the award of a personal decoration.

2. <u>Timeliness</u>. Timely recommendations are essential to a successful awards program. A recommendation should be submitted as soon as possible following the act, achievement, or service upon which it is based. However, due consideration must be given to security requirements, the time required to properly investigate the event, validation of facts, and processing. All recommendations must be appropriately justified and sufficiently detailed to allow proper evaluation and decision.

a. Award recommendations should be submitted to <u>arrive at the final awarding authority</u> for adjudication at least 60 days prior to the desired presentation date, to allow sufficient time for administrative processing. For awards requiring review by more levels in the chain of command, additional time should be allowed.

b. Process the recommendation for an award for meritorious service terminating with retirement or separation so presentation may be made at the individual's current duty station. Other meritorious awards may be processed for presentation at either the individual's current or new duty station.

c. Time limits are three years for submitting most personal military decorations and five years for awarding them.

Exceptions to this are the Distinguished Flying Cross, with time limits of two years for submission and three years for awarding, and the Purple Heart Medal and Combat Action Ribbon, which do not have submission time limits. Awards may be considered beyond these time limits under the following circumstances:

(1) If SECNAV determines an individual's superior submitted an appropriately documented award recommendation within the specified time limits, but the recommendation was not acted upon due to inadvertent loss during processing.

(2) If the award recommendation is made through a Member of Congress. Chapter 8 provides further information regarding this process.

3. Meritorious Service Recognition. An individual is recognized for sustained superior performance at the termination of the period during which that performance was demonstrated, such as at the end of an assigned tour of duty. Several factors must be considered:

a. End of Tour. A routine end of tour (EOT) award is not an integral part of the awards system. A copy of any personal awards received during the tour must be submitted to the awarding authority with the award recommendation.

b. Specific Achievement. A specific achievement (or impact) award may be authorized for exceptional performance over a period of short duration, which is generally no longer than twelve months. However, specific achievement awards may not support an EOT award; neither the Summary of Action nor the citation issued for the period of meritorious service shall mention the specific achievement previously recognized.

c. Sailor of the Year. The actions listed in a specific achievement award given in recognition of a competitive accomplishment, such as Sailor of the Year (SOY), may not support an EOT award. However, winning SOY, or other competitive accomplishments, may be mentioned in the EOT award. A copy of the SOY award citation must be enclosed with the EOT award submission. An individual shall only receive one award of this nature in any given year.

d. Mid-tour Awards. Mid-tour awards are not appropriate; commands should retain such recommendations for inclusion in the EOT award. A tour is normally designated by a set of orders to leave the command, not by a change of position within the command. This should not hinder a command from awarding an EOT award and/or an additional award for members who extend at arduous duty stations or operational commands.

      e. <u>Dual Responsibilities</u>. Members with dual responsibilities, i.e., "double-hatted," are normally viewed for an EOT award following completion of all duties, not each individually.

      f. <u>Detachment of Reporting Senior</u>. When a reporting senior is detaching and believes the service of a subordinate merits recognition, an Award Recommendation Form for the observed period should be completed and retained within the command, pending detachment of the individual. If at that time the current reporting senior feels the latter portion of the individual's tour merits recognition, the recommendation should be combined with the earlier one; if not, the recommendation of the predecessor shall be forwarded for consideration on its own merits.

    4. <u>Awards for Personal Staff</u>. Commanders may <u>not</u> approve awards for any member who is considered personal staff, such as aides, executive assistants, sergeants major, etc. These awards must be submitted to the immediate superior in command for approval.

    5. <u>Awards for Multiple Individuals for the Same Incident or Action</u>. In situations where multiple personal awards are recommended for the same incident or action, <u>all</u> of the recommendations shall be forwarded together to the highest awarding authority (such as CNO, CMC, or SECNAV) for consideration, even if only one of the recommendations would normally require that level of approval.

    6. <u>Awards Presented at the Time of Retirement</u>. DON does not have a retirement award, nor is it appropriate to recommend an award for the entire career of a service member. If an individual is recommended for an award upon retirement or transfer to the Fleet Reserve or Fleet Marine Corps Reserve, it shall only recognize service at the last duty station, or service that has not previously been recognized. However, it <u>is</u> appropriate to include a statement in the citation reflecting the member's total number of years of service. For example, "Gunnery Sergeant Smith's superior performance of duties

highlights the culmination of 20 years of honorable and dedicated service."

7. <u>Reconsideration of an Award Previously Considered</u>. Recommendations for awards previously considered by an awarding authority may be reconsidered <u>only</u> upon the presentation of new and relevant material evidence that was not available at the time the original recommendation was considered.

8. <u>Requirement for Honorable Service</u>. 10 U.S.C. §6249 provides that no medal, cross, bar, or associated emblem or insignia may be awarded or presented to any individual if the service after the distinguishing act or period has not been honorable.

a. Any approved award may be revoked <u>before</u> presentation by the awarding authority.

b. If the awardee's honorable service is questioned <u>after</u> presentation of an award, forward the entire case to NDBDM, via CNO or CMC, as appropriate, for a determination. If subsequently determined facts would have prevented the original approval of the award, or if the awardee's service after the presentation of the award has not been honorable, SECNAV may revoke the award.

9. <u>DoD and Joint Awards</u>. DoD has a personal awards program equivalent to that of DON. When DON personnel serve in a DoD agency or activity, or a Joint or Combatant Command, recognition by a DoD or Joint award, in lieu of a DON award, is appropriate. The only exception is for DON personnel retiring or transferring to the Fleet Reserve or Fleet Marine Corps Reserve while attached to another Service or Joint command; in such cases, if recognition is deemed appropriate, it is <u>preferred</u> that Navy or Marine Corps award a DON award. An individual may not receive two awards, i.e., DoD and/or other Service and also DON, for the same act or period of service.

a. In cases where the Secretary of the Navy (SECNAV) has been designated an "Executive Agent of a Joint Function," SECNAV has been delegated authority, per the DoD Awards Manual, to award the Joint Service Commendation Medal (JC) and the Joint Service Achievement Medal (JA) for personnel serving within that activity or command.

b. Recommendations for JC and JA medals forwarded to SECNAV shall be in the same format as DON awards; DON eligibility criteria are the same as that of the DoD. Use OPNAV 1650/3 for Navy personnel and NAVMC 11533 (EF) for Marine Corps personnel and submit recommendations through the chain of command to SECNAV. To be eligible for a Joint decoration, the individual must be permanently assigned to a Joint activity or a Joint Task Force Headquarters in a valid, verifiable Joint duty billet per manpower documentation.

10. Engraving at Government Expense. Except for the Medal of Honor, no military decorations will be engraved at Government expense. The Medal of Honor shall be engraved for all recipients with grade, name, branch of service and the words, "For action above and beyond the call of duty in (area) on (date)."

212. EXTRAORDINARY HEROISM. 10 U.S.C. §6330 provides that each enlisted member transferred to the Fleet Reserve or Fleet Marine Corps Reserve, who has been credited by SECNAV with Extraordinary Heroism (EH), is entitled to an increase of 10 percent in retainer pay. Additionally, §6330 states that the EH determination made by SECNAV is final and conclusive for all purposes. All awards for heroism, with the complete justification package, shall be forwarded to NDBDM for an EH determination.

1. Extraordinary Heroism Recommendations. Awards for heroism approved by delegated awarding authorities shall contain a recommendation as to the eligibility of the individuals for the benefits of EH. The awarding authority, in recommending an award recipient be accorded EH benefits, should compare the act(s) with other acts of heroism, and believe that it stands out well above ordinary acts of heroism. Therefore, individuals must have distinguished themselves beyond those who have already earned distinction for heroism. The following considerations are furnished to assist in making a recommendation.

a. Individuals must have performed a worthwhile act or an act that was considered worthwhile at the time. Needless and foolish risking of life or tempting of fate is not considered worthwhile.

b. The act must have been performed voluntarily. This requirement should not be applied so strictly as to exclude from consideration individuals, who in carrying out orders, do more of their own volition than could ordinarily be expected under the circumstances.

c. Whether the individual chose not to seek cover or leave a place of comparative safety to perform the act, without direct orders or without being forced into the more dangerous situation by circumstances over which the individual had no control.

d. Whether there would have been cause for censure or blame, had the individual not performed the action(s) cited. Individuals who failed to perform the duties expected of their grade and experience, and for which they had been trained, might be considered candidates for censure rather than praise.

e. The act performed by the individual must not have been motivated solely by a desire for self-preservation.

2. Adjudication of Extraordinary Heroism. NDBDM will review all awards for heroism and forward a recommendation to SECNAV for final determination. If there is no record of a previous EH determination for an award for heroism, adjudication will be made when the individual applies for transfer to the Fleet or Fleet Marine Corps Reserve. CNO or CMC, as applicable, will advise the member of SECNAV's decision. NDBDM will forward those cases in which EH is not considered justified to CNO or CMC for retention in the individual's record. If requested by an individual at the time of transfer to the Fleet or Fleet Marine Corps Reserve, NDBDM will review the awards correspondence submitted.

3. Responsibilities. The following procedures are effective for the determination of EH benefits:

a. Commanders possessing delegated awarding authority shall review all approved awards for heroism, and provide recommendations as to whether or not the individuals should receive EH benefits, in accordance with the criteria contained in this article.

b. CNO and CMC

(1) When an individual applies for transfer to the Fleet or Fleet Marine Corps Reserve, forward correspondence concerning any act of heroism to CNP (PERS-4823) for Navy personnel, or to CMC (MMSR-2) for Marine Corps personnel. Provide all supporting information, including copies of the award citation, award recommendation form, eyewitness

statements, and other documentation as appropriate.

(2) At the time of application for transfer to the Fleet or Fleet Marine Corps Reserve, advise applicants that award correspondence for heroism will be reviewed if they so request. If requested, forward the pertinent correspondence as described above.

(3) Provide notification to personnel whose acts of heroism have been affirmatively determined by SECNAV as qualifying for the benefits of EH.

213. EYEWITNESS STATEMENTS. For all combat and lifesaving awards, a minimum of two notarized eyewitness statements, with contact information for the eyewitnesses, shall be included in the recommendation package. The statements shall be in the eyewitnesses' own words and neither statement may be from the individual being recommended for the award. The following specific additional requirements also apply:

1. Medal of Honor Recommendations. For Medal of Honor recommendations, also include a summary of the recommendation in the following format:

Identifying Information

Name:
Rate or rank at time of action:
Organization:
Next of kin:
Person(s) who assisted:

Conditions Under Which Act Performed

Location:
Date:
Terrain:
Weather:
Enemy condition:
Friendly condition:

Narrative Description of Gallant Conduct

2. Lifesaving or Attempted Lifesaving Awards. For awards involving lifesaving or attempted lifesaving, include the following information. It is emphasized that recommendations

should include the following, but are not necessarily limited to this information.

a. The eyewitness statements, in addition to providing an account of the incident, should include an opinion as to whether the person for whom the award is sought imperiled his or her life. Police reports and/or other relevant, official documents may also be submitted.

b. The precise location of the rescue or attempted rescue.

c. The date, time of day, nature of weather, including amount and source of light if at night, force of the wind, condition and temperature of the water, if applicable.

d. The names of all persons rendering assistance and the nature of the assistance.

e. A diagram of the scene, including distances, location of assistance, and, when applicable, heights of terrain or relevant structures, such as piers or vessels from which rescue efforts were started.

f. A statement as to the swimming qualifications of the rescuer, if applicable. (See Article 6610120 of the MILPERS Manual for Navy personnel and MCO 1500.52C for Marine Corps personnel.)

g. An account of the cooperation or lack thereof on the part of the person being rescued.

h. A rescue from burning should be described in great detail, including the aid received by the rescuer, the extent of the burns, and a description of the outer clothing of the rescuer.

214. <u>SPECIAL CONSIDERATIONS FOR MEDAL OF HONOR RECIPIENTS</u>

1. <u>Medal of Honor Roll</u>. Applicable provisions of law relating to the Medal of Honor Roll are as follows:

a. 38 U.S.C. §1560 established the Medal of Honor Roll.

(1) There shall be in the Department of the Army, Department of the Navy, Department of the Air Force and Department of Homeland Security, respectively, a roll designated as the "Army, Navy, Air Force, and Coast Guard Medal of Honor Roll," hereafter referred to as the "Medal of Honor Roll."

(2) Upon written application to the Secretary concerned, the Secretary shall enter and record on such roll the names of all surviving individuals, who have served on active duty in the Armed Forces of the United States, and who have been awarded a Medal of Honor for conspicuously distinguishing themselves by gallantry and intrepidity at the risk of their lives, above and beyond the call of duty, while so serving.

(3) Applications for entry on such roll shall be made in the form, and under regulations prescribed by the Secretary concerned, and shall indicate whether or not the applicant desires to receive the special pension provided by §1562 of this law. The Secretary concerned shall furnish proper application forms and instructions without charge upon the request of any person claiming these benefits.

b. 38 U.S.C. §1561 established the Medal of Honor Roll Enrollment Certificate.

(1) The Secretary concerned shall determine whether or not each applicant is entitled to have his or her name entered on the Medal of Honor Roll. If the official award of the Medal of Honor to the applicant, or the official notice to him/her thereof, shows the Medal of Honor was awarded to the applicant for an act described in §1560 of this law, such award or notice shall be sufficient to entitle the applicant to have his/her name entered on such roll without further investigation. Otherwise, all official correspondence, orders, reports, recommendations, requests and other evidence on file in any public office or department shall be considered.

(2) All individuals whose names are entered on the Medal of Honor Roll shall be furnished enrollment certificates of service and of the act of heroism, gallantry, bravery, or intrepidity for which the Medal of Honor was awarded, and if they have executed the right to receive the special pension provided by §1562 of this law.

(3) The Secretary concerned shall deliver a certified copy of each certificate issued by him/her, under subparagraph (2) above, to the Secretary of Veteran Affairs, in which the right of the person named in the certificate to the special pension provided by §1562 of this law is set forth. Such copy shall authorize the Administrator to pay such special pension to the person named in the certificate.

c. 38 U.S.C. §1562 established the Special Pension Provision for those personnel on the Medal of Honor Roll.

(1) Upon receipt of a copy of the certificate per subparagraph b. above, the Secretary of Veterans Affairs shall pay each person, whose name has been entered on the Medal of Honor Roll, a special pension. The rate of the special pension shall be as adjusted annually in accordance with the provisions of 38 U.S.C. §1562. The special pension shall be paid beginning as of the date of application therefor under §1560. In addition, a lump sum shall be paid to each person eligible for the special pension equal to the total amount of special pension that would have been received from the first day of the first month after the act for which the Medal of Honor was awarded through the last day of the month preceding the actual commencement of the payment of the special pension. The lump sum amount payable shall be determined using the monthly rate that was in effect at the time for each month of eligibility.

(2) The receipt of special pension shall not deprive any person of any other pension or other benefit, right, or privilege to which he/she is or may hereafter be entitled under any existing or subsequent law. The special pension shall be paid in addition to all other payments under laws of the United States.

(3) The special pension shall not be subject to any attachment, execution, levy, tax, lien, or detention under any process whatsoever.

(4) If any individuals have been awarded more than one Medal of Honor, they shall not receive more than one special pension.

2. Service Academy Appointments. 10 U.S.C. §4342, §6954, and §9342 authorize the appointment of children of a person who has been awarded the Medal of Honor as cadets at the U.S.

Military Academy or the U.S. Air Force Academy, or as midshipmen at the U.S. Naval Academy, without regard to quota requirements. Applications for admittance to the Naval Academy under this provision should be sent to the Dean of Admissions, U.S. Naval Academy, regardless of the branch of Service in which the parent served. Applications should include the full name and date of birth of the applicant, and the full name and grade or rate of the person awarded the Medal of Honor.

3. Travel in Military Aircraft. Medal of Honor recipients are authorized to travel in U.S. military aircraft on a space-available basis, within the Continental United States, provided they certify the trip is not for personal gain or remuneration.

4. Duplicate Medal of Honor. 14 U.S.C. §504 provides that a living Medal of Honor recipient shall upon written application be issued, without charge, one duplicate Medal of Honor (marked "DUPLICATE") with ribbons and appurtenances.

5. Medal of Honor Flag. In accordance with Public Law 107-248 §8143, Medal of Honor recipients who were living as of 23 October 2002 shall be presented with the Medal of Honor Flag as designated in 36 U.S.C. §903.

SECTION 2 - ADMINISTRATIVE PROCEDURES

220. PREPARATION OF RECOMMENDATIONS

1. Award Recommendation Form

a. Prepare recommendations for personal decorations on the Personal Award Recommendation Form (Navy: OPNAV 1650/3; Marine Corps: NAVMC 11533 (EF)). Use a separate form for each award being recommended. General information on preparing the OPNAV 1650/3 and a sample form are contained in Appendix A to this chapter; the complete instructions are available online at https://awards.navy.mil, the Navy Department Awards Web Service (NDAWS). Marine Corps units shall use the electronic Awards Processing System (APS) to prepare, forward, and record all awards. This system provides the originator and awarding authority with all references and forms.

b. The following two-letter codes are applicable:

MH Medal of Honor
NX Navy Cross
DM Distinguished Service Medal
SS Silver Star Medal
LM Legion of Merit
LV Legion of Merit with "V"
DX Distinguished Flying Cross
DV Distinguished Flying Cross with "V"
NM Navy and Marine Corps Medal
BS Bronze Star Medal
BV Bronze Star Medal with "V"
PH Purple Heart Medal
MM Meritorious Service Medal
AS Air Medal (Strike/Flight)
AF Air Medal (Individual Action)
AH Air Medal (Individual Action with "V")
JC Joint Service Commendation Medal
NC Navy and Marine Corps Commendation Medal
CV Navy and Marine Corps Commendation Medal with "V"
JA Joint Service Achievement Medal
NA Navy and Marine Corps Achievement Medal
NV Navy and Marine Corps Achievement Medal with "V"
CR Combat Action Ribbon
XX Letter of Commendation (Navy)
LC Letter of Commendation (Marine Corps)

2. <u>Summary of Action</u>. Since each award recommendation is evaluated on the merits of the justification, the Summary of Action is critical. It is required in all cases except command-awarded Navy and Marine Corps Achievement Medals at Navy units; all Marine Corps awards require a detailed Summary of Action. Avoid generalities and excessive use of superlatives. Present an objective summary, giving specific examples of the performance and the manner in which it was accomplished, together with the results and benefits derived. The amount of detail and supporting documentation required depends upon the circumstances and the nature of the award being recommended; in general, <u>a single page will suffice</u>. When additional space is required, add sheets of standard size paper; however, use continuation pages sparingly.

3. <u>Citation</u>. A proposed citation, condensed from the Summary of Action, must accompany the recommendation. Although a citation is laudatory and formalized, it must be factual and contain no classified information. In most instances, the introduction to the citation is written, "The President takes <u>pleasure</u> in presenting . . ." However, in the case of

posthumous awards, the citation shall be written, "The President takes <u>pride</u> in presenting . . ." The body of the citation consists of three parts:

a. <u>Opening Sentence</u>. The body of the citation begins with a standard phrase describing the degree of meritorious or heroic service as specified for each award, duty assignment of the individual, inclusive dates of service on which the recommendation is based, and, if desired, a description of the operations of the unit to which the individual is attached. Note: The ending date on awards for personnel leaving Naval service is the last day of duty prior to the beginning of any period of terminal leave. The following opening phrases for specific decorations are exclusive to the respective award, and not used in others:

Medal of Honor: "For conspicuous gallantry and intrepidity at the risk of his/her life above and beyond the call of duty..."

Navy Cross: "For extraordinary heroism..."

Distinguished Service Medal: "For exceptionally meritorious service to the Government of the United States in a duty of great responsibility..."

Silver Star Medal: "For conspicuous gallantry and intrepidity in action..."

Legion of Merit: "For exceptionally meritorious conduct in the performance of outstanding service..."

Distinguished Flying Cross: "For heroism (or extra-ordinary achievement) while participating in aerial flight..."

Navy and Marine Corps Medal: "For heroism..."

Bronze Star Medal: "For heroic achievement (or meritorious achievement) (or meritorious service) (or heroic service) in connection with combat operations against the enemy (or operations involving conflict with an opposing foreign force)..."

Meritorious Service Medal: "For outstanding meritorious achievement or service..."

Air Medal: "For heroic (or meritorious) achievement in aerial flight..."

Joint Service Commendation Medal: "For meritorious service (or meritorious achievement) while serving as..."

Navy and Marine Corps Commendation Medal: "For meritorious service (or meritorious achievement) (or heroic service) (or heroic achievement) while serving as..."

Joint Service Achievement Medal: "For professional achievement in the superior performance of duties while serving as..."

Navy and Marine Corps Achievement Medal: "For professional achievement (or heroic achievement) in the superior performance of his/her duties while serving as..."

    b. <u>Statement of Heroic/Meritorious Achievement or Service</u>. The second part of the citation identifies the recipient by name, describes specific duty assignments, his/her accomplishments and the outstanding personal attributes displayed. The description of the individual's achievements must show clearly that they were sufficient to justify the award recommended. The value of results of achievements may also be included. If duty was performed in actual combat, the citation should so state. <u>No classified information may be included in the proposed citation</u>.

    c. <u>Commendatory Remarks</u>. The third part of the citation states that the outstanding attributes, mentioned or implied in the second part, "reflected credit upon himself/herself and were in keeping with the highest traditions of the United States Naval Service." If an award is given in the name of the President, then the individual has reflected "<u>great</u> credit" upon himself/herself (Air Medal and above). In the case of Marines, use "... traditions of the Marine Corps and the United States Naval Service." Note: The attributes used in the last sentence of the example citations are <u>not</u> mandatory for that award. Attributes appropriate to the individual and/or the act(s) or service being recognized should be used. There are two options for the format of the last sentence:

    (1) Beginning with the individual's name: "First Lieutenant Doe's bold leadership, wise judgment, and complete dedication to duty reflected great credit upon him and were in keeping with the highest traditions of the Marine Corps and the United States Naval Service."

    (2) Beginning with the three attributes: "By his

bold leadership, wise judgment, and complete dedication to duty, First Lieutenant Doe reflected great credit upon himself and upheld the highest traditions of the Marine Corps and the United States Naval Service."

       d. <u>Combat Distinguishing Device (Combat "V")</u>. If approved, the citation must contain the statement, "The Combat Distinguishing Device is authorized."

       e. <u>Citation Format</u>. Citations for the Air Medal and above shall be prepared in upper and lower case type, without the use of acronyms. The font used shall be Courier New, size 12. The citation is limited to 23 typewritten lines, with the following margins: left margin 0.7 inches, right margin 0.5 inches, top margin two inches, bottom margin one inch. Citations for the Navy and Marine Corps Commendation and Navy and Marine Corps Achievement Medals shall be prepared in all upper case letters in Courier New, size 10, and are limited to 7 1/2 typewritten lines with margins of one inch.

       (1) The opening line is formatted by type of award; follow instructions above and examples for noting subsequent awards.

       (2) The grade, name, and service are all capital letters and centered. In accordance with NAVADMIN 121/05, the "service" for all Navy personnel (whether active or reserve component) shall be "UNITED STATES NAVY." Due to the length of Navy enlisted rates, three lines are used; warfare designation is not required, but the primary designation is used when space is available; additional designations are never appropriate. Navy officers use two lines with rank and name combined; a third line, for staff corps designation is optional. For Marine Corps personnel, two lines shall be used for the individual's grade, name, and service.

       (3) There can be many varieties of style for the same award; awarding authorities may dictate specific guidance for awards under their authority, as long as they meet the basic requirements cited above.

       f. <u>Sample Citations</u>. See Appendix B to this chapter for examples of citations.

    4. <u>Required Signatures for Citations and Certificates</u>. Citations and certificates are signed as indicated in the following table:

Award	Citation	Certificate
MH	President in the name of Congress	President and SECNAV
NX, DM & SS	Awarding Authority	SECNAV in the name of the President
LM, DX, NM & BS	Awarding Authority	Awarding Authority in the name of the President
PH	No citation issued	Awarding Authority in the name of the President
MM & AM	Awarding Authority	Awarding Authority in the name of the President
JC & JA	Secretary of the Navy (Awarding Authority)	Awarding Authority in the name of SECDEF
NC & NA	Awarding Authority	Awarding Authority in the name of SECNAV

221. PROCESSING OF RECOMMENDATIONS

1. Submission. Address recommendations to the awarding authority who has jurisdiction over the individual at the time of the act or service. Award recommendations for the Air Medal and above must be submitted via the operational chain of command, with the first endorsement beginning no lower than the Echelon 3 level. A list of awarding authorities is provided in Appendix A to Chapter 1. Award recommendations shall be forwarded through all intermediate echelon commanders, who shall each make a recommendation regarding approval. Do not provide "advance copies" of proposed award recommendations to the chain

of command. An Immediate Superior in Command (ISIC) or a delegated awarding authority may require submission via a lower level chain of command; however, recommendations may <u>not</u> be terminated at any level below the final awarding authority.

2. <u>Premature Disclosure</u>. Premature public disclosure of information concerning award recommendations during their processing, including intermediate approval and/or disapproval recommendations, is a potential source of embarrassment and disappointment to both those recommended and the DON. Therefore, personnel involved in the submission and processing of awards shall <u>not</u> comment on any case under consideration, and all award recommendations shall be handled on a "FOR OFFICIAL USE ONLY" basis until the awards are officially announced or actually presented. In view of the additional sensitivity regarding Medal of Honor cases, exceptional care shall be exercised to avoid disclosure of any information, including but not limited to, the fact that an individual has been recommended for the award.

222. <u>RESPONSIBILITIES OF AWARDING AUTHORITIES</u>

1. <u>Initial Review of Awards</u>. Awarding authorities may take one of the following actions:

   a. Approve the award.

   b. Approve a lower award (downgrade).

   c. Disapprove the award.

   d. Approve a higher award (upgrade), if so empowered, or recommend a higher award to the appropriate awarding authority.

   e. Return the recommendation for further clarification or justification.

2. <u>Award Elements</u>. Once an award has been approved, issue the following award elements. Appendix C to this chapter contains information regarding procurement.

   a. Medal, if this is the first award for a living recipient, or if the award is being made posthumously.

   b. Gold or Silver Star, as appropriate, if award is a subsequent award of a medal.

c. Citation and certificate, or the combined citation-certificate in the case of the Navy and Marine Corps Commendation and Achievement Medals.

d. Presentation folder.

3. Actions After Award Presentation

a. An awarding authority may revoke an award he/she has approved that has not yet been presented. Once an award has been presented, only SECNAV has the authority to revoke it.

b. Awarding authorities are responsible for reissuing and/or correcting, as necessary, any awards they have approved.

4. Administrative Requirements

a. CNO (DNS-35) shall:

(1) Maintain the Navy Department Awards Web Service (NDAWS), which is the Navy's authoritative electronic awards system. NDAWS consists of a public website, a Navy-wide awards processing application, control of personal and unit award forms, and the Navy's authoritative awards database.

(2) Monitor NDAWS for database accuracy and ensure corrections are made, as necessary.

(3) Conduct weekly data transfer to the Master Awards File at NPC for further transfer to Navy electronic service records.

b. For Navy personnel, NDAWS authorities shall:

(1) Provide PERS-312 a copy of the signed award citation, or certificate in the case of Navy and Marine Corps Commendation and Achievement Medals, for entry into the member's electronic service record. The member's Social Security Number (SSN) shall be neatly printed in the upper right hand corner of the citation/certificate and, due to the member's name and SSN appearing on the document, these citations/certificates shall be marked "Privacy Sensitive."

(2) Enter approved awards into NDAWS. Award entry procedures may be found at the Navy Awards website.

(3) Enter missing awards into NDAWS as requested.

c. For Navy personnel, the awarding authority shall:

(1) Advise the recommending command of the action taken either by copy of appropriate correspondence or separate letter.

(2) Maintain a <u>permanent</u> record of all awards processed, including the OPNAV 1650/3, a signed copy of the citation, supporting documents, and any related correspondence. Award files shall <u>not</u> be disposed of in accordance with the standards used for other types of correspondence and records.

(3) Follow the procedures located on the Navy Awards website under "Reference Items." Documents must be transmitted to the appropriate NDAWS Authority in the chain of command. A list of NDAWS Authorities is available on the Navy Awards website. Do <u>not</u> send approved awards to SECNAV or CNO Awards for data entry; they will be returned with no action taken.

(4) In the case of Marine Corps personnel assigned to Navy commands, forward a copy of the adjudicated (approved or disapproved) OPNAV 1650/3, Summary of Action, and signed citation to CMC (MMMA) for recording in APS and entry in the Marine's official military record.

(5) For awards considered but not recommended for approval, the recommendation must be forwarded via the remaining chain of command to the appropriate awarding authority.

d. For Marine Corps personnel, use of the electronic Awards Processing System (APS) satisfies the above requirements. MMMA shall provide the Personnel Management Support Branch (MMSB) a copy of the award recommendation and citation for entry into the Marine's Official Military Personnel File.

223. <u>TRANSMITTAL OF AWARDS</u>

1. <u>Active duty recipients</u>

a. For awardees still attached to the command that originated the award, send award elements to that command for presentation.

b. For awardees who have transferred to another duty

station, send award elements to the new duty station for presentation.

2. Retired, released, or discharged awardees

a. If the awardee resides in the area of the originating command, send award elements to the originating command for presentation.

b. If the awardee no longer resides in the area of the originating command:

(1) For Navy personnel, send the award elements to the awardee's home address.

(2) For Marine Corps personnel, forward personal awards, as appropriate, to either a unit of the Marine Corps operating forces or to an Inspector-Instructor Staff nearest the individual's home address to allow a presentation ceremony to be arranged.

3. Posthumous awards

a. The awarding authority shall send the medal, citation, and certificate to the originating command if the next of kin is residing in the area, or to the USN/USMC activity closest to the next of kin; see Article 224 below.

b. For posthumous combat awards for Navy personnel, the individual's chain of command shall contact CNO (DNS-35) to make arrangements regarding award level and processing procedures.

4. Undeliverable Awards. In cases when the awardee or next of kin cannot be located or refuses to accept the award, forward the entire case to CNO (DNS-35) or CMC (MMMA) for disposition.

224. PRESENTATION OF DECORATIONS

1. Medal of Honor. The President usually presents the Medal of Honor to living recipients at the White House. Posthumous awards are usually presented to the next of kin in Washington, DC, by the President or his personal representative.

2. Other Personal Decorations. Other United States military decorations will be presented with appropriate

formality. Ceremonies may range from formal reviews to small office ceremonies at which the citation is read and the decoration presented to the recipient. DON personal decorations shall be presented by a commissioned officer or appropriate DoD official. Non-military personnel, such as elected officials, may participate in award ceremonies; however, the actual award presentation shall be made by the military officer or DoD official. In the act of presentation, the decoration is attached over the left breast pocket of the uniform or to the left side of a civilian jacket.

3. <u>Posthumous Awards</u>. 10 U.S.C. §6250 provides that if individuals who distinguish themselves die before presentation of an award to which entitled, the award shall be processed and the medal, cross, bar, associated emblem, or insignia presented to the next of kin. Make every effort to present posthumous awards within 90 days after the individual is declared dead. Such awards shall be presented at an appropriate ceremony to the next of kin, if they desire. Whenever possible, awards to personnel killed in action should be presented at graveside. Decorations shall not be pinned on the clothing of any next of kin; rather, the decoration should be handed to the next of kin in an opened decoration container.

SECTION 3 - REQUIREMENTS

230. <u>SPECIFIC MILITARY DECORATIONS</u>. Listed below are military decorations authorized for award to Navy and Marine Corps personnel that can be recommended by Navy and Marine Corps commands. DoD awards for Navy and Marine Corps personnel assigned to certain Joint assignments are addressed in the DoD Awards Manual.

    1. <u>Medal of Honor</u>

        a. Authorization. 10 U.S.C. §6241.

        b. Eligibility Requirements

        (1) Awarded by the President, in the name of Congress, to members of the Naval service who conspicuously distinguish themselves by gallantry and intrepidity at the risk of their lives above and beyond the call of duty.

        (a) While engaged in an action against an enemy of the United States;

(b) While engaged in military operations involving conflict with an opposing foreign force; or

(c) While serving with friendly foreign forces engaged in an armed conflict against an opposing armed force in which the United States is not a belligerent party.

(2) There must be no margin of doubt or possibility of error in awarding this honor. To justify the decoration, the individual's service must clearly be rendered conspicuous above his or her comrades by an act so outstanding that it clearly distinguishes his or her gallantry beyond the call of duty from lesser forms of bravery; and it must be the type of deed which if not done would not subject the individual to any justified criticism. The deed must be without detriment to the mission of the command or to the command to which attached.

c. Special Benefits for Medal of Honor Recipients. See Article 214 above.

2. Navy Cross

a. Authorization. 10 U.S.C. §6242.

b. Eligibility Requirements

(1) Awarded to individuals who, while serving in any capacity with the Navy or Marine Corps, distinguish themselves by extraordinary heroism, not justifying the award of the Medal of Honor.

(a) While engaged in an action against an enemy of the United States;

(b) While engaged in military operations involving conflict with an opposing foreign force; or

(c) While serving with friendly foreign forces engaged in an armed conflict against an opposing armed force, in which the United States is not a belligerent party.

(2) To warrant this distinctive decoration, the act or execution of duty must be performed in the presence of great danger, or at great personal risk, and must be performed in such a manner as to set individuals apart from their shipmates or fellow Marines. An accumulation of minor acts of heroism normally does not justify the award. The high standards

demanded must be borne in mind when recommending the award.

3. Distinguished Service Medal

a. Authorization. 10 U.S.C. §6243.

b. Eligibility Requirements. Awarded to individuals who, while serving in any capacity with the Navy or Marine Corps, distinguish themselves by exceptionally meritorious service to the United States, in a duty of great responsibility. To justify this decoration, exceptional performance of duty, clearly above that normally expected, which has contributed materially to the success of a major command or project, is required. In general, the Distinguished Service Medal will be awarded only to those officers in principal commands at sea, or in the field, whose service is such as to justify the award. However, this shall not be interpreted to preclude the award of the Distinguished Service Medal to any individual whose service meets the requirements. If there is any doubt as to the degree of service involved, the Legion of Merit is the more appropriate award.

4. Silver Star Medal

a. Authorization. 10 U.S.C. §6244.

b. Eligibility Requirements

(1) Awarded to a person who, while serving in any capacity with the Navy or Marine Corps, is cited for gallantry in action that does not warrant a Medal of Honor or Navy Cross.

(a) While engaged in an action against an enemy of the United States;

(b) While engaged in military operations involving conflict with an opposing foreign force; or

(c) While serving with friendly foreign forces engaged in an armed conflict against an opposing armed force in which the United States is not a belligerent party.

(2) The heroic act(s) performed must render the individual conspicuous and well above the standard expected. An accumulation of minor acts of heroism normally does not justify the award, but unusual or exceptional cases will be decided on their merits.

5. Legion of Merit

    a. Authorization. 10 U.S.C. §1121.

    b. Eligibility Requirements. Awarded to members of the Armed Forces of the United States who distinguish themselves by exceptionally meritorious conduct in performing outstanding service. To justify this decoration, the service rendered must have been comparable to that required for the Distinguished Service Medal, but in a duty of lesser, though considerable, responsibility. In general, the Legion of Merit will be awarded to officers in lesser commands at sea, or principal commands on shore, who have performed such exceptionally meritorious service as to justify the award of the Distinguished Service Medal, except as to degree of merit. However, this should not be interpreted to preclude the award of the Legion of Merit to any individual, regardless of grade or rate, whose acts or services meet the requirements. When the degree of achievement or service rendered, although meritorious, is not sufficient to warrant the award of the Legion of Merit, the Bronze Star Medal or the Meritorious Service Medal should be considered.

    c. Combat Distinguishing Device. The Combat Distinguishing Device was authorized for service subsequent to 17 July 1967. It was discontinued in April 1974, but reauthorized effective 17 January 1991.

6. Distinguished Flying Cross

    a. Authorization. 10 U.S.C. §6245.

    b. Eligibility Requirements. Awarded to individuals who, while serving in any capacity with the Navy or the Marine Corps, distinguish themselves by heroism or extraordinary achievement while participating in an aerial flight. To justify this decoration for heroism, an act in the face of danger, well above those actions performed by others engaged in similar flight operations, is required; for achievement, the results accomplished must be so exceptional as to render them conspicuous among those accomplished by others involved in similar circumstances.

    (1) In adjudging the appropriate awards for the various members of a flight crew, it is considered that the pilot responsible for flying the aircraft is sometimes eligible for a higher award than other members of the flight crew.

However, in a two-seat aircraft where the pilot and crewmember constitute a team, and function as an integral part of the weapons system, both would generally be eligible for the same award. A crewmember other than the pilot should not be precluded from receiving a higher award if circumstances so indicate. Each case will be considered on its own merits.

(2) Establishing a new record in aerial flight does not necessarily qualify as an extraordinary achievement.

c. Combat Distinguishing Device. The Combat Distinguishing Device may be authorized for service after 4 April 1974.

7. Navy and Marine Corps Medal

a. Authorization. 10 U.S.C. §6246.

b. Eligibility Requirements

(1) Awarded to individuals who, while serving in any capacity with the U.S. Navy or the U.S. Marine Corps, distinguish themselves by heroism not involving actual conflict with the enemy. For acts of lifesaving, or attempted lifesaving, it is required that the action be performed at the risk of one's own life.

(2) Navy Reserve or Marine Corps Reserve personnel involved in lifesaving or attempted lifesaving incidents may be considered for recognition of any heroic act(s) performed regardless of whether or not the Reservist was in a duty status at the time of the act.

c. Although the Navy and Marine Corps Medal is often awarded for heroism involving lifesaving, it is not a lifesaving medal. As the senior peacetime award for heroism, this award hinges on the actual level of personal "life threatening" risk experienced by the awardee. For heroic performance to rise to this level, it must be clearly established that the act involved very specific life-threatening risk to the awardee. When there is none, or at best very limited life-threatening risk, the award of the Navy and Marine Corps Commendation Medal may be more appropriate. See Article 213 for details regarding the required eyewitness statements.

8. <u>Bronze Star Medal</u>

    a. Authorization. E.O. 9419 of 4 February 1944, as amended by E.O. 11046 of 24 August 1962 and 10 U.S.C. §1133.

    b. Eligibility Requirements

        (1) Awarded to individuals who, while serving in any capacity with the Armed Forces of the United States, distinguish themselves, on or after 7 December 1941, by heroic or meritorious achievement or service, not involving participation in aerial flight, under the following circumstances:

            (a) While engaged in an action against an enemy of the United States;

            (b) While engaged in military operations involving conflict with an opposing foreign force; or

            (c) While serving with friendly foreign forces engaged in an armed conflict against an opposing armed force in which the United States is not a belligerent party.

        (2) The Bronze Star Medal may only be awarded to members of the Armed Forces who are in receipt of Imminent Danger Pay at the time of the actions or service for which they are being recognized. To merit this award, the acts or services must be performed in a manner significantly above that normally expected, and sufficient to distinguish the individual above those performing similar acts or services. The award may be authorized as follows:

            (a) Heroic Achievement or Service. A single act of heroism worthy of special recognition, although not to the degree required for the Silver Star Medal, or several minor acts of heroism. An award for Heroic Service may cover an extended period of time; such award does not preclude receipt of an additional award for a specific act within that period, if warranted.

            (b) Meritorious Achievement or Service in Connection with Combat Operations. A single achievement or a period of service worthy of special recognition, although not to the degree required for the Legion of Merit. An award for Meritorious Service may cover an extended period of time; such award does not preclude receipt of an additional award for a specific act within that period, if warranted.

c. Combat Distinguishing Device. The Combat Distinguishing Device may be authorized for this award.

9. Purple Heart Medal

a. Authorization. E.O. 9277 of 3 December 1942, E.O. 10409 of 12 November 1952, E.O. 11016 of 25 April 1962 as amended by E.O. 12464 of 23 February 1984, 10 U.S.C. §1129, and Public Laws 98-525, 104-106, and 105-851.

b. Eligibility Requirements. Awarded to members of the Armed Forces of the United States who, while serving under competent authority in any capacity with an Armed Force of the United States after 5 April 1917, have been killed or wounded.

(1) In action against an enemy of the United States.

(2) In action with an opposing armed force of a foreign country, in which the Armed Forces of the United States are or have been engaged.

(3) While serving with friendly foreign forces engaged in an armed conflict against an opposing armed force, in which the United States is not a belligerent party.

(4) As the result of an act of any such enemy or opposing armed force.

(5) As the result of an act of any hostile foreign force.

(6) As the result of friendly weapons fire while actively engaging the enemy.

(7) As the indirect result of enemy action (e.g., injuries resulting from parachuting from a plane brought down by enemy or hostile fire.)

(8) As the result of maltreatment inflicted by their captors while a prisoner of war.

(9) After 28 March 1973, as a result of international terrorist attack against the U.S. or a foreign nation friendly to the U.S.

(10) After 28 March 1973, as a result of military operations while serving outside the territory of the United States, as part of a peacekeeping force.

c. An individual must have been wounded either as a direct or indirect result of enemy action. A "wound" is defined as an injury to any part of the body from an outside force or agent, sustained while in action as described in the eligibility requirements. A physical lesion is not required, provided the concussion or other form of injury received was a result of the action in which engaged.

d. Except in the case of a prisoner of war, the wound for which the award is made must have required treatment by a medical officer at the time of injury. Only one award is authorized for more than one wound or injury received at the same instant, from the same missile, force, explosion, or agent. Prisoners of war, if entitled, will be limited to a single Purple Heart covering the entire period of their captivity.

e. Chapter 8 contains information regarding eligibility determinations for prior service personnel.

10. Meritorious Service Medal

a. Authorization. E.O. 11448 of 16 January 1969, as amended by E.O. 12312 of 2 July 1981.

b. Eligibility Requirements. Awarded to members of the Armed Forces of the United States, or members of the armed forces of a friendly foreign nation, who distinguish themselves by outstanding meritorious achievement or service to the United States. To justify this decoration, the acts or services rendered by an individual, regardless of grade or rate, must have be comparable to that required for the Legion of Merit, but in a duty of lesser responsibility. The Meritorious Service Medal is the counterpart of the Bronze Star Medal for the recognition of meritorious non-combat service. When the degree of meritorious achievement or service rendered is not sufficient to warrant the award of the Meritorious Service Medal, the Navy Commendation Medal, when appropriate, should be considered.

11. Air Medal

a. Authorization. E.O. 9158 of 11 May 1942, as amended by E.O. 9242-A of 11 September 1942.

b. Eligibility Requirements. In adjudging the appropriate awards for the various members of a flight crew, the pilot responsible for flying the aircraft is sometimes eligible for a higher award than other members of the flight crew. However, in a two-seat aircraft where the pilot and crewmember constitute a team, and function as an integral part of the weapons system, both would generally be eligible for the same award. A crewmember other than the pilot should not be precluded from receiving a higher award if circumstances so indicate. Each case will be considered on its own merits. The Air Medal may be awarded in two categories:

(1) Individual Award. Awarded to individuals who, while serving in any capacity with the Armed Forces of the United States, distinguish themselves by heroic or meritorious achievement while participating in aerial flight, under flight orders. Gold Arabic numerals (5/16 inch) are worn to denote total number of Individual awards of the Air Medal. Numerals are positioned to the wearer's right on the ribbon bar and suspension ribbon. The Combat Distinguishing Device may be authorized for Individual Air Medals after 4 April 1974.

(2) Strike/Flight Award. Awarded to individuals who, while serving in any capacity with the Armed Forces of the United States, distinguish themselves by meritorious achievement while participating in sustained aerial flight operations, under flight orders. Bronze Arabic numerals (5/16 inch) are worn to denote the total number of Strike/Flight awards. Numerals are positioned to the wearer's left on the ribbon bar and suspension ribbon. Strike/Flight awards may only be approved within the parameters (area, dates, etc.) established by SECNAV; delegated authority of this award is specific in nature and always in writing.

(a) Definitions

1 Strike. Those sorties that deliver ordnance against the enemy, insert or extract assault personnel, or engage in Search and Rescue (SAR) operations that encounter enemy opposition.

2 Flight. Those sorties that deliver ordnance against the enemy, insert or extract assault personnel, or engage in SAR operations that encounter no enemy opposition.

3 Direct Combat Support Mission. Those

missions which may include reconnaissance, combat air patrol, electronic countermeasures (ECM) support, psychological warfare, patrol operations in support of coastal surveillance, etc., which do not necessarily involve delivery of ordnance against the enemy, inserting or extracting assault personnel, or engaging in SAR operations. However, direct combat support missions that encounter enemy opposition equivalent to that encountered by a strike, should be considered as a strike sortie. Examples are photo reconnaissance, combat air patrol, and electronic counter-measures aircraft that are endangered by anti-aircraft artillery (AAA) or surface to air missiles (SAMs). Administrative and logistical flights between established airbases or secure areas and/or ships are not considered to be direct combat support sorties.

4 Awarding authorities are authorized to deviate from the above criteria, when appropriate, with due regard to hazard and exposure incurred in sustained aerial flight operations.

(b) Periods for Award of Strike/Flight Air Medals. Appendix D to this chapter lists the areas in which Strike/Flight Air Medals may be authorized.

(c) Requirements. The award of the Air Medal on a Strike/Flight basis shall require 20 points.

1 10 strikes (1 strike = 2 points); or

2 20 flights (1 flight = 1 point); or

3 50 missions (1 mission = .4 points); or

4 250 flight hours in direct combat support missions that do not encounter enemy opposition (25 hours = 2 points); or

5 A combination of these, using the appropriate ratios, e.g.:

```
     3 strikes  =  6 points
     8 flights  =  8 points
   *10 missions =  4 points
    25 hours    =  2 points
                  20 total points = 1 S/F AM
```

*Note: Time flown on 'missions' are not counted as 'hours'.

(d) Special Provisions

<u>1</u> Only personnel participating in aerial flight, under competent flight orders, are eligible to receive the Strike/Flight award of the Air Medal. The Combat Distinguishing Device (Combat "V") may <u>not</u> be authorized for Strike/Flight Air Medals.

<u>2</u> Award of an Individual Air Medal, or other personal decoration for a particular sortie, does not preclude that sortie from counting toward eligibility for a Strike/Flight award of the Air Medal.

<u>3</u> Officers of the rank of captain/colonel or above shall not be eligible for the award of the Air Medal on a Strike/Flight basis, unless the sorties involved were actually required in the performance of their regular duties. Recommendations involving officers in this category, regardless of the current extent of delegated awarding authority, <u>shall be forwarded via the chain of command to SECNAV for approval</u>.

12. <u>Navy and Marine Corps Commendation Medal</u>

a. Authorization. ALNAV 11 of 11 January 1944 authorized the Navy Commendation Ribbon, and on 22 March 1950 SECNAV established the medal pendant for this award. On 21 September 1960, SECNAV changed the name of the award to the Navy Commendation Medal. On 19 August 1994, SECNAV changed the name of the award to the Navy and Marine Corps Commendation Medal.

b. Eligibility Requirements. Awarded to individuals (including foreign military personnel) who, while serving in any capacity with the U.S. Navy or Marine Corps, distinguish themselves on or after 7 December 1941, by heroic or meritorious achievement or service. To merit this award, the acts or services must be accomplished or performed in a manner above that normally expected, and sufficient to distinguish the individual above those performing similar services as set forth in the following:

(1) Heroic Achievement or Service. Act(s) of heroism worthy of special recognition, but not to the degree required for the Bronze Star Medal when combat is involved, or the Navy and Marine Corps Medal when combat is not involved.

(2) Meritorious Achievement or Service. A single achievement or a period of service worthy of special

recognition, but not to the degree required for the Bronze Star Medal or Air Medal when combat is involved, or the Meritorious Service Medal or Air Medal when combat is not involved.

(a) An award for meritorious service may cover an extended period of time; such award does not preclude an additional award for a specific act within that period, if warranted. The criteria, however, should not be the period of service involved, but rather the circumstances and conditions under which the service was performed.

(b) The performance should be well above that usually expected of an individual commensurate with his or her grade or rate, and above that degree of excellence that can be appropriately reflected in the individual's fitness report, performance evaluation, or personnel record.

c. Combat Distinguishing Device. The Combat Distinguishing Device may be authorized for this award.

13. Navy and Marine Corps Achievement Medal

a. Authorization. SECNAVINST 1650.16 of 1 May 1961, re-designated by SECNAVNOTE of 17 July 1967. On 19 August 1994, SECNAV changed the name of the award to the Navy and Marine Corps Achievement Medal.

b. Eligibility Requirements. Awarded to members of the Armed Forces of the grade of lieutenant commander or major and junior thereto, for service performed on or after 1 May 1961. The award may be authorized for meritorious service or achievement in a combat or non-combat situation, based on sustained performance or specific achievement of a superlative nature, and shall be of such merit as to warrant more tangible recognition than is possible by a fitness report or performance evaluation, but which does not warrant a Navy and Marine Corps Commendation Medal.

(1) Professional achievement that merits the award must:

(a) Clearly exceed that which is normally required or expected, considering the individual's grade or rate, training, and experience; and,

(b) Be an important contribution of benefit to the United States and the Naval Service.

(2) Leadership achievement that merits the award
must:

(a) Be noteworthy;

(b) Be sustained so as to demonstrate a high
state of development or, if for a specific achievement, be of
such merit as to earn singular recognition for the act(s); and,

(c) Reflect most creditably on the efforts of
the individual toward the accomplishment of the unit mission.

c. Limitations. The Navy and Marine Corps
Achievement Medal will not be awarded for service involving
participation in aerial flight after 1 January 1969. The Air
Medal is the more appropriate recognition for meritorious
achievement while participating in aerial flight. This does not
preclude award of the Navy and Marine Corps Achievement Medal to
individuals who meet the eligibility requirements for service
during which participation in aerial flight was incidental.

d. Combat Distinguishing Device. The Combat
Distinguishing Device was authorized for service subsequent to
17 July 1967, and discontinued in April 1974; it was
reauthorized on 17 January 1991.

14. Combat Action Ribbon

a. Authorization. SECNAVNOTE 1650 of 17 February
1969.

b. Eligibility Requirements

(1) Awarded to members of the Navy, Marine Corps,
and Coast Guard (when the Coast Guard, or units thereof, operate
under the control of the Navy) in the grade of captain/colonel
and junior thereto, who have actively participated in ground or
surface combat.

(2) The principal eligibility criterion is,
regardless of military occupational specialty or rating, the
individual must have rendered satisfactory performance under
enemy fire while actively participating in a ground or surface
engagement. Neither service in a combat area nor being awarded
the Purple Heart Medal automatically makes a service member
eligible for the Combat Action Ribbon (CR). The following
amplifying guidance is provided:

(a) Direct exposure to the detonation of an Improvised Explosive Device (IED) used by an enemy, with or without the immediate presence of enemy forces, constitutes active participation in a ground or surface engagement. Eligibility under this criterion is retroactive to 7 October 2001.

(b) Personnel who serve in clandestine or special operations, who by the nature of their mission, are restricted in their ability to return fire, and who are operating in conditions where the risk of enemy fire was great and expected to be encountered, may be eligible for the CR.

(c) The CR will not be awarded to personnel for aerial combat, since the Strike/Flight Air Medal provides recognition for aerial combat exposure; however, a pilot or crewmember forced to escape or evade, after being forced down, may be eligible for the award.

(d) Current DON personnel who were formerly in the U.S. Army and earned the Combat Infantryman Badge or Combat Medical Badge, upon submission of official military documentation to their commanding officer, may be authorized to wear the CR.

(e) Under Public Law 106-65, the CR may be awarded retroactively to 7 December 1941. See Chapter 8 for information regarding retroactive eligibility determinations.

c. Eligible Operations. SECNAV, or his designee, determines which operations meet the criteria for this award. Appendix E to this chapter lists the operations for which award of the CR has been authorized. An individual, whose eligibility has been established in combat in any of the operations listed in Appendix E, may be awarded the CR. Only one award per operation is authorized. The listing is not all inclusive, as the CR has been awarded in minor operations, as well as for specific actions. Chapter 8 contains information regarding requests for eligibility determinations for personnel no longer on active duty.

USN ELECTRONIC AWARD SUBMISSION PROCEDURES

1. All Navy organizations, including those that report directly to the Secretary of the Navy (SECNAV), shall submit both personal and unit award recommendations electronically. Submission requirements are highlighted in this appendix; however, the Navy Awards Website, https://awards.navy.mil, should be reviewed for full details. The following documents must be included in all submissions:

    a. An Electronic Award Recommendation Form, OPNAV 1650/3 for personal awards or OPNAV 1650/14 for unit awards. The forms are available at https://awards.navy.mil or on CD/ROM from the Navy Publications Center. Both forms contain data fields which are directly imported into the Navy Department Awards Web Service (NDAWS) database and, therefore, must be downloaded according to website directions to maintain formatting. The forms include the Summary of Action. Block-by-block instructions for completing the forms are available on the Navy Awards Website through the "Reference Items" link.

    b. Proposed citation in Microsoft Word format.

    c. Scanned 1650/3 or 1650/14 cover page, showing hand-written signatures; PDF format is recommended. The originator's, endorsers', and approval authority's original hand-written signatures shall be obtained and retained on file.

    d. Other supporting documentation, as required.

2. The Summary of Action is part of the electronic form and shall be completed for all award recommendations, except Navy command-approved Navy and Marine Corps Achievement Medals.

3. Endorsements on award recommendations shall be made as required by the chain of command. Endorsers shall make their recommendations on the paper form using the appropriate two-letter code for the level of award, check the appropriate boxes, sign, and date the form.

4. Once an originator or endorser has hand-signed the paper form, an electronic signature shall be recorded on the electronic form. An electronic signature consists of typing the individual's signature in the appropriate block on the form, as they sign their name, preceded by "/s/"; for example, /s/ J. R. DOE. The date of the signature shall be recorded in the

appropriate block, per the electronic award submission guidelines on the website.

5.   In cases when multiple awards are emailed, each award package shall be transmitted in a separate email.

6.   Email procedures for Navy award recommendations requiring CNO endorsement or adjudication, or final adjudication by SECNAV, are available at https://awards.navy.mil. Only CNO and SECNAV level awards shall be emailed as described on the Navy Awards Website.

7.   All Navy award recommendations shall be uploaded into NDAWS by the appropriate NDAWS Authority, as listed on the Navy Awards Website under the "NDAWS Authorities" link. Awards approved at any level below the CNO shall not be sent to SECNAV (NDBDM) or CNO Awards for data or service record entry, but rather to the appropriate NDAWS Authority.

PERSONAL AWARD RECOMMENDATION
FOR OFFICIAL USE ONLY

ENSURE ALL BLOCKS ARE FILLED IN, SIGNED AND DATED.
COMPLETE MAILING ADDRESSES ARE REQUIRED

1. FROM: ADDRESS:		1a. UIC / RUC	2. TO (Awarding Authority) : ADDRESS:	2a. UIC / RUC

3. COMMAND POC: NAME: EMAIL:	4. PHONE: (DSN): (COM):	5. EXP DATE OF ACTIVE DUTY (DD-MMM-YYYY):
		5.a. IF RETIREMENT/SEPARATION, NUMBER OF YEARS:

6. SSN	7. DESIG/NEC/MOS	8. DETACHMENT OR CEREMONY DATE (EARLIER DATE):

9. NAME (LAST, FIRST, MIDDLE, SUFFIX)	10. ☐ RETIREMENT ☐ TRANSFER ☐ SEPARATION ☐ SPECIFIC ACHIEVEMENT

11. COMPONENT	12. NEW DUTY STATION ADDRESS (Home address for retirement/separation)
13. PAYGRADE AND RATING	

14. WARFARE QUALIFICATION	15. UNIT AT TIME OF ACTION/SERVICE	16. DUTY ASSIGNMENT

17. UIC/RUC	18. CAMPAIGN	18a. OPERATION :	19. PREVIOUS PERSONAL DECORATIONS AND PERIOD RECOGNIZED (exclude Combat Action Ribbon)

20. RECOMMENDED AWARD

21. ☐ HEROIC ☐ MERI-TORIOUS ☐ HEROIC POSTHUMOUS ☐ MERITORIOUS POSTHUMOUS ☐ MIA	22. PERSONAL AWARDS RECOMMENDED-NOT YET APPROVED

23. RECOMMENDED AWARD NUMBER (EX: 1,2,3 ...)	24. OTHER PERSONNEL BEING RECOMMENDED FOR SAME ACTION:

25. ACTION DATE/MERITORIOUS PERIOD -	26. (FOR O-6 AND ABOVE) RANK AND NAME OF PREDECESSOR:

27. GEOGRAPHIC AREA OF ACTION/SERVICE	28. IF FOREIGN NATIONAL, INDICATE FOREIGN SERVICE AND COUNTRY:

29. I CERTIFY THAT THE FACTS CONTAINED IN THE SUMMARY OF ACTION ARE ☐ KNOWN TO ME ☐ A MATTER OF RECORD

30a. NAME, RANK/GRADE, COMPONENT, TITLE OF ORIGINATOR	30b. SIGNATURE	30c. DATE

31. FORWARDING ENDORSEMENTS BY VIA ADDRESSEE(S)

VIA	COMMAND (To be completed by originator) (Include Telephone Number)	RECOMMENDED AWARD	COMBAT "V"	SIGNATURE, GRADE	DATE FWD
1			☐ YES ☐ NO		
2			☐ YES ☐ NO		
3			☐ YES ☐ NO		

32. TO BE COMPLETED BY AWARDING AUTHORITY

DISPOSITION OF BASIC RECOMMENDATION	COMBAT "V"	EXTRAORDINARY HEROISM RECOMMENDED	SIGNATURE, GRADE, TITLE	DATE APPROVED
	☐ YES ☐ NO	☐ YES ☐ NO		

33. CNO / CMC AWARDS BRANCH USE ONLY SERIAL NO: DATE RECEIVED:

34. NDBDM USE ONLY FROM: SECNAV (NDBDM)   DATE: TO: CNO (DNS-37/N09B13)   CMC (CODE MMMA) 1. Extraordinary heroism recommended: ☐ YES ☐ NO ☐ NOT APPLICABLE 2. Reviewed and recorded.

_____
By direction

INSTRUCTIONS

1. Before completing this form see SECNAVINST 1650.1. For the electronic form, help for each Block can be accessed by placing the cursor over the data entry field and pressing the F1 key.
2. The Summary of Action (item 35) is requested (except for Command approved NAMs). In addition, attach a double spaced proposed citation
3. Two (2) letter codes to be used in Blocks 19, 20, 31 and 32
4. All dates should be entered in the DD-3-letter month ID-YYYY format (EX: 23-FEB-2004)

MH	Medal of Honor	NM	Navy and Marine Corps Medal	JC	Joint Service Commendation Medal
NX	Navy Cross	BS	Bronze Star Medal	NC	Navy & Marine Corps Commendation Medal
DM	Distinguished Service Medal	BV	Bronze Star w/ V Medal	CV w/ V	Navy & Marine Corps Commendation Medal
SS	Silver Star	PH	Purple Heart Medal	JA	Joint Service Achievement Medal
LM	Legion of Merit	MM	Meritorious Service Medal	NA	Navy & Marine Corps Achievement Medal
LV	Legion of Merit w/ V	AS	Air Medal (Strike/Flight)	NV w/ V	Navy & Marine Corps Achievement Medal
DX	Distinguished Flying Cross	AF	Air Medal (Individual Action)	CR	Combat Action Ribbon
DV	Distinguished Flying Cross w/ V	AH	Air Medal (Individual Action w/ V)	XX	Letter of Commendation

35. Summary of Action *(not required for Command approved NAMs)*

The President of the United States in the name of The Congress takes pride in presenting the MEDAL OF HONOR posthumously to

SERGEANT
JOHN D. DOE
UNITED STATES MARINE CORPS

for service as set forth in the following

CITATION:

For conspicuous gallantry and intrepidity at the risk of his life above and beyond the call of duty while serving as a machine gunner with Company F, First Battalion, Seventh Marines on 17 March 1967. During a reconnaissance operation, Sergeant Doe's squad was suddenly hit by enemy sniper fire. The squad immediately deployed to a combat formation and advanced to a strongly fortified enemy position, when it was again struck by small arms and automatic weapons fire, sustaining numerous casualties. Although wounded, Sergeant Doe boldly remained in the open, delivering a devastating volume of accurate fire on the numerically superior force. The enemy was intent upon annihilating the small Marine force and directed the preponderance of their fire on his position. He was again wounded, this time in the right hand, which prevented him from operating his vitally needed machine gun. Suddenly and without warning, an enemy grenade landed in the midst of the few surviving Marines. Unhesitantly and with complete disregard for his personal safety, Sergeant Doe threw himself upon the grenade, absorbing with his body the full force of the explosion. In a final act of bravery, he crawled to the side of a wounded comrade and administered first aid before succumbing to his grievous wounds. By his undaunted courage, intrepid fighting spirit, and unwavering devotion to duty in the face of certain death, Sergeant Doe saved his comrades from further injury or possible death, thereby reflecting great credit upon himself and upholding the highest traditions of the Marine Corps and the United States Naval Service. He gallantly gave his life for another.

President of the United States

Appendix B to
Chapter 2

The President of the United States takes pleasure in presenting the NAVY CROSS to

SERGEANT
JOHN L. DOE
UNITED STATES MARINE CORPS

for service as set forth in the following

CITATION:

For extraordinary heroism while serving as Fire Team Leader, 2nd Platoon, Bravo Company, 3d Battalion, 1st Marine Regiment, Regimental Combat Team 1, 1st Marine Division, U.S. Marine Corps Forces, Central Command, in support of Operation IRAQI FREEDOM on 10 June 2004. While conducting security patrols, Sergeant Doe's platoon secured two buildings from which to observe enemy movement. Suddenly, a numerically superior enemy force attacked the platoon with rocket-propelled grenades and machinegun fire from three directions. Almost immediately, the enemy closed to within 30 meters of the platoon, wounding many Marines on the rooftop position. After ensuring wounded platoon members received medical treatment, Sergeant Doe rushed to reinforce the critical rooftop position. After enemy fire wounded one of his comrades, he courageously exposed himself to enemy fire to move the Marine to safety and was himself wounded in the arm, face and leg. Despite his injuries, he again exposed himself to enemy fire and continued to attack the enemy with grenades and by firing his rifle with his uninjured arm. Sergeant Doe halted the determined enemy assault and enabled the evacuation of wounded Marines. By his decisive actions, bold initiative, and complete dedication to duty, Sergeant Doe reflected great credit upon himself and upheld the highest traditions of the Marine Corps and the United States Naval Service.

For the President,

Secretary of the Navy

The President of the United States takes pleasure in presenting the DISTINGUISHED SERVICE MEDAL to

REAR ADMIRAL JOHN L. DOE
UNITED STATES NAVY

for service as set forth in the following

CITATION:

For exceptionally meritorious service to the Government of the United States in a duty of great responsibility while serving as Chief of Legislative Affairs from May 2003 through March 2006. Rear Admiral Doe produced unprecedented levels of success with the Navy's legislative agenda through his extraordinary foresight and keen understanding of military issues and the legislative process. He carefully forged strong personal bonds with Members of Congress and key staff members that translated into support for Navy's most critical personnel and programmatic priorities. Rear Admiral Doe provided outstanding counsel to the Secretary of the Navy and the Chief of Naval Operations for initiatives that significantly enhanced the readiness and capabilities of the Department of the Navy's current and future forces. Rear Admiral Doe's unparalleled leadership and strong vision ensured the Navy's legislative strategy remained on course. Through his decisive action, he ensured favorable Congressional consideration across the entire spectrum of Navy programs, including numerous high profile issues. By his superior leadership, wise judgment, and deep devotion to duty, Rear Admiral Doe reflected great credit upon himself and upheld the highest traditions of the United States Naval Service.

For the President,

Secretary of the Navy

The President of the United States takes pride in presenting the SILVER STAR MEDAL posthumously to

LANCE CORPORAL
JOHN L. DOE
UNITED STATES MARINE CORPS

for service as set forth in the following

CITATION:

For conspicuous gallantry and intrepidity in action against the enemy as Machine Gun Team Leader, Company B, 3d Battalion, 1st Marines, Regimental Combat Team-1, 1st Marine Division, I Marine Expeditionary Force, U.S. Marine Forces Central Command in support of Operation IRAQI FREEDOM on 13 June 2004. Attacking from different directions, a numerically superior enemy force engaged Lance Corporal Doe's platoon, firing dozens of rocket-propelled grenades, thousands of machinegun rounds, and assaulting near his position. During the initial attack, several of his fellow Marines were wounded. After ensuring his wounded platoon members received medical treatment, Lance Corporal Doe rallied the few remaining members of the platoon, and rushed to the critical defensive position. Braving withering enemy machine gun and rocket-propelled grenade fire, he reached the position and prepared to throw a hand grenade. As he moved into a position from which to throw his grenade, enemy fire struck Lance Corporal Doe multiple times. Undaunted by his significant injuries, Lance Corporal Doe heroically threw his grenade, which halted the determined attack. Mortally wounded, Lance Corporal Doe continued to fire his weapon until he succumbed to his injuries. By his bold initiative, undaunted courage, and complete dedication to duty, Lance Corporal Doe reflected great credit upon himself and upheld the highest traditions of the Marine Corps and the United States Naval Service.

For the President,

Secretary of the Navy

The President of the United States takes pleasure in presenting the LEGION OF MERIT (Gold Star in lieu of the Third Award) to

CAPTAIN JOHN V. DOE III
UNITED STATES NAVY

for service as set forth in the following

CITATION:

For exceptionally meritorious conduct in the performance of outstanding service as Chief, Space and Global Strike Operations Division, United States Strategic Command from April 2004 to May 2006. Captain Doe's extraordinary leadership was instrumental in achieving quantum improvements to the Command. As a true visionary, he reorganized his division to closely align it with the Command's new structure. Under Captain Doe's direction, his division devised and implemented non-nuclear Global Strike Command and Control procedures that integrated conventional munitions, space control, information operations, and nuclear operations. Captain Doe directed teams of Mission Area Experts and provided Time Sensitive Planning and Crisis Action Planning for real world and exercise Global Strike support to various geographic combatant commands. Standing on the frontline of our Nation's strategic nuclear deterrence, he was prepared to advise the President of immediate strategic response options in the event of a ballistic missile, space, computer network, or nuclear attack. Captain Doe's superior performance of duties highlights the culmination of 24 years of honorable and dedicated service. By his dynamic direction, keen judgment, and loyal devotion to duty, Captain Doe reflected great credit upon himself and upheld the highest traditions of the United States Naval Service.

For the President,

Secretary of the Navy

2-43

The President of the United States takes pleasure in presenting the
DISTINGUISHED FLYING CROSS to

CAPTAIN JOHN P. DOE
UNITED STATES MARINE CORPS

for service as set forth in the following

CITATION:

For heroism while participating in aerial flight as the
Pilot of an AH-1W aircraft attached to Marine Light Attack
Helicopter Squadron 951, Marine Aircraft Group 75, 3d Marine
Aircraft Wing, I Marine Expeditionary Force in support of
Operation IRAQI FREEDOM on 23 March 2003. Captain Doe performed
courageously while providing close air support to Marines during
an attack in Iraq. Having operated continuously for fifteen hours,
Captain Doe continued to expertly employ his aircraft to maximize
its firepower. Responding to calls from a ground forward air
controller, he provided screening fire in support of Marine tanks
that were moving to rescue Soldiers who had been ambushed. Captain
Doe's accurate, lethal fires destroyed troops, trucks, and heavy
weapons that were engaging Marines and hindering the rescue effort
of the isolated Army unit. His efforts saved the lives of numerous
Army Soldiers and protected the Marines of the rescue force.
Continuing to fly a battle damaged aircraft, he was able to engage
and destroy an enemy tank platoon. By his superb airmanship,
inspiring courage, and loyal devotion to duty in the face of
hazardous flying conditions, Captain Doe reflected great credit
upon himself and upheld the highest traditions of the Marine Corps
and the United States Naval Service.

The Combat Distinguishing Device is authorized.

For the President,

Secretary of the Navy

2-44

The President of the United States takes pleasure in presenting the DISTINGUISHED FLYING CROSS to

LIEUTENANT COMMANDER JOHN C. DOE JR.
UNITED STATES NAVY

for service as set forth in the following

CITATION:

For extraordinary achievement while participating in aerial flight as the Pilot of an F/A-18 Aircraft in Fighter Attack Squadron 999 embarked in USS NEVERSAIL (CVN 90) on 13 November 2007. During the early afternoon hours, Lieutenant Commander Doe launched in Aircraft 205 for a post-maintenance check flight in the Central Arabian Gulf. At 25,000 feet and .8 mach, the radome of the aircraft separated, destroying the windscreen and canopy of the aircraft, breaking his left collarbone and blinding his left eye. Despite excruciating pain, near blindness, and virtually no use of his left arm, compounded with a total loss of verbal communication with the ship, he was able to capably regain control of the aircraft. Through exceptional presence of mind, courageous airmanship, and superior fortitude, Lieutenant Commander Doe successfully landed on board the ship. By his steadfast efforts, superb airmanship, and unexcelled dedication to duty in the face of hazardous flying conditions, Lieutenant Commander Doe reflected great credit upon himself and upheld the highest traditions of the United States Naval Service.

For the President,

Secretary of the Navy

The President of the United States takes pleasure in presenting the NAVY AND MARINE CORPS MEDAL to

MACHINIST'S MATE SECOND CLASS
JANE L. DOE
UNITED STATES NAVY

for service as set forth in the following

CITATION:

For heroism while serving at the Naval Diving and Salvage Training Center, Panama City, Florida on 7 January 2007. During an evolution to recharge oxygen from a delivery truck to the command's storage tanks, the oxygen charging lead ruptured with a loud blast, and an oxygen fire ensued. Of the six personnel present, only Petty Officer Doe had the presence of mind to secure the delivery truck's main oxygen supply valve, despite being burned and hit at least twice by the whipping charging lead. She did not leave the charging station until the valve was closed and the situation safe. Petty Officer Doe single-handedly prevented an explosion with grave potential for destruction and loss of life. By her courageous and prompt actions in the face of great personal risk, Petty Officer Doe prevented the loss of life, thereby reflecting great credit upon herself and upholding the highest traditions of the United States Naval Service.

For the President,

Secretary of the Navy

The President of the United States takes pleasure in presenting the BRONZE STAR MEDAL to

STAFF SERGEANT
JOHN S. DOE
UNITED STATES MARINE CORPS

for service as set forth in the following

CITATION:

For heroic achievement in connection with combat operations against the enemy as Team Leader, Company B, 3d Battalion, 3d Marines, in connection with operations against enemy forces in Afghanistan, in support of Operation ENDURING FREEDOM on 29 June 2006. While returning from a patrol, Staff Sergeant Doe's team came under heavy fire from a numerically superior enemy. Outnumbered and separated from friendly forces, Staff Sergeant Doe returned a heavy volume of accurate, direct fire, and coordinated indirect fire in response to the enemy's ambush, allowing the wounded to seek cover. Ignoring the rounds impacting around him, he retrieved vital first aid supplies from the ambush site in order to administer first aid to the wounded. His heroic actions and outstanding leadership were inspirational to his team, and undoubtedly saved the lives of his team members. By his extraordinary guidance, zealous initiative, and total dedication to duty, Staff Sergeant Doe reflected great credit upon himself and upheld the highest traditions of the Marine Corps and the United States Naval Service.

The Combat Distinguishing Device is authorized.

For the President,

Secretary of the Navy

The President of the United States takes pleasure in presenting the BRONZE STAR MEDAL (Gold Star in lieu of the Second Award) to

COMMAND MASTER CHIEF
JOHN R. DOE
UNITED STATES NAVY

for service as set forth in the following

CITATION:

For meritorious service in connection with combat operations against the enemy while serving as Command Master Chief, 1st Marine Division, I Marine Expeditionary Force in support of Operation IRAQI FREEDOM from March 2004 to March 2005. Master Chief Petty Officer Doe led Sailors of the Division during 12 months of combat operations. As the senior naval enlisted advisor, he provided the Commanding General sound advice on all Navy enlisted issues. Master Chief Petty Officer Doe's attention to his Sailors' career development and his mentoring resulted in an unprecedented reenlistment rate. To monitor and mentor the Sailors, he made dozens of site visits by air or ground convoy to every forward operating base and nearly all outposts in the area of operation. During two enlistment cycles, every eligible Sailor participated in advancement exams, and one in three Sailors in the Division was promoted. Master Chief Petty Officer Doe conducted hundreds of Fleet Marine Force (FMF) qualification boards, and more than 250 Sailors were qualified to wear FMF pins. His selfless dedication to the Sailors assured a well-trained and mentally prepared cadre of Sailors to accompany the warfighters into the fight. Master Chief Petty Officer Doe's distinctive contributions, unrelenting perseverance, and steadfast devotion to duty reflected great credit upon him and were in keeping with the highest traditions of the United States Naval Service.

For the President,

Secretary of the Navy

2-48

The President of the United States takes pleasure in presenting the MERITORIOUS SERVICE MEDAL (Gold Star in lieu of the Second Award) to

COMMANDER JANE L. DOE
UNITED STATES NAVY

for service as set forth in the following

CITATION:

For outstanding meritorious service or achievement while serving as Congressional Liaison for Intelligence, Office of Legislative Affairs from January 2003 to August 2006. Commander Doe consistently performed her demanding duties in a highly professional manner. She distinguished herself as a highly respected and effective liaison officer through her keen understanding of Navy intelligence systems and programs. Commander Doe's professional acumen and ability to communicate effectively across widely varying communities and committees helped secure Congressional approval for key Navy initiatives across the broad spectrum of General Defense Intelligence, Joint Military Intelligence and Tactical Intelligence and Related Activity Programs. Her interface with Members of Congress and their staffs was critical in informing them on a range of issues, including the Navy's involvement in the Global War on Terrorism, the impact of Intelligence Community Reform legislation, and key Intelligence, Surveillance and Reconnaissance initiatives. Commander Doe's exceptional professionalism, personal initiative, and loyal devotion to duty reflected great credit upon her and were in keeping with the highest traditions of the United States Naval Service.

For the President,

Secretary of the Navy

The President of the United States takes pleasure in presenting the AIR MEDAL (with Bronze Star for the First Award) to

LIEUTENANT JOHN B. DOE
UNITED STATES NAVY

for service as set forth in the following

CITATION:

  For heroic achievement while participating in aerial flight as a Radar Intercept Officer of an F-14A aircraft assigned to Fighter Squadron NINE FOUR FIVE, Detachment BRAVO deployed with Commander, United States FIFTH Fleet in support of Operation IRAQI FREEDOM on 10 June 2004. Lieutenant Doe launched as the Strike Coordination and Reconnaissance Mission Commander supporting an airborne assault on a suspected Weapons of Mass Destruction facility located north of Baghdad, Iraq. While ensuring the infiltration routes were clear, he expertly assessed the conditions for the assault. Despite anti-aircraft artillery fire in the area, Lieutenant Doe relentlessly attacked and suppressed several enemy artillery threats directly engaging the assault force. Through aggressive spirit and determination to shape the battlefield, he directly contributed to the success of the high-risk strategic mission with zero friendly losses. By his skillful airmanship, steadfast aggressiveness, and exemplary devotion to duty in the face of hazardous flying conditions, Lieutenant Doe reflected great credit upon himself and upheld the highest traditions of the United States Naval Service.

The Combat Distinguishing Device is authorized.

For the President,

Secretary of the Navy

2-50

The President of the United States takes pleasure in presenting the AIR MEDAL (First through Third Strike/Flight Awards) to

LIEUTENANT COMMANDER JOHN R. DOE
UNITED STATES NAVY

for service as set forth in the following

CITATION:

For meritorious achievement while participating in aerial flight as a Pilot of an F/A-18C aircraft, Marine Fighter Attack Squadron 725, U.S. Marine Corps Forces, Central Command, Kuwait during combat missions in support of Operation SOUTHERN WATCH and Operation IRAQI FREEDOM from 10 June 1994 to 23 April 2006. Commander Doe flew with his squadron in the successful enforcement of the Iraqi Southern No-Fly Zone and in direct support of combat missions. His leadership and efforts resulted in the destruction of enemy targets, successful suppression and destruction of Iraqi integrated air defenses, and disruption of communications and command nodes without the loss of coalition aircraft. By his superior airmanship, perseverance, and loyal devotion to duty in the face of hazardous flying conditions, Lieutenant Commander Doe reflected great credit upon himself and upheld the highest traditions of the United States Naval Service.

The Numeral "3" to represent Three Strike/Flight Awards is authorized.

For the President,

Secretary of the Navy

SECNAVINST 1650.1H
AUG 2 2 2006

DEPARTMENT OF THE NAVY

THIS IS TO CERTIFY THAT
THE SECRETARY OF THE NAVY HAS AWARDED THE

NAVY AND MARINE CORPS COMMENDATION MEDAL
(GOLD STAR IN LIEU OF THE SECOND AWARD WITH COMBAT "V")

TO

HOSPITAL CORPSMAN THIRD CLASS JOHN D. DOE, UNITED STATES NAVY

FOR

HEROIC ACHIEVEMENT WHILE SERVING AS A CORPSMAN FOR 2D SQUAD, WEAPONS PLATOON, COMPANY B, 4TH BATTALION, 99TH MARINES, 1ST MARINE DIVISION, I MARINE EXPEDITIONARY FORCE, U.S. MARINE CORPS FORCES, CENTRAL IN SUPPORT OF OPERATION IRAQI FREEDOM ON 14 FEBRUARY 2005. WHILE ON PATROL, PETTY OFFICER DOE LEARNED AN IRAQI CIVILIAN HAD BEEN SHOT AND LEFT IN A CAR RIGGED WITH AN IMPROVISED EXPLOSIVE DEVICE (IED). DISREGARDING HIS OWN SAFETY, HE RAN TO THE CAR AND EXTRACTED THE CIVILIAN. SUDDENLY, THE IED DETONATED, WOUNDING PETTY OFFICER DOE. UNDAUNTED, HE CONTINUED TO SAFETY, SAVING THE CIVILIAN'S LIFE. BY HIS UNSWERVING DETERMINATION, WISE JUDGMENT, AND COMPLETE DEDICATION TO DUTY, PETTY OFFICER DOE REFLECTED CREDIT UPON HIMSELF AND UPHELD THE HIGHEST TRADITIONS OF THE UNITED STATES NAVAL SERVICE.

2-52

Appendix B to
Chapter 2

SECNAVINST 1650.1H
AUG 22 2005

DEPARTMENT OF THE NAVY

THIS IS TO CERTIFY THAT
THE SECRETARY OF THE NAVY HAS AWARDED THE

NAVY AND MARINE CORPS ACHIEVEMENT MEDAL
(SILVER STAR IN LIEU OF THE SIXTH AWARD)
TO

CHIEF YEOMAN (SURFACE WARFARE) JOHN L. DOE, UNITED STATES NAVY

FOR

PROFESSIONAL ACHIEVEMENT AS RECORDER FOR THE PHYSICAL EVALUATION BOARD, SECRETARY OF THE NAVY COUNCIL OF REVIEW BOARDS FROM MAY 2005 TO AUGUST 2007. CHIEF PETTY OFFICER DOE'S INSPIRING LEADERSHIP AND PERSONAL INITIATIVE WERE INSTRUMENTAL IN THE EFFICIENT AND TIMELY PROCESSING OF MORE THAN 50,000 NAVY AND MARINE CORPS ACTIVE DUTY AND RESERVE DISABILITY CASES, AND COMBAT RELATED SPECIAL COMPENSATION (CRSC) CASES. HE CONTINUALLY EDUCATED PERSONNEL ON THE INTRICACIES OF THE CRSC SYSTEM. CHIEF PETTY OFFICER DOE'S EXCEPTIONAL PROFESSIONALISM, UNRELENTING PERSEVERANCE, AND LOYAL DEVOTION TO DUTY REFLECTED CREDIT UPON HIM AND WERE IN KEEPING WITH THE HIGHEST TRADITIONS OF THE UNITED STATES NAVAL SERVICE.

Appendix B to
Chapter 2

PROCUREMENT INFORMATION

FORMS AND BINDERS

1. The following forms are available in the Navy Supply System and may be requisitioned per CD ROM NAVSUP P600 (NLL):

    a. OPNAV 1650/3 (7-04), Personal Award Recommendation, S/N 0107-LF-128-0900

    b. OPNAV 1650/14, Unit Award Recommendation, S/N 0107-LF-127-1300

    c. OPNAV 1650/6 (2-96), Naval Reserve Meritorious Service Medal Certificate, S/N 0107-LF-020-3100

    d. NAVSO 1650/11 (7-99), Navy and Marine Corps Commendation Medal Certificate, S/N 0104-LF-982-1800 (for issue only by those commanders with authority to award the medal)

    e. NAVSO 1650/12 (7-99), Navy and Marine Corps Achievement Medal Certificate, S/N 0104-LF-982-3000 (for issue only by those commanders with authority to award the medal)

    f. NAVPERS 1650/1 (6-81), Navy Good Conduct Medal Certificate, S/N 0106-LF-016-5006

    g. NAVMC 11416, Marine Corps Good Conduct Medal Certificate, S/N 0109-LF-982-5000

2. The following forms are authorized for purchase by the appropriate delegated awarding authorities:

    a. NAVSO 1650/9 (7-99), Air Medal Certificate (Individual), S/N 0104-LF-982-0600

    b. OPNAV 1650/130 (12-99), Meritorious Service Medal Certificate, S/N 0107-LF-986-7400

3. The following binders may be requisitioned through the General Services Administration using the GSA Catalog:

    a. Navy Certificate Binders (Blue), S/N 7510-00-482-2994

    b. Marine Corps Certificate Binders (Red), S/N 7510-01-056-1927

STOCK NUMBERS FOR MEDALS, RIBBON BARS, AND DEVICES

MEDAL	FSN
Medal of Honor	Only CNO/CMC may order
Navy Cross	8455-00-680-0705
Distinguished Service Medal	8455-00-680-0703
Silver Star Medal	8455-00-269-5758
Legion of Merit	8455-00-262-3469
Distinguished Flying Cross	8455-00-269-5748
Navy and Marine Corps Medal	8455-00-817-0305
Bronze Star Medal	8455-00-269-5749
Purple Heart Medal	8455-00-269-5757
Meritorious Service Medal	8455-00-450-3728
Air Medal	8455-00-269-5747
Navy and Marine Corps Commendation Medal	8455-00-680-0617
Navy and Marine Corps Achievement Medal	8455-00-926-6784
Combat Action Ribbon	8455-00-411-0117
Presidential Unit Citation	8455-00-334-7965
Navy Unit Commendation	8455-00-334-7967
Meritorious Unit Commendation	8455-00-935-6664
Navy "E" Ribbon	8455-01-043-9711
"E" Attachment	8455-01-043-9712
Prisoner of War Medal	8455-01-251-2096
Navy Good Conduct Medal	8455-00-753-2906
Marine Corps Good Conduct Medal	8455-00-261-4501
Naval Reserve Meritorious Service Medal	8455-00-926-6783
Selected Marine Corps Reserve Medal	8455-00-641-8968
Navy Expeditionary Medal	8455-00-820-8138
Marine Corps Expeditionary Medal	8455-00-082-5609
China Service Medal	8455-00-261-4499
Navy Occupation Service Medal	8455-00-890-2166
National Defense Service Medal	8455-00-281-3214
Korean Service Medal	8455-00-269-5771
Antarctica Service Medal	8455-00-965-1708
Armed Forces Expeditionary Medal	8455-00-082-5638
Vietnam Service Medal	8455-00-926-1664
Southwest Asia Service Medal	8455-01-334-9513
Kosovo Campaign Medal	8455-01-475-6856
Afghanistan Campaign Medal	8455-01-527-8027
Iraq Campaign Medal	8455-01-527-8023
Global War on Terrorism Expeditionary Medal	8455-01-506-7144
Global War on Terrorism Service Medal	8455-01-506-7170
Korea Defense Service Medal	8455-01-512-7138

Appendix C to
Chapter 2

Armed Forces Service Medal	8455-01-426-5479
Humanitarian Service Medal	8455-01-063-4674
Military Outstanding Volunteer Svc Medal	8455-01-400-3295
Sea Service Deployment Ribbon	Not stocked
Navy Arctic Service Ribbon	Not stocked
Navy and Marine Corps Overseas Svc Ribbon	Not stocked
Navy Recruit Training Service Ribbon	Not Stocked
Navy Recruiting Service Ribbon	Not Stocked
Marine Corps Recruiting Ribbon	8455-01-442-3876
Marine Corps Drill Instructor Ribbon	8455-01-449-6765
Marine Corps Security Guard Ribbon	8455-01-449-6760
Armed Forces Reserve Medal	8455-00-753-2908
United Nations Service Medal	8455-00-269-5778
NATO Medal	8455-01-426-5479
Kuwait Liberation Medal (Saudi Arabia)	8455-01-349-7517
Kuwait Liberation Medal (Kuwait)	8455-01-421-0067
Republic of Korea War Service Medal	Not stocked
Expert Rifleman Medal	8455-00-577-5878
Expert Pistol Shot Medal	8455-00-577-5877
Gold Stars (5/16 in.)	8455-00-141-0888
Silver Stars (3/16 in.)	8455-00-261-4507
Silver Stars (5/16 in.)	8455-00-141-0889
Bronze Stars (3/16 in.)	8455-00-261-4506
"M" Device	8455-01-437-2834
"V" Device	8455-00-249-0190
PUC Civilian Lapel Device	8455-00-134-9123
NUC Civilian Lapel Device	8455-00-134-9125
MUC Civilian Lapel Device	8455-00-134-9124

AIR MEDAL (STRIKE/FLIGHT) ELIGIBILITY PERIODS

Following are the geographic areas and time periods during which personnel may have been eligible to earn Strike/Flight awards of the Air Medal:

Vietnam	4 Jul 65 - 28 Mar 73
Grenada	23 Oct - 2 Nov 83
Lebanon	1 Oct 83 - 31 Oct 84
Libya	Mar - Apr 86
Operation PRAYING MANTIS	18 - 19 Apr 88
Panama	20 Dec 89 - 31 Jan 90
Operation DESERT STORM	17 Jan - 28 Feb 91
Operation SOUTHERN WATCH	Aug 92 - 18 Mar 03
Operation DENY FLIGHT	1 Jul 92 - 20 Dec 95
Operation JOINT ENDEAVOR	15 Dec 95 - 16 Dec 96
Kosovo	24 Mar 99 - TBD
Operation ENDURING FREEDOM	11 Sep 01 - TBD
Operation IRAQI FREEDOM	19 Mar 03 - TBD

Note: The operational commander receives specific delegated Air Medal (Strike/Flight) awarding authority from SECNAV. Specifications for each area of operations must be adhered to, in addition to the basic guidance in Chapter 2.

COMBAT ACTION RIBBON ELIGIBILITY PERIODS

An individual whose eligibility has been established in combat in any of the following listed operations may be authorized award of the Combat Action Ribbon. Only one award per operation is authorized. This listing is not all-inclusive, as the Combat Action Ribbon has been awarded in minor operations, as well as for specific actions.

    1. Southeast Asia: 1 Mar 61 to 15 Aug 73.

    2. Dominican Republic: 28 Apr 65 to 21 Sep 66. (No ships qualified.)

    3. USS LIBERTY (AGTR 5): 8 Jun 67 to 9 Jun 67.

    4. USS PUEBLO (AGTR 2): 23 Jan 68.

    5. Operation FREQUENT WIND (Saigon evacuation): 29 to 30 Apr 75. (No ships qualified.)

    6. Operation MAYAGUEZ: 15 May 75. (No ships qualified.)

    7. Grenada: 24Oct83 to 2 Nov 83. (No ships qualified.)

    8. Lebanon: 20Aug82 to 1 Aug 84. (No ships qualified.)

    9. Persian Gulf

        (a) COMNAVSPECWAR Task Unit Tango: 22 Sep 87.

        (b) USS SAMUEL B. ROBERTS (FFG 58): 14 Apr 88.

        (c) Operation PRAYING MANTIS: 18 Apr 88.

                SAG BRAVO
                COMDESRON NINE STAFF embarked on (DD 976)
                USS MERRILL (DD 976)
                HSL-35 DET 1
                USS LYNDE MCCORMICK (DDG 8)
                USS TRENTON (LPD 14)
                CONTINGENCY MAGTF 2-88
                HSL 44, DET 5

SAG CHARLIE
USS WAINWRIGHT (CG 28)
USS BAGLEY (FF 1069)
HSL-35, DET 7
USS SIMPSON (FFG 56)
HSL-42, DET 10
COMMANDER, NAVAL SPECIAL WARFARE TASK
 GROUP MIDDLE EAST FORCE
SEAL TEAM TWO, THIRD PLATOON

SAG DELTA
COMDESRON TWENTY-TWO
USS JACK WILLIAMS (FFG 24)
HSL-32, DET 2
USS JOSEPH STRAUSS (DDG 16)
USS O'BRIEN (DD 975)
HSL-33, DET 2
CC, SPEC BOAT UNIT TWELVE
SEAL TEAM 5, PLATOON C

     (d) USS ELMER MONTGOMERY (FF 1082) and USS VINCENNES (CG 49): 3 Jul 88.

     (e) Persian Gulf MCM Operations: Specific units during the periods 19 Nov 87 to 1 Apr 88; 14 to 20 Apr 88; 20 to 23 Apr 88; and 2 Aug 90 to 10 Sep 91.

     10. Operation JUST CAUSE (Panama): 20 Dec 89 to 31 Jan 90. (No ships qualified.)

     11. Operation SHARP EDGE: 5 to 24 Aug 90. (No ships qualified.)

     12. Operation DESERT STORM: 17 Jan 91 to 28 Feb 91.

     (a) The Secretary of the Navy approved the CAR as an exception to policy for the following ships that operated north of 28.30N and west of 49.30E from 17 Jan 91 to 28 Feb 91:

USS ADROIT (MSO 509)	USS AVENGER (MCM 1)
USS BEAUFORT (ATS 2)	USS BUNKER HILL (CG 52)
USS CARON (DD 970)	USS CURTS (FFG 38)
USS DURHAM (LKA 114)	USS FIFE (DD 991)
USS FORD (FFG 54)	USS FORT MCHENRY (LSD 43)
USS PAUL F. FOSTER (DD964)	USS HAWES (FFG 53)
USNS HASSAYAMPA (T-AO 145)	USS HORNE (CG 30)
USS IMPERVIOUS (MSO 449)	USS JARRETT (FFG 33)

USS KIDD (DDG 993)   USS LASALLE (AGF 3)
USS LEADER (MSO 490)   USS LEFTWICH (DD 984)
USS MACDONOUGH (DDG 39)   USS MCINERNEY (FFG 8)
USS MISSOURI (BB 63)   USS MOBILE BAY (CG 53)
USS NASSAU (LI-IA 4)   USS NIAGARA FALLS (AFS 3)
USS NICHOLAS (FFG 47)   USS OKINAWA (LPH 3)
USS OLDENDORF (DD 972)   USNS PASSUMPSIC (T-AO 107)
USS PORTLAND (LSD 37)   USS PRINCETON (CG 59)
USS RALEIGH (LPD 1)   USS TRIPOLI (LPH 10)
USS VREELAND (FF 1068)   USS WISCONSIN (BB 64)
USS WORDEN (CG 18)

(b) The following ships were approved for the dates indicated:

USNS COMFORT (T-AH 20)	26 Feb 91
USS GUAM (LPH 9)	25 to 26 Feb 91
USS IWO JIMA (LPH 2)	26 Feb 91
USS OGDEN (LPD 5)	25 to 26 Feb 91
USS MISSOURI (BB 63)	12 Feb 91 and 25 Feb 91
VC-6 Detachment	
EODMU Detachments	
USS RICHMOND K. TURNER (CG 20)	19 to 24 Feb 91
USS VALLEY FORGE (CG 50)	16 to 28 Feb 91
USS LEADER (MSO 490)	23 Mar 91

13. El Salvador: 1 Jan 81 to 1 Feb 92.

14. Operation RESTORE HOPE (Somalia): 5 Dec 92 to 31 Mar 95. (No ships qualified.)

15. Cambodia: 1 Jun 92 to 15 Nov 93.

16. Operation ASSURED RESPONSE (Monrovia, Liberia): 7 to 18 Apr 96. (No ships qualified.)

17. Kosovo Campaign: 24 Mar 99 to 27 Jan 00.

18. Operation ENDURING FREEDOM: 11 Sep 01 to TBD.

19. Operation IRAQI FREEDOM: 19 Mar 03 to TBD.

CHAPTER 3 - UNIT AWARDS

SECTION 1 - GENERAL

310. DEFINITION. A unit is any ship, aircraft squadron, shore command, or military organizational element, composed of military personnel, under control of a military command and charged with carrying out a military mission or function.

311. POLICY CONSIDERATIONS

    1. Purpose. To foster morale, esprit de corps, and provide incentive, unit awards recognize entire organizations for outstanding heroism or achievement performed during periods of war, international tension, national emergencies, or extraordinary situations that involve national interests. They are restricted to the recognition of acts or services that clearly and distinctly, by nature and magnitude, place the unit's performance significantly above that of other units performing similar missions. They are not intended to recognize individual actions, but rather to acknowledge the combined efforts of the organization. The unit's performance should be such that it cannot be adequately recognized in any other way.

    2. Unit Awards from Other Services. Naval personnel may participate in unit awards tendered by the U.S. Army, U.S. Air Force, or U.S. Coast Guard, provided CNO, CMC, or SECNAV, as appropriate, has concurred. See the appropriate uniform regulations for the correct wear of the ribbons, if authorized.

    3. DON Unit Awards to Other Services. Units of the U.S. Army, U.S. Air Force, and U.S. Coast Guard, with concurrence of their parent Service, may participate in DON unit awards.

    4. Participation of Civilians in Unit Awards. Subsequent to 16 March 1969, DON civilian U.S. citizen employees assigned to a unit recommended for a Presidential Unit Citation (PU), Navy Unit Commendation (NU), or Meritorious Unit Commendation (MU) may be nominated for participation in the award, provided the officer recommending the award certifies the civilian employees played a key role in the achievement for which the award is being recommended.

    5. DON Unit Awards to Foreign Units. The PU, NU, and MU may be awarded to units of the armed forces of friendly foreign nations, serving with the Armed Forces of the United States, for

outstanding performance, in accordance with the same criteria applicable for such awards to U.S. units.

6. <u>Foreign Unit Awards to DON Units</u>. Foreign unit awards tendered to units of the Naval service by friendly foreign nations will be forwarded to SECNAV for approval of acceptance. See Chapter 7 for information regarding foreign unit awards that have been accepted and authorized for wear.

312. <u>ELIGIBILITY TO PARTICIPATE IN UNIT AWARDS</u>. When a unit award is issued, component, reinforcing and/or supporting units authorized to participate in the award will be designated. The commanding officer of the unit determines individual eligibility to participate in unit awards. Eligibility criteria for participation in PU, NU, and MU awards are as follows:

1. Military personnel:

a. All personnel <u>permanently</u> assigned to the cited unit, who were actually present and participated in the action(s) for which the unit was cited, are authorized to wear the ribbon permanently. Eligibility may be established by evidence in service records for Navy personnel and by information contained in the Marine Corps Total Force System for Marine Corps personnel. In cases where a determination cannot be made at the local level, requests for award eligibility shall be submitted to NPC (PERS-312) or CMC (MMMA).

b. Transient, limited active duty for training or special active duty (less than 30 days), and temporary duty personnel assigned to the cited unit are <u>normally ineligible</u>. However, exceptions may be made for individuals temporarily attached to the cited unit to provide direct support through the particular skills they possess. The award recommendation must specifically mention that such personnel are recommended for participation in the award, and include certification from the cited unit's commanding officer that the individual(s) made a direct, recognizable contribution to the performance of the services that qualified the unit for the award. Such personnel will be authorized for participation by the awarding authority upon approval of the award.

c. Reserve personnel and Individual Augmentees (IAs) assigned to a unit are eligible to receive unit awards and should be specifically considered by commanding officers for inclusion, as appropriate, based on the contributory service provided.

2. Civilian personnel, when specifically authorized, may wear the appropriate lapel device (point up). The command is responsible for ordering lapel devices for civilians eligible for the award.

3. Reservists who receive unit awards as civilians are not eligible to wear the ribbon bars on their military uniforms.

4. Students are not eligible.

SECTION 2 - ADMINISTRATIVE PROCEDURES

320. <u>PREPARATION OF RECOMMENDATIONS</u>. For Navy units, recommendations for the PU, NU, and MU shall be prepared by completing OPNAV Form 1650/14 in its entirety. Appendix A to this chapter contains a sample 1650/14. General guidance for completing the form is contained in Appendix A to Chapter 2. The complete instructions are available on the Navy Awards website at https://awards.navy.mil. Marine Corps recommendations shall be prepared in naval letter format by the Immediate Superior in Command (or another more senior officer within the chain of command). It is not appropriate for the "recommended unit" to originate the nomination for a unit award. All recommendations shall include the following:

1. A narrative justification containing sufficient data, in light of the eligibility criteria, to enable the reviewing and approving authorities to consider them adequately. The narrative should be specific and direct in establishing why the unit has earned this distinction and exactly what sets this unit apart from its peers.

2. A complete list of all units recommended for participation, including staffs when appropriate, with dates of attachment to the unit recommended for citation. Navy units shall use Page 3 of OPNAV Form 1650/14 to list the recommended units. Identify any previous unit awards that have been approved or recommended for any units on the list. If there have been no previous unit awards for the period of the recommendation, a statement to this effect should be included.

3. An estimate of the total number of personnel (officers, enlisted, and civilians) who would be eligible to participate in the award if approved.

4. If civilians are nominated for participation, include a by-name list of nominees, the total number of civilians nominated, certification that they played a key role in the achievement for which the award is being recommended, and a statement that they are U.S. citizens and DON employees. Neither contractors nor foreign nationals are eligible.

5. For PU recommendations only, include an unclassified concise summary of the justification for the award in narrative form, no more than three pages long, including figures on friendly and enemy casualties, number and types of personal awards issued as a result of the action, and a description of damage incurred by both sides.

6. A double-spaced, unclassified proposed citation in upper and lower case, not longer than 27 lines. Acronyms may be used if spelled out the first time. Appendix B to this chapter provides sample citations. Following is guidance regarding the format of unit citations:

   a. The font shall be Courier New, size 12.

   b. The margins shall be: top 2.5, bottom 1.0, left .7, and right .5.

   c. The name of the unit in the title line shall be in all capital letters, and the name in the title must be exactly as used in the first and last sentence of the citation. If the unit being cited is a ship, the format shall be "USS SHIP NAME (HULL NUMBER)." The ship's name may be used without the hull number or "USS" in the remainder of the citation.

   d. The opening sentence is formatted by type of award. Note: If the cited actions occur within the same year, the year is only mentioned once; for example, 10 February to 30 June 2006.

      (1) PU: "For extraordinary heroism in action against enemy forces from (day, month, year) to (day, month, year). NAME OF UNIT . . ."

      (2) NU: "For exceptionally meritorious (service or achievement) during assigned missions from (day, month, year) to (day, month, year). The personnel of NAME OF UNIT . . . "

(3) MU: "For meritorious (service or achievement) from (day, month, year) to (day, month, year). The personnel of NAME OF UNIT . . ."

e. The word "great" shall only be used in the last sentence of PU and NU citations. Civilian employees are mentioned in the last sentence when appropriate. Note: The three descriptive phrases used in the last sentences of the sample citations in Appendix B are examples only and are <u>not</u> the only phrases that may be used. The words used should be appropriate to the actions of the unit(s) being cited.

321. <u>SUBMISSION OF RECOMMENDATIONS</u>

1. Recommendations for all PU, NU, and MU awards shall be forwarded to the awarding authority through either the administrative (for sustained performance) or operational (for deployment) chain of command, as appropriate. If a type commander and/or fleet commander are part of the appropriate chain of command, the recommendation shall be forwarded through them for comment and recommendation. CNO or CMC, as appropriate, will endorse the recommendation when SECNAV is the approval authority. Delegation of authority to approve unit awards is delineated in Appendix A to Chapter 1.

2. If the recommended unit has operated under a Combatant Commander for any portion of the meritorious period, the recommendation must be forwarded via the Combatant Commander for endorsement and to prevent duplication of awards. All recommendations for the PU shall be processed via the appropriate Combatant Commander.

3. For reserve units, include an endorsement by the active component command the unit regularly reports to/mobilizes with. Also include an endorsement by the commander under whom the service or act was performed, if it is other than the active command to which the unit is regularly assigned.

4. For units commanded by a staff corps officer who reports for primary or additional duty to a line commander, the line commander must endorse the recommendation.

5. Recommendations that include participation of units of other U.S. Armed Forces shall be forwarded as follows by CNO or CMC, as appropriate, to obtain parent Service concurrence, prior to final approval.

Department of the Army
Commander, U.S. Army Human Resources Command
AHRC-PDO-PA
200 Stovall Street
Alexandria, VA 22332-0471

Department of the Air Force
Headquarters AFPC/DPPPRA
550 C Street West, Suite 12
Randolph AFB, TX 78150-4712

Commandant (CG-1221), U.S. Coast Guard
2100 Second Street SW, Room 5501
Washington, DC 20593-0001

6. Recommendations that include participation of units of friendly foreign nations require the specific concurrence of the American Ambassador and the Defense Attaché to the country of the proposed recipient(s) prior to forwarding the recommendation to CNO, CMC, and/or SECNAV.

7. All submissions must include a command point of contact and applicable telephone numbers and email addresses.

322. LIMITATIONS

1. No unit, or part thereof, may be awarded more than one unit award, regardless of type (including Joint unit awards), for the same act or period of service.

2. PU, NU, and MU recommendations must be submitted within three years from the date of the action or service, and the award must be made within five years thereof. When a recommendation has been initiated and placed in official channels within the time limits prescribed and has become lost, a certified copy of the original recommendation may be resubmitted. If a copy is not available, the originator may submit a statement to that effect, and the case will be considered on its merits.

323. AWARD ELEMENTS AND ATTACHMENTS

1. Commanding officers shall procure and issue the appropriate ribbon bars for the PU, NU, or MU to eligible military personnel. Appendix C to Chapter 2 contains information regarding procurement. When authorized, civilian personnel will

be issued a 9/16-inch triangular lapel device and citation copy.
There are no medals authorized for these awards.

2. Cited units hold the original citations, and either
CNO (DNS-35) or CMC (MMMA), as appropriate, will hold electronic
and/or paper copies.

3. The appropriate documentation will be forwarded to
ensure the service records of Navy personnel are updated. For
Marine Corps personnel, ensure Unit Diary/Marine Integrated
Personnel System (UD/MIPS) entries are made on all eligible
personnel.

324. INSIGNIA FOR SHIPS AND UNITS

1. Each separate activity that was part of or attached to
a cited unit and participated in one or more of the actions for
which the unit was cited, is authorized to display insignia as
follows:

a. Pennant. May be flown from the fore truck of a
ship from sunrise to sunset when not underway. Shore commands or
commands based ashore may fly the pennant from such standard as
the commanding officer may designate. The flagship of the cited
unit is entitled to fly the pennant irrespective of whether the
flagship was a part of the unit and participated in any of the
actions for which the unit was cited. A replica of this pennant
may be painted in a suitable place on individual ships, aircraft,
tanks, etc., in accordance with type commander instructions.

b. Streamer. Authorized for display per current CNO
or CMC directives. A list of battle streamers is available on
the Navy Awards website under "Unit Awards."

2. Disposition. Ships and units being decommissioned
will turn over all streamers and pennants to the Naval Historical
Center, Curator Branch, 805 Kidder Breese Street SE, Washington
Navy Yard, DC 20374-5060, or to Director of Marine Corps History,
2014 Anderson Avenue, Quantico, Virginia 22134-5002, as
appropriate. A reactivated or re-commissioned unit previously
cited is authorized to obtain and display appropriate pennants or
streamers.

325. LISTS OF CITED UNITS. Consolidated lists of unit awards
are maintained online by CNO (DNS-35) and by CMC (MMMA) at
https://awards.navy.mil and http://awards.manpower.usmc.mil.

The service record remains the authoritative source for verification of individual receipt of a unit award.

SECTION 3 - REQUIREMENTS

330. <u>SPECIFIC UNIT AWARDS</u>. Navy and Marine Corps commands may recommend units for the following awards.

1. <u>Presidential Unit Citation</u>

a. Authorization. E.O. 9050, 6 February 1942.

b. Eligibility Requirements. Awarded in the name of the President of the United States to units of the U.S. Armed Forces and friendly foreign nations for extraordinary heroism in action against an armed enemy. The unit must have displayed such gallantry, determination, and esprit de corps in accomplishing its mission, under extremely difficult and hazardous conditions, to have set it apart from and above other units participating in the same campaign. The degree of heroism required is the same as that which would be required for award of a <u>Navy Cross</u> to an individual.

2. <u>Navy Unit Commendation</u>

a. Authorization. ALNAV 224 of 18 December 1944.

b. Eligibility Requirements. Awarded by SECNAV to any unit of the Navy or Marine Corps that has distinguished itself by outstanding heroism in action against the enemy, but not sufficient to justify the award of the Presidential Unit Citation; or to any such unit that has distinguished itself by extremely meritorious service, not involving combat, but in support of military operations, rendering the unit outstanding compared to other units performing similar service. This award may also be conferred upon units of the other branches of the U.S. Armed Forces, and of armed forces of friendly foreign nations serving with the U.S. Armed Forces, provided such units meet the standards established for Navy and Marine Corps units. To justify this award, the unit must have performed service of a character comparable to that which would merit the award of a <u>Silver Star Medal</u> for heroism, or a <u>Legion of Merit</u> for meritorious service to an individual. Normal performance of duty or participation in a large number of combat missions does not, in itself, justify the award. An award will not be made to a unit for actions of one or more of its component parts, unless the unit performed uniformly as a team, in a manner justifying collective recognition.

3. Meritorious Unit Commendation

a. Authorization. SECNAV Notice 1650 of 17 July 1967.

b. Eligibility Requirements. Awarded by SECNAV, CNO, or CMC to any unit of the Navy or Marine Corps that has distinguished itself, under combat or non-combat conditions, by either valorous or meritorious achievement, which renders the unit outstanding compared to other units performing similar service, but not sufficient to justify award of the Navy Unit Commendation. This award may also be conferred upon units of the other branches of the U.S. Armed Forces, and the armed forces of friendly foreign nations serving with U.S. Armed Forces, provided such units meet the standards established for Navy and Marine Corps units. To justify this award, the unit must have performed service of a character comparable to that which would merit the award of a Bronze Star Medal, or achievement of like caliber in a non-combat situation, to an individual. Normal performance of duty or participation in a large number of combat missions does not, in itself, justify the award. An award will not be made to a unit for actions of one or more of its component parts, unless the unit performed uniformly as a team in a manner fully justifying collective recognition.

4. Navy "E" Ribbon

a. Authorization. SECNAV letter Ser 210 of 31 March 1976.

b. Eligibility Requirements. This ribbon denotes permanent duty on ships or in squadrons that won Battle Efficiency competitions after 1 July 1974. There is no medal, citation, or certificate to accompany this award. Documentation for Navy service records and Marine Corps UD/MIPS will be made as appropriate. Following are the specific eligibility criteria:

(1) Military Personnel

(a) Navy personnel permanently attached to and serving with cited ships and units during the competitive cycle for which the award was given, or any part thereof, are entitled to the award as of 1 July 1974.

(b) Marine Corps personnel serving as part of the ship's Marine detachment or otherwise designated as "ship's company" are eligible. Personnel assigned to embarked Marine Corps units are not eligible for the award; e.g., aircraft squadrons, Battalion Landing Teams, Regimental Landing Teams, Marine Expeditionary Units, etc.

(c) All Selected Reserve personnel permanently attached to and serving with the mobilization augmentation Navy Reserve unit(s) during the competitive cycle for which the award was given, or any part thereof, are entitled to the award provided the individuals concerned performed active duty for training aboard the unit during that competitive cycle.

(d) Reservists performing active duty for training aboard units awarded the "E" who are not members of the dedicated Reserve unit(s), and Reservists who were members of the dedicated Reserve unit(s), but who did not perform active duty for training aboard, are not eligible for the award.

(e) Transients and temporary duty personnel are not eligible for this award.

(f) Embarked personnel, staffs, squadrons, or detachments are also not eligible.

(2) Civilian personnel are not eligible for the Navy "E" ribbon.

(3) Type Commanders, the awarding authority for the Navy "E," must adhere to these rules when issuing local directives. Type Commanders are also responsible for updating the Navy Department Awards Web Service (NDAWS).

c. Subsequent Awards. The first, second, and third award of the Navy "E" are denoted by a Silver "E." Four or more awards are denoted by one wreathed "E."

UNIT AWARD RECOMMENDATION
FOR OFFICIAL USE ONLY

ENSURE ALL BLOCKS ARE FILLED IN, SIGNED AND DATED.
COMPLETE MAILING ADDRESSES ARE REQUIRED

1. FROM: ADDRESS:	1a. UIC / RUC	2. TO (Awarding Authority) : ADDRESS:	2a. UIC / RUC

3. COMMAND POC: NAME: EMAIL:	4. PHONE: (DSN) (COM)	5. IS LIST OF PARTICIPATING COMMANDS INCLUDED IN THIS SUBMISSION? YES ☐ NO ☐

6. CITED UNIT:	7. UIC/RUC OF CITED UNIT:

8. CITED UNIT COMPONENT:	9. SHIP ? YES ☐ NO ☐	10. RECOMMENDED AWARD NUMBER (EX: FIRST)

11. RECOMMENDED AWARD	12. PREVIOUS UNIT AWARDS AND DATES RECOGNIZED:
13. UNIT AWARDS RECOMMENDED-NOT YET APPROVED	

14. CAMPAIGN	14a. OPERATION	15. OTHER UNITS BEING RECOMMENDED FOR SAME ACTION:

16. GEOGRAPHIC AREA OF ACTION/SERVICE	17. ACTION DATE/MERITORIOUS PERIOD -

18a. NAME, RANK/GRADE, COMPONENT, TITLE OF ORIGINATOR	18b. SIGNATURE	18c.DATE

19. FORWARDING ENDORSEMENTS BY VIA ADDRESSEE(S)

VIA	COMMAND (To be completed by originator) (Include Telephone Number)	RECOMMENDED AWARD	SIGNATURE, GRADE	DATE FWD
1				
2				
3				
4				
5				

20. TO BE COMPLETED BY AWARDING AUTHORITY

DISPOSITION OF BASIC RECOMMENDATION	SIGNATURE, GRADE, TITLE	DATE APPROVED

21. CNO / CMC AWARDS BRANCH USE ONLY
SERIAL NO: DATE RECEIVED:

22. NDBDM USE ONLY

FROM: SECNAV (NDBDM)   DATE:

TO: CNO (DNS 37/N09B13)   CMC (CODE MMMA)

1. Extraordinary heroism recommended: ☐YES ☐NO ☐NOT APPLICABLE
2. Reviewed and recorded.

_____
By direction

INSTRUCTIONS

1. Before completing this form see SECNAVINST 1650.1. For the electronic form, help for each Block can be accessed by placing the cursor over the data entry field and pressing the F1 key.
2. The Summary of Action (item 23) is requested. In addition, attach a double spaced proposed citation
3. Two (2) letter codes to be used in Blocks 11, 12, 13, 19 and 20
4. All dates should be entered in the DD-3-letter month ID-YYYY format (EX: 23-FEB-2004)

EM	Navy Expeditionary Medal	NU	Navy Unit Commendation	LC	Cmdr in Chief, US Atl Flt LOC
AE	Armed Forces Expeditionary Medal	MU	Meritorious Unit Commendation	PC	Cmdr in Chief, Pac Flt LOC
HS	Humanitarian Service Medal	NE	Navy "E" Ribbon	EC	Cmdr in Chief, USN Forces, Europe LOC
CR	Combat Action Ribbon	SC	SECNAV LOC	CF	Cmdr, US Naval Forces Central Cmd LOC
PU	Presidential Unit Citation	CT	CMC COC	XX	Letter of Commendation
JU	Joint Meritorious Unit Award	CL	CNO LOC		

23. Summary of Action

PARTICIPATING COMMANDS ENTRY FORM

P1. CITED UNIT NAME:	For Multiple Forms Entry: Participating Commands Entry Page#
P2. CITED UNIT RECOMMENDED AWARD	P3. CITED UNIT ACTION DATE/MERITORIOUS PERIOD -

List Participating Commands for the Unit Awards; fill in Merit Dates and/or Component ONLY if they are different than the Primary Cited Unit's.

	PARTICIPATING COMMAND	MERIT START	MERIT END	COMPONENT
1				
2				
3				
4				
5				
6				
7				
8				
9				
10				
11				
12				
13				
14				
15				
16				
17				
18				
19				
20				
21				
22				
23				
24				
25				
26				
27				
28				
29				
30				
31				
32				
33				

UNIT AWARD RECOMMENDATION SUPPLEMENT

PARTICIPATING COMMANDS ENTRY FORM			

P1. CITED UNIT NAME:	For Multiple Forms Entry: Participating Commands Entry Page #
P2. CITED UNIT RECOMMENDED AWARD	P3. CITED UNIT ACTION DATE/MERITORIOUS PERIOD -

List Participating Commands for the Unit Awards; fill in Merit Dates and/or Component ONLY if they are different than the Primary Cited Unit's.

	PARTICIPATING COMMAND	MERIT START	MERIT END	COMPONENT
1				
2				
3				
4				
5				
6				
7				
8				
9				
10				
11				
12				
13				
14				
15				
16				
17				
18				
19				
20				
21				
22				
23				
24				
25				
26				
27				
28				
29				
30				
31				
32				
33				

The President of the United States takes pleasure in presenting the PRESIDENTIAL UNIT CITATION to

<u>NAME OF UNIT OR UNITS</u>

for service as set forth in the following

CITATION:

For extraordinary heroism and outstanding performance of duty in action against enemy forces from (<u>day, month, year</u>) to (<u>day, month, year</u>). <u>NAME OF UNIT</u> conducted the longest sequence of coordinated combined arms overland attacks in the history of the Marine Corps. From the border between Kuwait and Iraq to the culmination of hostilities north of Baghdad, <u>NAME OF UNIT</u> advanced nearly 800 kilometers under sustained and heavy combat. Utilizing the devastating combat power of organic aviation assets, coupled with the awesome power resident in the ground combat elements, and maintaining momentum through the herculean efforts of combat service support elements, <u>NAME OF UNIT</u> destroyed nine Iraqi Divisions. This awesome display of combat power was accomplished while simultaneously freeing the Iraqi people from more than 30 years of oppression and reestablishing basic infrastructure in the country. During the 33 days of combat to the transition to civil-military operations, <u>NAME OF UNIT</u> sustained a tempo of operations never before seen on the modern battlefield, conducting four major river crossings, maintaining the initiative, and sustaining forces. The ferocity of the campaign was made possible through the skills and determination of the Soldiers, Sailors, Airmen, Marines, and Coalition Partners comprising <u>NAME OF UNIT</u> at all levels, all echelons, and in all occupational fields. By their outstanding courage, aggressive fighting spirit, and untiring devotion to duty, the officers and enlisted personnel of <u>NAME OF UNIT</u> reflected great credit upon themselves and upheld the highest traditions of the Marine Corps and the United States Naval Service.

For the President,

Secretary of the Navy

3-15

The Secretary of the Navy takes pleasure in presenting the NAVY UNIT COMMENDATION to

NAME OF UNIT OR UNITS

for service as set forth in the following

CITATION:

For exceptionally meritorious service (achievement) during assigned missions from (day, month, year) to (day, month, year). The personnel of NAME OF UNIT conducted challenging support missions in an outstanding fashion, leading the way in operational employment, professional innovation and tactical development. NAME OF UNIT mobilized, deployed and began combat operations within ten days of receiving their mobilization orders in support of Operation IRAQI FREEDOM. Assigned to various Joint commands, the NAME OF UNIT completed more than 1,500 combat flight hours and 850 combat sorties in direct support of U.S. and multi-national forces. Their exceptional efforts significantly impeded enemy forces from taking action against Coalition forces. NAME OF UNIT'S unparalleled record of achievement affirms the outstanding technical ability and esprit de corps of the NAME OF UNIT. By their truly distinctive achievements, extensive enthusiasm, and unfailing devotion to duty, the officers, enlisted personnel and civilian employees of NAME OF UNIT reflected great credit upon themselves and upheld the highest traditions of the United States Naval Service.

Secretary of the Navy

The Secretary of the Navy takes pleasure in presenting the MERITORIOUS UNIT COMMENDATION to

<u>NAME OF UNIT</u>

for service as set forth in the following

CITATION:

<u>For meritorious service</u> from (<u>day, month, year to day, month, year</u>). The personnel of <u>NAME OF UNIT</u> consistently demonstrated unparalleled success in providing regional presence, power projection, and strategic deterrence in the Central Command area. <u>NAME OF UNIT</u> expediently developed doctrine to support transformational concepts, and quickly demonstrated its full lethality and agility, exceeding all operational requirements and expectations, in support of Operations IRAQI FREEDOM and ENDURING FREEDOM. Traversing the entire Central Command littoral area, <u>NAME OF UNIT</u> assigned units aggressively engaged in sensitive national tasking, regional engagement, surveillance and reconnaissance, maritime interdiction, and humanitarian operations. Specifically, they seized at sea more than 2,000 metric tons of smuggled crude oil and 15 million dollars of illicit drugs, detained two suspected Al Qaeda operatives, and led a first-of-its kind exercise involving 16 coalition nations. <u>NAME OF UNIT</u>'s monumental drive greatly impacted the stabilization of Southern Iraq, the improvement of relations with important allies, and the development of a land-sea interface intelligence picture. Operating in concert with the NEVERSAIL Carrier Strike Group, <u>NAME OF UNIT</u> played a pivotal role in developing command and control structures for integrated Expeditionary Strike Force operations. By their truly distinctive accomplishments, unrelenting perseverance, and unfailing devotion to duty, the officers and enlisted personnel of <u>NAME OF UNIT</u> reflected credit upon themselves and upheld the highest traditions of the United States Naval Service.

Secretary of the Navy

3-17

CHAPTER 4 - CAMPAIGN AND SERVICE AWARDS

SECTION 1 - GENERAL

410. <u>DEFINITION</u>. A campaign or service award is issued to an individual to denote participation in a campaign, armed conflict, national emergency, or expedition, or to denote service requirements fulfilled in a creditable manner.

411. <u>AUTHORIZED AWARDS</u>. This chapter contains information regarding campaign and service awards currently authorized for issue. See Chapter 8 for information regarding selected campaign and service awards for which the eligibility period has ended.

412. <u>ISSUANCE OF AWARDS</u>

1. When a campaign or service award is available for initial distribution, CNO and CMC shall issue instructions to inform commanding officers of the eligibility requirements. Appendix C to Chapter 2 contains information regarding procurement.

2. No more than one of any campaign or service medal shall be issued to an individual. A 3/16-inch bronze star is issued and worn on the suspension ribbon and ribbon bar to denote subsequent awards. A 3/16-inch silver star is worn in lieu of the sixth award.

3. 3/16-inch bronze stars are also used as engagement and battle stars, when authorized, and indicate participation in actual combat. (Note: The terms "engagement star" and "battle star" have historically been used interchangeably, and have the same meaning.)

4. Unless specifically prohibited in the individual award requirements below, all campaign and service awards may be presented posthumously to such representative of the deceased as deemed appropriate.

5. Commanding officers shall ensure appropriate service record entries are made concerning campaign and service awards earned by personnel under their command. Marine Corps commanding officers shall make appropriate entries in the Marine Corps Total Force System (MCTFS).

SECTION 2 - REQUIREMENTS

420. <u>SPECIFIC CAMPAIGN AND SERVICE AWARDS</u>. The authorization, eligibility requirements, and special provisions for campaign and service awards are delineated in the following paragraphs. Unit commanders, members of their staffs, and personnel attached to other units derive their eligibility for service medals and engagement stars in the same manner as personnel regularly assigned to the ship or unit to which they are attached.

1. Prisoner of War Medal

    a. <u>Authorization</u>. 10 U.S.C. §1128.

    b. <u>Eligibility Requirements</u>. Awarded to any person who, while serving in any capacity with the Armed Forces of the United States, was declared a prisoner of war and held captive after 5 April 1917.

    (1) Civilians and Foreign Nationals. The Prisoner of War (POW) Medal will only be issued to U.S. and foreign civilians who have received credit for U.S. military service, as determined by the Department of Defense Civilian/Military Service Review Board and Advisory Panel (DoD Directive 1000.20 of 11 September 1989). The period of creditable military service must include the period of captivity from date of capture through date of release.

    (2) Missing in Action. The POW Medal will only be issued to the legal next of kin of military personnel or civilians who have received credit for U.S. military service and whose status as POWs has been officially confirmed and recognized as such by the Military Departments and DoD. The next of kin of persons listed as missing, but for whom there is no evidence of having been a POW, will not be issued the medal. Return of remains, in and of itself, does not constitute evidence of POW status. The next of kin of POWs who die in captivity may be issued the medal regardless of the length of the period of captivity.

    (3) Hostages, Detainees, and Internees. The medal will be issued only to those taken prisoner by an enemy during armed conflict. For the purpose of this medal, armed conflicts are defined as World Wars I and II, the Korean and Vietnam

Conflicts, and Operations DESERT STORM, ENDURING FREEDOM, and IRAQI FREEDOM. Hostages of terrorists and persons detained by governments with which the United States is not actively engaged in armed conflict are not eligible for the medal.

    c. Character of Service. Any person convicted by a U.S. military tribunal of misconduct or a criminal charge, or whose discharge is less than honorable based upon actions while a POW, is ineligible for the medal. Furthermore, POWs whose conduct is documented by U.S. military records as not being in accord with the Code of Conduct are ineligible for the medal. SECNAV will resolve any questionable cases.

    d. Subsequent Awards. A period of captivity terminates upon return to U.S. military control. Escapees who do not return to U.S. military control, and are subsequently recaptured by an enemy, do not begin a new period of captivity for the purpose of a subsequent award of the medal.

2. Navy Good Conduct Medal

    a. Authorization. The Navy Good Conduct Medal (NGCM) was established by SECNAV on 26 April 1869 to recognize the "all-around" good Navy enlisted person, well qualified in all phases of conduct and performance. Effective 1 February 1971, commanding officers were delegated authority to award the NGCM. The CNO has review authority over the NGCM and designates specific criteria for the award.

    b. Eligibility Requirements

        (1) Period of Service. In accordance with NAVADMIN 305/95, subsequent to 1 January 1996, any three years of continuous active service as an enlisted person in the Regular Navy or Navy Reserve. For the period 1 November 1963 through 31 December 1995, inclusive, the qualifying eligibility period is four years. This requirement may be fulfilled by:

            (a) Continuous active service during a minority (see note) enlistment, provided the member served on active duty to the day preceding his/her 21st birthday, even though he/she extended the enlistment and remained on active duty. Note: The term "minority" as used in this paragraph and paragraph (b) below refers to being under the age of 18 and not to any particular racial or ethnic background.

(b) Continuous active service during a minority enlistment, provided the member served on active duty within three months of the day preceding his/her 21st birthday.

(c) Continuous active service during a three-year first enlistment. For first-term personnel who meet all eligibility requirements except length of service, the NGCM may be awarded up to three months prior to the eligibility date if the member is discharged or released to inactive duty; i.e., the last three months of service may be waived. This does not apply to members who are discharged for the purpose of immediate reenlistment.

(d) A member not eligible for the NGCM who reenlists or reports for active duty within three months after discharge or release to inactive duty, is considered to be serving under "continuous active service" conditions. While the time between the date of separation and date of return to active duty is not counted as an interruption of active service, it may not be included in computing time served. A member who reenlists or reports for active duty more than three months after separating must begin a new three-year qualification period.

(e) An enlisted member appointed a temporary warrant or commissioned officer may include such temporary service, upon reverting to an enlisted status, regardless of the purpose (including discharge to accept appointment as a permanent officer). Naval Academy midshipmen who are not commissioned, but are retained in the service in an enlisted status, may include such midshipman service for the purpose of earning the NGCM. Except as provided above, service in warrant, commissioned, or Naval Academy midshipman status may not be included in computing time served.

(2) Conduct. Within the required period of active service, the individual must have a clear record (no convictions by court-martial, no non-judicial punishment (NJP), no lost time by reason of sickness-misconduct, no civil convictions for offenses involving moral turpitude).

(a) If confinement as a result of conviction by any court-martial (general, special, or summary) is involved, a new qualifying period shall begin with the date of restoration to duty on a probationary basis. If confinement is not included in the approved sentence of the court-martial, a new qualifying period shall begin with the date of convening authority action.

(b) If the service record contains record of NJP, a new qualifying period shall begin with the date following the date of the offense. If the date of the offense cannot be determined, the new qualifying period shall begin with the date following the NJP.

(c) If convicted by civil authorities for an offense involving moral turpitude, a new qualifying period shall begin with the date of return to active duty status.

(d) If the record contains a disqualifying mark that is not the result of NJP, the new qualifying period shall begin with the date following the date of the mark.

(3) Performance marks required during period of eligibility.

(a) Subsequent to 1 January 1996, no mark below 2.0 in any trait.

(b) Between 31 August 1983 and 31 December 1995, no mark below 3.0 in Military Knowledge/Performance, Rating Knowledge/Performance, Reliability, Military Bearing, Personal Behavior, and Directing.

(c) Prior to 31 August 1983:

1 E-4 and below. No mark below 3.0 in any trait.

2 E-5 and E-6. No mark below EEL (Typically Effective-Lower) in Directing, Individual Productivity, Reliability or Conduct.

3 E-7 to E-9. No mark below the bottom 50 percent in Performance, Reliability, Conduct or Directing. If an individual receives a disqualifying trait mark, a new period of eligibility shall begin on the day following the ending date of the performance evaluation report that contains the disqualifying trait mark.

c. Waivers. Subsequent to 17 May 1974, for the first award only, the NGCM may be awarded in the following cases, provided conduct and performance requirements are met:

(1) For individuals who are killed in combat against an opposing armed force, or die as a direct result of wounds received in combat against an opposing armed force, the award may be presented posthumously to the next of kin.

(2) For individuals who are separated from the Naval Service for physical disability as a result of wounds incurred in combat against an opposing armed force, or in the line of duty where such wounds were directly related to action against the enemy.

(3) For individuals who die while in a POW status, the NGCM may be presented posthumously to the next of kin, provided it has been determined the member's conduct while a POW was acceptable.

d. Limitations

(1) When the requirements have been met, but it is evident the individual is not deserving of the NGCM due to a repeated record of valid letters of indebtedness, or other acts which are not in keeping with the high moral standards required of all Navy personnel, the commanding officer will make an appropriate recommendation to CNO (DNS-35) stating the reasons.

(2) Although the period of qualifying service was revised to three years effective 1 January 1996, in accordance with Navy Uniform Regulations, this change does not affect the four-year requirement for service stripes.

(3) Active service in a Reserve status credited toward the Naval Reserve Meritorious Service Medal may not also be credited for the NGCM.

e. Certificates. A certificate shall be prepared for each award. The member's rate, name, branch of Service, and number of the award shall be centered in the appropriate spaces. The ending date of the period of service for which the award was earned shall be centered after "Awarded for service completed on." The commanding officer's name, grade, and branch of Service shall be typed above "Commanding Officer" and his/her signature affixed.

3. Marine Corps Good Conduct Medal

a. Authorization. Special Order No. 49 of 20 July 1896 established the Marine Corps Good Conduct Medal (MCGCM) to recognize good behavior and faithful service in the Marine Corps. The CMC has review authority over the MCGCM and designates specific criteria for the award.

b. Eligibility Requirements

(1) Service

(a) Any three years of continuous active service after 10 December 1945, regardless of expiration or extension of enlistments and any previous or subsequent disciplinary action, except as indicated in subparagraph (b) for enlisted personnel, Regular or Reserve, including service in temporary warrant or temporary commissioned status, provided such temporary officer reverts to enlisted status. Also, if reenlisted within a period of 90 days from date of discharge, it will not be construed as an interruption of continuous service, but the period between discharge and reenlistment will not be counted.

(b) Individual Ready Reservists, mobilized for three continuous years, may elect the MCGCM in lieu of continuing their eligibility for the Selected Marine Corps Reserve Medal. Administrative units should make an appropriate entry in the Marine's official military record (OMPF), which indicates the Marine was mobilized under Title 10, specifies the dates of the mobilization period, and that the Marine elected to receive the MCGCM for the period of active duty. A copy of the Marine's orders and the award certificate should be filed in the Marine's OMPF for historical purposes.

(c) Provided the individual is otherwise qualified, an MCGCM shall be authorized for any three years of enlisted service consisting of a combination of periods of active service in a war, national emergency, or armed hostilities in which the United States is engaged. When the first period of such service terminated prior to 10 December 1945, a total of four years of enlisted service is required. In establishing eligibility for the MCGCM under this paragraph, service performed during World War II, Korea, and Vietnam will not be creditable unless entry or reentry to active service occurred during the inclusive periods 8 September 1939 to 31 December 1946; 27 June 1950 to 27

July 1954; and/or 3 July 1965 to 30 September 1975.

(d) For the first award only, the MCGCM may be awarded, provided conduct requirements are met, to the next of kin in cases when a service member is killed in combat against an opposing armed force, or dies as a direct result of wounds received in combat against an opposing armed force, or dies in the line of duty when such death was directly related to actions against the enemy. In addition, for the first award only, the MCGCM is authorized for individuals who are separated from the Naval Service for physical disability, as a result of wounds incurred in combat against an opposing armed force, or in the line of duty when such wounds resulted directly from action against the enemy, provided conduct requirements are met. For the first award only, the MCGCM may be presented posthumously to the next of kin of POWs if the service member's death occurs while in a POW status, provided it has been determined the individual's conduct while a POW was acceptable.

(e) The three-year requirement for the MCGCM may be waived upon a Marine's completion of Officer Candidate School (OCS), as long as the period waived does not exceed 90 days. Upon completion of OCS, requests for waiver of the three-year requirement shall be submitted to CMC (MMMA) for consideration.

(2) Conduct

(a) The MCGCM shall be earned for otherwise qualifying service, involving no convictions by courts-martial or non-judicial punishment (NJP) under the Uniform Code of Military Justice, Article 15, and no lost time by reason of sickness-misconduct or injury-misconduct. Prior to 27 April 1990, not more than one NJP was allowed.

(b) When NJP or a court-martial voids creditability of service, a new good conduct period shall commence effective on the date of approval of the NJP, or on the date of the convening authority's action on the court-martial, except when the offense occurred within the three-year period and the date of approval of the NJP or of the convening authority's action is after the expiration of the three-year period; under these circumstances, the date of the offense shall be the commencement date for the new period. Offenses committed in a previous period will not be considered when determining eligibility during the current three-year period.

4-8

(c) When sentenced to confinement as a result of conviction by any court-martial, a new period shall begin with the date of restoration to duty, even though in a probationary status. The date of approval by the convening authority on all courts-martial, not involving confinement, shall be the new commencement date. (See also Individual Records Administration Manual (IRAM), Para. 4008, MCO P1070.12K.)

(d) In cases of time lost due to sickness-misconduct or injury-misconduct, the date of return to duty shall be the new commencement date for MCGCM qualifying service.

(e) In the case of individuals placed on the Temporary Disability Retired List (TDRL) who subsequently return to active duty, the period spent on the TDRL does not count as a break in service, nor does it count as active service for computing eligibility for the MCGCM.

(f) When the foregoing requirements have been met, but it is evident the individual is not deserving of the MCGCM due to a repeated record of valid letters of indebtedness, conviction(s) by civil court for major offense(s), or other acts not in keeping with the high moral standards of the Marine Corps, the commanding officer will make the appropriate recommendation to CMC (MMMA) stating the reasons.

c. Certificates. A Good Conduct Award Certificate (NAVMC-11416(11-02)) will be completed by the commanding officer at the time entitlement is confirmed for presentation to the member.

4. Naval Reserve Meritorious Service Medal

a. Authorization. The Naval Reserve Meritorious Service Medal (NRMSM) was authorized by SECNAV on 22 June 1964. Originally SECNAV approved a National Naval Reserve Policy Board Item in 1960 for the award as a ribbon, in recognition of Navy Reservists on inactive duty for fulfilling certain requirements with distinction. The NRMSM is intended to provide Navy Reservists an award equivalent to the Navy Good Conduct Medal.

b. Eligibility Requirements. The initial date for computation of service is 1 July 1958. From 1 July 1958 through 31 December 1995, the period of eligibility was four years.

Beginning 1 January 1996, the period of eligibility is three years. The medal may be awarded to an enlisted Navy Reservist who meets the following minimum requirements:

(1) Performs three periods of active duty of not less than 12 consecutive days each, unless Commander, Navy Reserve Force or his delegated authority waives any period or portion of a period. Any combination of Annual Training (AT), Active Duty for Training (ADT), and/or Active Duty for Special Work (ADSW) satisfies the annual requirement. AT completed prior to 31 August 1994 must have been for periods of not less than 12 consecutive days, unless waived by competent authority for reasons not initiated by the individual reservist.

(2) Attends a minimum of 90 percent of all scheduled drills each year prior to 1 October 1997, and a minimum of 85 percent thereafter, with an organized unit of the Navy Reserve, for three consecutive years (authorized equivalent instruction or duty may be credited in lieu of drills). Assignments to Records Review of six months or less may be counted toward eligibility for this award, provided the member maintains eligibility for a satisfactory year toward retirement by completing correspondence courses. A period of eligibility interrupted for six months or more will result in a new three-year period beginning with the date of return to a drilling status. Situations not covered in this article should be addressed to NPC (PERS—913) for resolution.

(3) When a member of the Navy Reserve is ordered to active duty, temporary active duty, or initial active duty for training, such period(s) will be credited toward fulfillment of the requirements prescribed in paragraphs 3b(1) and (2) of this article under the following conditions:

(a) The active duty consists of at least 30 days;

(b) The member must have earned some credit toward an award while in an inactive duty drilling status, except for personnel enlisted in reserve programs with no drilling obligation prior to reporting to active duty. These programs include Two Year General Detail (GENDET), Three Year Enlistment Apprenticeship, Sea/Air Mariner (SAM), or TAR Enlistment (TEP) Programs. Personnel enlisted in these programs may receive credit toward the NRMSM for periods of active duty or active duty for training (ACDUTRA) performed, provided such a period is less than three years.

(c) Upon completion of the three-year eligibility requirement for the award while on continuous active duty, the member may not qualify for subsequent awards without returning to an inactive duty drill status. Continuous active duty may be applied toward the award of a Navy Good Conduct Medal.

(d) Active duty time credited toward the award of the Navy Good Conduct Medal may not be credited toward eligibility for the NRMSM. Active duty time not credited toward award of the NGCM may be credited toward the NRMSM provided the member affiliates with the Selected Reserve within 90 days of discharge or release from active duty and has met all other requirements for the NGCM.

(4) Conduct and Performance

(a) Member must have a clear record for the period of eligibility (no convictions by courts-martial or NJP). If a member's service record indicates convictions by either court-martial or NJP, the three-year period shall begin with the date of completion of the court-martial sentence or NJP.

(b) No enlisted performance evaluation mark below 2.0 in any trait subsequent to 31 December 1995, or below 3.0 in military knowledge/performance, rating knowledge/performance, reliability, military bearing, personal behavior, and directing between 31 August 1983 and 31 December 1995 (or equivalent when other than numerical values are assigned).

c. Certificates. A certificate shall be prepared for each award earned. The member's rate, name, branch of service, and number of the award shall be centered in the appropriate spaces. The ending date of the period of the service for which the award was earned shall be centered after "Awarded for service completed on." The commanding officer's name, rank, and branch of service shall be typed above "Commanding Officer," and his/her signature affixed.

5. Selected Marine Corps Reserve Medal

a. Authorization. The Selected Marine Corps Reserve Medal (SMCRM) was established by a SECNAV directive of 19 February 1939.

b. <u>Eligibility Requirements</u>. Awarded to members of the Selected Marine Corps Reserve (SMCR) who, effective 1 January 1996, fulfilled designated service requirements within any three-year period of service in the Organized Marine Corps Reserve. For the period 1 July 1925 through 31 December 1995, inclusive, a four-year period of service is required. The following are specific eligibility requirements for this medal:

(1) Attendance with an SMCR unit, including duty in an Individual Mobilization Augmentee (IMA) billet in Training Category A, at three consecutive annual field training periods. A period of active duty for training which was authorized to be performed in lieu of a regular annual field training period will fulfill this requirement.

(2) Effective 24 April 1961, attendance with an SMCR unit, including duty in an IMA billet in Training Category A, of 90 percent of all scheduled drills each year for four consecutive years. Eligibility for the medal prior to that date is based on 80 percent attendance of all scheduled drills. (Appropriate duty or equivalent instruction-or-duty may be credited in lieu of drills.)

(3) In the case of officers and noncommissioned officers (sergeant or above), the commanding officer (or the Commander, Marine Corps Mobilization Command (MOBCOM) in the case of IMA Category A) is responsible for determining whether the individual's service and performance of duty warrant the award. Enlisted personnel in the grade of corporal and below must have obtained a combined average of conduct and proficiency markings of 4.0 or above for the first three-year period. For subsequent three-year periods, enlisted personnel must have obtained a combined average of conduct and proficiency markings of 4.5 or above. When it is evident an individual who otherwise fulfills the eligibility criteria is not deserving of this award because of a repeated record of valid indebtedness or other acts which are not in keeping with the high moral standards required of all Marines, the commanding officer (or Commander, MOBCOM in the case of IMA Category A) will make an appropriate recommendation to CMC (MMMA) stating the reasons.

(4) When called to active duty in time of war or national emergency, SMCR members (including IMA Category A) may be credited, while on active duty, with the annual field

training and required drill attendance, provided they have
served not less than one month on active duty during each
qualification year. Such active service may be credited only
for the purpose of qualification for the medal or bronze star
toward which the reservist is working at the time of
mobilization. When the reservist's three-year period is
completed, active duty subsequently performed may not be
credited toward the issuance of a medal or star. If the period
of active duty is of such duration that the reservist is ordered
to inactive status prior to completion of the reservist's three-
year period, the time spent on active duty may be credited
toward the award of the medal, but credit for active duty will
not be allowed for any three-year period which began with the
reservist on active duty. Once the award is earned after
mobilization, the reservist must return to drill and training
status in the SMCR (including IMA category "A") before a new
qualification period begins.

        (5) When a member of the SMCR is unable to attend drills
due to absence from the place of drill, or for causes beyond
his/her control, exclusive of sickness, the reservist should
request a leave of absence for such period, in order that the
absence from the regular drill period will not count against the
record of attendance for eligibility for the Selected Marine
Corps Reserve Medal.

        (6) Retroactive to 12 January 1961, the medal will be
awarded to officers prohibited by the rotation system, due to
the lack of billets, from serving in the SMCR (including service
as an IMA category A) for a three-year period, provided they
have completed any continuous five anniversary years of
satisfactory Federal service in the Marine Corps Reserve
(including IMA Training Categories A, B, C, and D) as defined by
regulations. This must include a minimum of two consecutive
years of satisfactory participation as a member of an SMCR unit,
or as an IMA Category A, during which attendance at drills and
periods of annual field training meets the requirements cited
above.

        (7) Any period of qualifying service beginning with SMCR
membership, interrupted by duty with the Active Reserve (AR)
Program, shall not be considered a break in said period of three
consecutive years for eligibility. Furthermore, any such period
of active duty may be credited with the annual field training
and required drill attendance for the purpose of completing

qualification only for the medal or bronze star toward which the reservist was working at the time of active duty in the AR Program.

(8) When enlisted Marine Corps reservists are assigned to active duty in the AR Program, they must elect whether to continue their eligibility for the SMCRM for which they have accumulated qualifying service, or commence qualifying service for the MCGCM. Officers may continue to earn qualifying service toward SMCRM. Under no circumstances may a Reservist commence an eligibility period for the SMCRM while on the AR Program. MCO P1070.12K (IRAM) contains administrative instructions.

(9) Individual Ready Reservists mobilized for three continuous years may elect the MCGCM in lieu of continuing their eligibility for the SMCRM. Administrative units should make an appropriate entry in the Marine's official military record (OMPF), which indicates the Marine was mobilized under Title 10, specifies the dates of the mobilization period, and that the Marine elected to receive the MCGCM for the period of active duty. A copy of the Marine's orders and the award certificate should be filed in his/her OMPF for historical purposes.

c. Certificates. At the time eligibility is confirmed, a Selected Marine Corps Reserve Certificate (NAVMC 10592) will be completed by the commanding officer for presentation to the member.

6. Navy Expeditionary Medal

a. Authorization. Navy Department General Order (N.D.G.O.) No. 84 of 5 August 1936.

b. Eligibility Requirements. Awarded to U.S. Navy service members who have actually landed on foreign territory and engaged in operations against armed opposition, or operated under circumstances deemed to merit special recognition, and for which no service or campaign medal was awarded. Only personnel attached to one of the approved ships or units during the eligibility period, and who actually participated in the given operation, are eligible for the Navy Expeditionary Medal (NEM). This includes personnel attached to a squadron or unit embarked in a ship during the eligible period for that ship. Members of rear echelons, transients, observers, and personnel assigned for short periods of Temporary Additional Duty (TAD) or Training Duty (TD) are not normally eligible for the award. However, an individual will be given consideration in those instances when the local commander certifies a particular and significant contribution. Such certification should be submitted to the CNO/CMC, via the fleet commander who exercised operational control in the area involved. CNO maintains a list of eligible ships/units.

    c. <u>Authorized Operations</u>. The following are the most recently authorized expeditions:

CUBA	03 Jan 61-23 Oct 62
THAILAND	16 May 62-10 Aug 62
INDIAN OCEAN/IRAN/YEMEN	08 Dec 78-06 Jun 79
IRAN/INDIAN OCEAN	21 Nov 79-20 Oct 81
LEBANON	20 Aug 82-31 May 83
LIBYA	20 Jan 86-27 Jun 86
PERSIAN GULF	01 Feb 87-23 Jul 87
LIBERIA (SHARP EDGE)	05 Aug 90-21 Feb 91
RWANDA (DISTANT RUNNER)	07 Apr 94-18 Apr 94
ERITERA (SAFE DEPARTURE)	06 Jun 98-25 Jun 98
USS COLE (DETERMINED RESPONSE)	12 Oct 00-15 Dec 02

    d. <u>Awarding Authority</u>. Commanding officers shall ensure appropriate service record entries are made for eligible enlisted personnel, and issue letters of eligibility for eligible officer personnel. No citation or certificate will be issued.

    e. <u>Limitations</u>. The NEM may only be awarded cases in which Navy units were the sole participants in the designated operation. In cases where an operation involved participation of units from other branches of the U.S. Armed Forces, the Armed Forces Expeditionary Medal (AFEM) shall be considered the more appropriate award. See paragraph 10 below for further details regarding the AFEM.

7. <u>Marine Corps Expeditionary Medal</u>

    a. <u>Authorization</u>. M.C.G.O. No. 33 of 8 May 1919.

    b. <u>Eligibility Requirements</u>. Awarded to U.S. Marine Corps personnel per the requirements listed above for the Navy Expeditionary Medal. CMC maintains listings of eligible units.

c. <u>Limitations</u>. The Marine Corps Expeditionary Medal (MCEM) may only be awarded when Navy and Marine Corps units were the <u>sole</u> participants in the designated operation. In cases where an operation involved the participation of units from other branches of the U.S. Armed Forces, the AFEM shall be considered the more appropriate award. See paragraph 10 below for further details regarding the AFEM.

d. <u>Branch of Service</u>. In cases where Navy personnel are assigned to units of the Marine Corps operating forces that have been awarded the MCEM, Navy personnel will wear the NEM in lieu of the MCEM. Conversely, Marines assigned to units of the Navy operating forces that have been awarded the NEM will wear the MCEM in lieu of the NEM.

8. <u>National Defense Service Medal</u>

a. <u>Authorization</u>. E.O. 10448, E.O. 12776, and E.O. 13293.

b. <u>Eligibility Requirements</u>

(1) Honorable active service as a member of the Armed Forces for any of the following periods, all dates inclusive: 27 June 1950 to 28 July 1954; 1 January 1961 to 14 August 1974; 2 August 1990 to 30 November 1995; and 12 September 2001 to a date to be determined.

(2) Categories of personnel listed below are ineligible, except as noted:

(a) Guard and Reserve force personnel on short tours of active duty to fulfill training obligations under an inactive duty training program, including drill periods and two-week training. However, effective 8 October 1991, the President of the United States expanded criteria to include all members of the National Guard and Reserve who were part of the Selected Reserve in good standing during the periods 2 August 1990 to 30 November 1995, and from 12 September 2001 to a date to be determined. Consequently, all members of the Navy and Marine Corps Reserve who were part of the Selected Reserve in good standing during said periods are eligible.

(b) Any person on temporary active duty to serve on boards, courts, commissions and like organizations.

(c) Any person on active duty for the sole purpose of undergoing a physical examination.

(d) Any person on active duty for purposes other than extended active duty.

(3) Subparagraph (2) above shall not bar award of the National Defense Service Medal (NDSM) to members of the Guard or Reserve forces, who, after 31 December 1960, become eligible for award of the Armed Forces Expeditionary Medal or the Vietnam Service Medal, who serve for 30 days or more on temporary active duty. Such persons shall be considered to be performing active service for the purpose of eligibility for the NDSM.

(4) Midshipmen attending the Naval Academy during the above periods are eligible for this medal.

(5) Naval Reserve Officers Training Corps (NROTC) Midshipmen are only eligible if they participated in a summer cruise in an area that qualified for a campaign medal.

9.   Antarctica Service Medal

a.   Authorization.   P.L. 86-600 of 7 July 1960.

b.   Eligibility Requirements.   Subsequent to 1 January 1946 until a date to be determined, each person who meets the qualifications of any of the subparagraphs below shall be eligible to receive the award. For the purpose of this paragraph, Antarctica is defined as the area south of latitude 60 degrees south.

(1) Any member of the U.S. Armed Forces or civilian citizen, national or resident alien of the United States who participates in scientific, direct support, or exploration operations in Antarctica as a member of a U.S. expedition.

(2) Any member of the U.S. Armed Forces or civilian citizen, national or resident alien of the United States who participates in a foreign Antarctic expedition, in coordination with a U.S. Antarctic expedition, and who is under the sponsorship and approval of competent U.S. government authority.

(3) Any member of the U.S. Armed Forces who participates in flights as a crew member of an aircraft flying to or from the Antarctic Continent, in support of operations in Antarctica.

(4) Any member of the U.S. Armed Forces or civilian citizen, national or resident alien of the United States who serves in a United States ship operating south of latitude 60 degrees south, in support of U.S. programs in Antarctica.

(5) The Secretary of the Department, under whose cognizance the expedition falls, may approve the award for any person, including a citizen of a foreign nation, who does not fulfill the qualifications under subparagraphs (1) through (4) above, or the following paragraphs establishing the time requirements of participation, but who participates in a U.S. Antarctic expedition at the invitation of a participating U.S. agency, provided the commander of the military support force, as senior U.S. representative in Antarctica, determines that the individual shared the hardships and hazards of the expedition, and that his/her service was outstanding and exceptional.

(6) Prior to 1 June 1973, there is no period of service requirement for award eligibility. Beginning 1 June 1973, the requirement is 30 days under competent orders to duty at sea or ashore, south of latitude 60 degrees south. Days do not have to be consecutive. The following exceptions apply:

(a) Each day of duty under competent orders at any remote, outlying station on the Antarctic Continent will count as two days when determining award eligibility.

(b) Effective 1 July 1987, flight crews of aircraft providing logistics support from outside the Antarctic area may earn the medal based on 15 missions into the area. One "mission" consists of one flight in and one flight out of the area. When an aircrew is required to remain overnight due to weather or other circumstances, members earn one day for each actual day spent in the area of eligibility (AOE). A combination of missions flown and days in the AOE may be used to establish award eligibility, with one mission equal to two days.

c. Medal Attachments

(1) Clasps. Personnel who stay on the Antarctic Continent during the winter months shall be eligible to wear a bronze clasp with the words "Wintered Over" on the suspension ribbon of the large medal only. A gold clasp is authorized for the second wintering over period, and a silver clasp is worn to denote the third or subsequent wintering over period. Not more

than one clasp shall be worn on the suspension ribbon of the medal. The winter period is from mid-March to early October. The summer period is from early October to mid-March.

(2) Disks. The first wintering over eligibility will be denoted by a 5/16-inch bronze disk with an outline of the Antarctic Continent inscribed thereon worn on the miniature medal suspension ribbon or ribbon bar representing the medal. (Disk is worn with peninsula pointing up.) A gold disk will represent the second wintering over period. A silver disk will represent the third or subsequent wintering over period. Not more than one disk shall be worn on the ribbon bar.

d. Awarding Authority. CNO (DNS-35) is the awarding authority and maintains the list of eligible ships and units.

e. Subsequent Awards. Subsequent awards are not authorized.

10. Armed Forces Expeditionary Medal

a. Authorization. E.O. 10977 of 4 December 1961.

b. Eligibility Requirements

(1) Personnel. Awarded to personnel of the U. S. Armed Forces who, after 1 July 1958:

(a) Participate as members of U.S. military units in a U.S. military operation in which personnel of any military department participate in significant numbers, in the opinion of the Joint Chiefs of Staff (JCS).

(b) Encounter, during such participation, foreign armed opposition, or are otherwise placed in such position that hostile action by foreign armed forces was imminent, in the opinion of the JCS, even though such hostile action did not materialize.

(2) Categories of Operations. The Armed Forces Expeditionary Medal (AFEM) may be authorized for three categories of operations:

(a) U.S. military operations.

(b) U.S. operations in direct support of the United Nations.

(c) U.S. operations of assistance to friendly

foreign nations.

(3) Definitions

(a) The "Area of Operations" is defined as:

<u>1</u> The foreign territory upon which U.S. Armed Forces have actually landed, or are present, and specifically deployed for the direct support of the designated military operation.

<u>2</u> Adjacent water areas in which U.S. ships are operating, patrolling or providing direct support of operations.

<u>3</u> The airspace above and adjacent to the area in which operations are being conducted. Ships and units present in an area solely for training purposes are not eligible for the award.

(b) "Direct Support" is defined as furnishing fire, patrol, guard, reconnaissance or other military support, and the supply by ground units, ships and aircraft, of services and/or supplies and equipment to combat forces in the area of operations, provided such support involves actually entering the designated area.

(4) Degree of Participation. Personnel must be bona fide members of a unit engaged in the operation, or meet one or more of the following criteria:

(a) Serve not less than 30 consecutive days in the area of operations.

(b) Engage in direct support of the operation for 30 consecutive days or 60 non-consecutive days, provided such support involves entering the area of operations.

(c) Serve for the full period when an operation is less than 30 days.

(d) Engage in actual combat or duty equally as hazardous as combat duty, during an operation against armed opposition, regardless of time in the area.

(e) Participate as a regularly assigned crewmember of an aircraft flying into, out of, within or over the area in support of the military operation.

(f) Be recommended or attached to a unit recommended for the award by the appropriate Combatant Commander, although the criteria above may not have been fulfilled.

(g) Personnel are entitled to the award if they were attached to or served onboard a ship or unit for at least one day during the period(s) for which that ship or unit is listed as eligible. This includes personnel attached to a squadron or unit embarked in a ship during the period(s) for which that ship is listed as eligible. Members of rear echelons, transients, observers and personnel assigned for short periods of TAD and training duty are normally not eligible for the award; however, consideration will be given in those instances where the cognizant commander certifies a particular and significant contribution by an individual. Such certification should be submitted to CNO/CMC, via the fleet commander who exercised operational control in the area involved.

(5) Eligible Operations. Appendix A to this chapter contains the operations designated by JCS as qualifying for the AFEM.

(6) Eligible Ships and Units. Ships and units present in an area solely for training purposes, or transiting the area are not eligible for the award. Squadrons or units embarked in a ship during the period for which that ship is listed as eligible are automatically eligible for the medal.

(7) Limitations. The AFEM shall be awarded only for operations for which no other U.S. campaign medal is approved. However, this does not preclude AFEM eligibility for subsequent on-going operations if the associated campaign medal has been terminated. No individual shall be eligible for both the AFEM and a campaign medal during a single tour or deployment in the designated operation. For operations in which personnel of only one military department participate, the medal shall be awarded only if there is no other suitable award available to that department. In the case of an operation in which Navy and Marine Corps units were the sole participants and another campaign medal has not been authorized, the Navy Expeditionary Medal and Marine Corps Expeditionary Medal shall be considered the more appropriate awards for the Naval personnel assigned or attached to the participating units.

(8) Election of AFEM or Vietnam Service Medal. The AFEM shall not be issued for service in Vietnam after 3 July 1965. Personnel who earned the AFEM for service in Vietnam during the period 1 July 1958 to 3 July 1965, inclusive, may elect to

receive the Vietnam Service Medal in lieu of the AFEM. No individual may be issued both medals for service in Vietnam during the period 1 July 1958 to 28 March 1973.

(9) Election of the AFEM or the Navy Expeditionary Medal/Marine Corps Expeditionary Medal. Members of the Naval service may elect one expeditionary medal for the following operations:

Lebanon	25 Aug 82
Libya	20 Jan 86 to 27 Jun 96
Persian Gulf	24 Jul 87 to 01 Aug 90
Panama	20 Dec 89 to 31 Jan 90

c. Approval of Operations. The JCS shall designate operations that qualify for the AFEM. Recommendations for military operations to be designated shall be submitted through joint channels to the JCS.

d. Subsequent Awards. Service stars are authorized for participation in each subsequent operation. Participation in two or more engagements within the same operation does not entitle the individual to wear a service star on the AFEM.

11. Kosovo Campaign Medal

a. Authorization. E.O. 13154 of 3 May 2000.

b. Eligibility requirements. Issued to officer and enlisted personnel of the U.S. Armed Forces participating in or in direct support of Kosovo operations within the established areas of eligibility (AOE).

(1) Personnel must have served in one or both of the following campaign AOEs:

(a) Kosovo Air Campaign AOE (24 March to 10 June 1999): total land and air space of Serbia (including Kosovo), Montenegro, Albania, Macedonia, Bosnia, Croatia, Hungary, Romania, Greece, Bulgaria, Italy, Slovenia, and the waters and air space of the Adriatic and Ionian Seas north of the 39th latitude.

(b) Kosovo Defense Campaign AOE (11 June 1999 to TBD): total land and air space of Serbia (including Kosovo), Montenegro, Albania, Macedonia, and the waters and air space of the Adriatic Sea within 12 nautical miles of the Montenegro,

Albania, and Croatia coastlines south of 42 degrees 52 minutes north latitude.

(c) The above campaign AOEs include the following operations in which personnel may have participated or served in direct support of:

ALLIED FORCE	24 Mar 99 to 10 Jun 99
NOBLE ANVIL	24 Mar 99 to 20 Jul 99
Task Force SABER	31 Mar 99 to 08 Jul 99
Task Force HUNTER	01 Apr 99 to 01 Nov 99
SUSTAIN HOPE	04 Apr 99 to 10 Jul 99
SHINING HOPE	04 Apr 99 to 10 Jul 99
ALLIED HARBOR	04 Apr 99 to 01 Sep 99
Task Force HAWK	05 Apr 99 to 24 Jun 99
JOINT GUARDIAN	11 Jun 99 to TBD
Task Force FALCON	11 Jun 99 to TBD per JOINT GUARDIAN

(2) While engaged in direct support of the operation or as members of an operational unit participating in the operation, personnel must serve 30 consecutive or 60 non-consecutive days in the AOE or meet one of the following criteria:

(a) Be engaged in actual combat with armed opposition, or duty equally as hazardous, during the operation, regardless of time in the AOE; or

(b) Be wounded, injured, or require medical evacuation from the AOE regardless of time in the AOE; or

(c) Participate as regularly assigned aircrew members flying sorties into, out of, within or over the AOE in direct support of military operations; for example, reconnaissance, combat air patrol, or electronic surveillance missions subject to anti-aircraft fire and surface-to-air missiles, vice administrative or logistical flights within secure areas. Each day that one or more sorties are flown, into, out of, within or over the AOE shall count as one day toward the 30 or 60-day requirement.

c. Definition. Direct support is defined as service supplied by ground units, ships, or aircraft, provided it actually involves entering the AOE. Such service may include ships and aircraft providing fire, patrol, guard, reconnaissance, or other military support. A unit that was not specifically assigned to support the above listed operations, or was not subject to combat conditions, must request approval via their operational command to Commander, U.S. Naval Forces, Europe (COMUSNAVEUR).

   d. Awarding Authority

      (1) Commanding officers exercising Navy and Marine Corps Achievement Medal authority are authorized to award the Kosovo Campaign Medal (KCM). COMUSNAVEUR is the final authority for questions of eligibility.

      (2) SECDEF approved the award to the following naval vessels, as an exception to policy, for the period of the Kosovo Air Campaign (24 March to 10 June 1999): USS NORFOLK, USS MIAMI, USS ALBUQUERQUE, USS NICHOLSON, USS PHILIPPINE SEA, and USS GONZALEZ.

   e. Engagement Stars. A maximum of two service stars may be earned for the KCM, one for the Air Campaign and one for the Defense Campaign. The eligibility periods for the service stars may not overlap. Service stars shall not be awarded for participation in the individual operations listed above.

12. Afghanistan Campaign Medal

   a. Authorization. E.O. 13363 of 29 November 2004, as amended by Public Law 109-163.

   b. Eligibility Requirements

      (1) Service by military personnel in direct support of Operation ENDURING FREEDOM (OEF), in the designated area of eligibility (AOE), which encompasses the entire land area of the country of Afghanistan, and all air space above the land. The period of eligibility is 11 September 2001 to a date to be determined. Effective 1 May 2005, the Afghanistan Campaign Medal (ACM) is the only award authorized for service in the Afghanistan AOE. See paragraph 14(f) below for guidelines to determine eligibility for the Global War on Terrorism Expeditionary Medal (GWOTEM) and ACM prior to 1 May 2005.

      (2) Service members must have been assigned, attached, or mobilized to units operating in the AOE for 30 consecutive or 60 non-consecutive days, or meet one of the following criteria:

(a) Be engaged in actual combat during an armed engagement, regardless of time in the AOE.

(b) Be wounded, killed, or injured requiring medical evacuation from the AOE, while participating in an operation or on official duties. Non-combat medical evacuation meets the qualification criteria.

(c) Participate as a regularly assigned aircrew member flying sorties into, out of, within, or over the AOE in direct support of military operations. Each day that one or more sorties are flown, into, out of, within, or over the AOE shall count as one day toward the 30 or 60-day requirement.

c. Subsequent Awards. There will be no subsequent awards of the ACM; therefore, service stars are not authorized.

d. Awarding Authority

(1) Navy Personnel. Commanding officers exercising Navy and Marine Corps Achievement Medal authority are authorized to award the ACM. Commands shall make the appropriate service record entries and issue the medals. The miniature bronze Fleet Marine Force Combat Operation emblem may be authorized for qualified Navy personnel who have engaged in actual combat; see Chapter 1, Article 123.

(2) Marine Corps Personnel. Unit commanders are authorized to issue the ACM to personnel assigned to their command who meet the eligibility criteria.

(3) Navy personnel attached to DoD, Joint, or other non-DON commands who believe they meet the eligibility criteria should have their command confirm eligibility and submit the appropriate service record documentation. Marines shall submit confirming documentation to their administrative chain of command for recording in MCTFS and entry into their Official Military Personnel File.

e. Participating Unit Lists. Navy Commanding Officers whose units meet the criteria for the ACM must submit their unit name with start and end dates in the AOE to CNO (DNS-35). Email a scanned PDF copy of the signed request to navyawards@navy.mil, using "ACM participating unit (your unit name)" as the subject line. CNO (DNS-35) will post a list of qualified units on the

Navy Awards Website. Future command input will be via command direct entry into the CESMEL (Campaign, Expeditionary, and Service Medal Eligibility List) section of NDAWS. This change will be announced via a NAVADMIN. Marine Corps unit commanders are not required to submit lists of participating units.

13. Iraq Campaign Medal

    a. Authorization. E.O. 13363 of 29 November 2004.

    b. Eligibility Requirements

        (1) Service by military personnel in direct support of Operation IRAQI FREEDOM (OIF) in the designated area of eligibility (AOE), which encompasses all land area of the country of Iraq, the contiguous waters of Iraq out to 12 nautical miles, and all air space above these waters and land area. The period of eligibility is 19 March 2003 to a date to be determined. Effective 1 May 2005, the Iraq Campaign Medal (ICM) is the only award authorized for service in the Iraq AOE. See paragraph 14(f) below for guidelines to determine eligibility for the Global War on Terrorism Expeditionary Medal (GWOTEM) and ICM prior to 1 May 2005. Personnel who deployed in support of Operation SOUTHERN WATCH and subsequently transitioned into OIF on or after 19 March 2003, must elect to receive either the Armed Forces Expeditionary Medal, the GWOTEM, or the ICM. Personnel may not be authorized more than one of these medals for a single deployment.

        (2) Service members must have been assigned, attached, or mobilized to units operating in the AOE for 30 consecutive or 60 non-consecutive days, or meet one of the following criteria:

        (a) Be engaged in actual combat during an armed engagement, regardless of time in the AOE.

        (b) Be wounded, killed, or injured requiring medical evacuation from the AOE, while participating in an operation or on official duties. Non-combat medical evacuation does meet the qualification criteria.

        (c) Participate as a regularly assigned aircrew member flying sorties into, out of, within, or over the AOE in direct support of military operations. Each day that one or more sorties are flown, into, out of, within, or over the AOE shall count as one day towards the 30 or 60-day requirement.

c. Subsequent Awards. There will be no subsequent awards of the ICM; therefore, service stars are not authorized.

d. Awarding Authority

(1) Navy Personnel. Commanding officers exercising Navy and Marine Corps Achievement Medal authority are authorized to award the ICM. Commands shall make the appropriate service record entries and issue the medals. The miniature bronze Fleet Marine Force Combat Operation emblem may be authorized for qualified Navy personnel who have engaged in actual combat; see Chapter 1, Article 123.

(2) Marine Corps Personnel. Unit commanders are authorized to issue the ICM to personnel assigned to their command who meet the eligibility criteria.

(3) Navy personnel attached to DoD, Joint, or other non-DON commands who believe they meet the eligibility criteria should have their command confirm eligibility and submit the appropriate service record documentation. Marines shall submit confirming documentation to their administrative chain of command for recording in MCTFS and entry into their Official Military Personnel File.

e. Participating Unit Lists. Navy Commanding Officers whose units meet the criteria for the ICM must submit their unit name with start and end dates in the AOE to CNO (DNS-35). Email a scanned PDF copy of the signed request to navyawards@navy.mil, using "ICM participating unit (your unit name)" as the subject line. CNO (DNS-35) will post a list of qualified units on the Navy Awards Website. Future command input will be via command direct entry into the CESMEL (Campaign, Expeditionary, and Service Medal Eligibility List) section of NDAWS. This change will be announced via a NAVADMIN. Marine Corps unit commanders are not required to submit lists of participating units.

14. Global War on Terrorism Expeditionary Medal

a. Authorization. E.O. 13289 of 12 March 2003.

b. Eligibility Requirements

(1) Service in direct support of the Global War on Terrorism by military personnel deployed abroad for designated operations in a specified area of eligibility (AOE). The period of eligibility is 11 September 2001 to a date to be determined.

(2) Service members must be assigned, attached, or mobilized to a unit participating in designated operations for 30 consecutive or 60 non-consecutive days, or meet one of the following criteria:

(a) Be engaged in actual combat against the enemy, regardless of time in the AOE.

(b) Be wounded, killed, or injured requiring medical evacuation from the AOE, while participating in the designated operation, regardless of time in the AOE.

(c) Participate as a regularly assigned aircrew member flying sorties into, out of, within, or over the AOE in direct support of the designated operations. Each day that one or more sorties are flown, into, out of, within, or over the AOE shall count as one day towards the 30 or 60-day requirement.

c. Designated Operations. The initial approved operations are Operations ENDURING FREEDOM and IRAQI FREEDOM. SECDEF, in consultation with the Chairman, Joint Chiefs of Staff (CJCS), has the authority to designate future operations as eligible for award of the Global War on Terrorism Expeditionary Medal (GWOTEM). Requests for future operation designation must be submitted from the Combatant Commander to SECDEF, via CJCS. Note: Personnel are only eligible for the GWOTEM for service in the Afghanistan and Iraq AOEs through 30 April 2005. Qualifying service after that date will be recognized by the ACM or ICM, as appropriate.

d. Specified Areas of Eligibility. Appendix B to this chapter provides a list of the qualifying AOEs. Updated lists will be posted at https://awards.navy.mil and http://awards.manpower.usmc.mil. Under no circumstances will units or personnel within the 50 United States or within 200 nautical miles of the shores of the United States be eligible for the GWOTEM.

e. <u>Awarding Authority</u>. The Combatant Commanders are the awarding authority for personnel and units deployed within their AOEs. U.S. Central Command delegated the authority to award the GWOTEM to U.S. Marine Corps Forces Central Command (MarCent) for units/personnel operating in the MarCent area of operations. U.S. Pacific Command delegated the authority to award the GWOTEM to Commander, Fleet Marine Forces Pacific (FMFPac) for units/personnel operating in the FMFPac area of operations.

(1) Unit commanding officers shall nominate qualified participating units or personnel, including location within the AOE and specific dates served in the designated operation, to the awarding authority, via their appropriate chain of command, for approval.

(2) Once the awarding authority approves the request, notification shall be provided to CNO (DNS-35) or CMC (MMMA), as appropriate, and the units will be added to the Navy and Marine Corps master lists posted at https://awards.navy.mil and http://awards.manpower.usmc.mil, respectively.

(3) Commanding officers shall ensure personnel assigned to qualifying units during the appropriate time period are issued the medal, and that proper service record documentation is completed.

(4) For Navy personnel only, the miniature bronze Fleet Marine Force Combat Operation emblem may be authorized for qualified personnel who have engaged in actual combat; see Chapter 1, Article 123.

(5) The DoD has a long-standing policy that U.S. campaign and service medals shall not be awarded to members of foreign militaries. Therefore, coalition partners <u>are not</u> eligible to receive the GWOTEM.

f. <u>Medal Election Guidelines</u>

(1) Eligibility for the GWOTEM for service in Afghanistan and Iraq terminated on 30 April 2005; beginning 1 May 2005, personnel are eligible only for the ACM or ICM, respectively. Personnel who earned the GWOTEM for qualifying service in Afghanistan or Iraq prior to 1 May 2005 shall remain qualified for the GWOTEM; however, they may elect to receive the ACM or ICM <u>in lieu</u> of the GWOTEM for such service. The election

of the ACM or ICM shall be documented with an appropriate service record entry signed by the member. Personnel who met the eligibility criteria for the GWOTEM and ACM, or the GWOTEM and ICM, during a single deployment must elect <u>one</u> of these medals. <u>No individual may be issued both medals for the same period of service.</u> A period of service is defined as a single tour or deployment.

(2) Personnel who elect to retain the GWOTEM for qualifying service in Afghanistan or Iraq prior to 1 May 2005 are eligible to earn the ACM or ICM, respectively, for subsequent deployments within the ACM or ICM AOE. <u>Under no circumstances shall an individual be eligible for both medals for the same action, time period, or service.</u>

   g. <u>Subsequent Awards and Battle Stars</u>. Subsequent awards of the GTOWEM are not authorized; therefore, service stars are not authorized. However, the CJCS, upon the request of a Combatant Commander, may approve battle stars at a future date to recognize personnel who were engaged in actual combat against the enemy, under circumstances involving grave danger of death or serious bodily injury. Commanding officers may identify units or personnel meeting the criteria for battle stars, and forward a request to the Combatant Commander for submission to the CJCS for determination. In addition to the specific unit(s) and/or individual(s) involved, the request shall contain the duration of the actual combat and a detailed description of the actions against the enemy.

15. <u>Global War on Terrorism Service Medal</u>

   a. <u>Authorization</u>. E.O. 13289 of 12 March 2003.

   b. <u>Eligibility Requirements</u>

      (1) Military personnel who participate in or serve in support of the Global War on Terrorism for specified operations on or after 11 September 2001 to a date to be determined.

      (2) Service members must be assigned, attached, or mobilized in CONUS or overseas, to a unit participating in or serving in support of (including indirect support) specified operations for 30 consecutive or 60 non-consecutive days, or meet one of the following criteria:

(a) Be engaged in actual combat, regardless of the time period of service in the operation.

(b) While participating in the specified operation, regardless of time, be killed, wounded, or injured requiring medical evacuation.

(3) Personnel in initial accession training, including follow-on career specific training, are not eligible. Eligibility begins for these personnel once assigned to their first permanent duty station.

(4) The DoD has a long-standing policy that U.S. campaign and service medals shall not be awarded to members of foreign militaries. Therefore, coalition partners are not eligible to receive the Global War on Terrorism Service Medal (GWOTSM).

c. Specified Operations. SECDEF, in consultation with the Chairman, Joint Chiefs of Staff (CJCS), has the authority to designate future qualifying GWOTSM operations. The initial approved operations are as follows:

(1) Airport security (27 Sep 01 through 31 May 02)

(2) Operation NOBLE EAGLE (11 Sep 01 through TBD)

(3) Operation ENDURING FREEDOM (11 Sep 01 through TBD)

(4) Operation IRAQI FREEDOM (19 Mar 03 through TBD)

d. Awarding Authority

(1) Navy Units. Awarding authority rests with the CNO and Combatant Commanders.

(a) Combatant Commanders have awarding authority for personnel assigned to units within their command, and Joint activities and forces directly under their operational control.

(b) CNO authorizes award of the GWOTSM for Navy personnel attached to commands that either directly or indirectly supported the designated operations. Support is defined as administrative, logistical, planning, operational, technical, readiness, and any other support services related to the designated operations.

(c) Echelon 2 commands shall submit a list of organizations deemed qualified for the GWOTSM to CNO for approval. Send all information electronically, to include a list in Excel format, with a signed cover letter in a PDF file to navyawards@navy.mil with the subject line "GWOTSM Qualified List Attached." Approved organizations will be posted on the Navy Awards website.

(d) Organizations reporting directly to SECNAV shall follow the procedures in subparagraphs (b) and (c) above to ensure proper documentation for qualified Navy personnel.

(e) Commanding officers shall ensure personnel eligible for the GWOTSM currently assigned to their command are issued the medal and that proper service record entries are completed.

(2) Marine Corps Units. The awarding authorities are:

(a) Combatant Commanders for personnel assigned to units within their command, and Joint activities and forces directly under their operational control.

(b) The CJCS for personnel assigned to the Joint Staff and those Joint activities that report directly to the CJCS.

(c) The directors of defense agencies for service members assigned to their agencies. The Director of Administration and Management, Office of the DoD Field Activities is responsible for the Joint DoD activities that report directly to an OSD principal staff assistant; multilateral and bilateral organizations; and other offices in the Executive Branch, the executive agencies and departments, and independent establishments and government corporations.

(d) The CMC for personnel assigned to headquarters or direct subordinate commands and activities, direct reporting units, and field operating agencies. The CMC may also approve the award for service members assigned to forces directly under his operational control, who fall outside the jurisdiction of the Combatant Commanders. The CMC has approved the GWOTSM for personnel assigned to HQMC, all operating forces, supporting establishments, and external elements that meet the eligibility criteria in subparagraph b. above.

(e) Commanders who have Marines assigned to the respective agencies, departments, and commands outlined in subparagraphs (a) through (d) above, will coordinate with these agencies, departments, and commands to ensure approval of the GWOTSM is documented in the service record of eligible Marines.

e. Subsequent Awards and Battle Stars. Subsequent awards of the GWOTSM are not authorized; therefore, service stars are not authorized. However, although qualifying circumstances will be extremely rare, the CJCS, upon the request of a Combatant Commander, may approve battle stars at a future date to recognize personnel who were engaged in actual combat against the enemy, under circumstances involving grave danger of death or serious bodily injury.

f. Multiple GWOT Medal Guidance. Personnel may receive both the GWOTSM and the Global War on Terrorism Expeditionary Medal (GWOTEM) provided they meet the requirements for both awards and the qualifying periods used to establish eligibility do not overlap.

16. Korea Defense Service Medal

a. Authorization. Public Law 107-314 §532.

b. Eligibility Requirements

(1) Members of the Armed Forces must have served in support of the defense of the Republic of Korea from 28 July 1954 to a date to be determined.

(2) The area of eligibility (AOE) encompasses all land area of the Republic of Korea, and the contiguous waters out to 12 nautical miles, and all air space above the land and water areas.

(3) Service members must have been assigned, attached, or mobilized to units operating in the AOE and have been physically deployed in the AOE for 30 consecutive or 60 non-consecutive days or meet one of the following criteria:

(a) Be engaged in actual combat during an armed engagement, regardless of time in the AOE.

(b) Be wounded or injured in the line of duty and require medical evacuation from the AOE, regardless of time in the AOE.

(c) While participating as a regularly assigned aircrew member flying sorties into, out of, within, or over the AOE in support of military operations. Each day that one or more sorties are flown in accordance with these criteria shall count as one day toward the 30 or 60-day requirement.

(4) Personnel who serve in operations and exercises conducted in the AOE are considered eligible for the award, provided the basic time criteria is met.

(5) Although the eligibility time period is extensive, the 60-day non-consecutive service requirement remains cumulative throughout the entire award period.

c. Awarding Authority. Commanding officers exercising Navy and Marine Corps Achievement Medal awarding authority are authorized to award the Korea Defense Service Medal (KDSM) to personnel who meet the eligibility criteria. Commanding officers shall issue the medals and ensure the appropriate service record entries are made. In the absence of supporting documentation to establish KDSM eligibility, qualified personnel may complete the self-certification document available online at https://awards.navy.mil or http://awards.manpower.usmc.mil. A copy of this form shall be filed in the individual's service record.

d. Subsequent Awards. Only one award of the KDSM is authorized for any individual; therefore, no service stars are authorized.

17. Armed Forces Service Medal

a. Authorization. E.O. 12985 of 11 January 1996.

b. Eligibility Requirements. Participate as members of U.S. military units, in a U.S. military operation deemed to be significant activity, and encounter no foreign armed opposition or imminent threat of hostile action. Personnel must be members of a unit participating in the operation for the delineated time period, within the designated area of eligibility (AOE), or meet one or more of the following criteria:

(1) Be engaged in direct support for 30 consecutive days in the AOE (or for the full period when an operation is of less than 30 days' duration) or for 60 non-consecutive days, provided such support involves entering the AOE.

(2) Participate as a regularly assigned crewmember of an aircraft flying into, out of, within, or over the area of eligibility in support of the operation.

   c. Qualifying Operations

(1) The Armed Forces Service Medal (AFSM) may be authorized for significant U.S. military activities for which no other U.S. campaign or service medal is appropriate, such as:

      (a) Peacekeeping operations.

      (b) Prolonged humanitarian operations.

(2) The AFSM may be awarded for U.S. military operations in direct support of the United Nations (UN) or the North Atlantic Treaty Organization (NATO), and for operations of assistance to friendly foreign nations.

   d. Guidelines

(1) The AFSM provides recognition to participants who deploy to the designated AOE for the qualifying operation. Non-deployed or remotely located support units and individuals are not eligible for the AFSM. Such performance may be recognized by appropriate unit and/or individual decorations.

(2) Because the AFSM may be awarded for a prolonged humanitarian operation, distinction between the AFSM and Humanitarian Service Medal (HSM) must be maintained.

      (a) The HSM is an individual award, presented to individuals who are physically present at the site of immediate relief and who directly contribute to and influence the humanitarian action. The HSM is only awarded for service during the identified period of immediate relief; eligibility for the

HSM terminates once the humanitarian action evolves into an established ongoing operation beyond the initial emergency condition.

(b) The AFSM is a theater award, authorized for presentation to all participants who meet eligibility requirements established for a designated operation.

(c) For operations in which all deployed participants are awarded the HSM, and for which the period of immediate relief coincides with the duration of significant deployed operations, award of the AFSM is not authorized.

(d) The AFSM may be awarded for humanitarian operations for which some (or all) participants are awarded the HSM, when the operation continued beyond the period of immediate relief.

e. Definitions

(1) Significant activity is defined as a United States military operation considered to be of such a high degree of scope, impact, and international significance as to warrant the permanent commemoration and recognition afforded by award of a campaign or service medal.

(2) Area of eligibility (AOE) is defined as follows:

(a) The foreign territory on which troops have actually landed or are present and specifically deployed for the operation.

(b) Adjacent water areas in which ships are operating, patrolling, or providing direct support of the operation.

(c) The air space above and adjacent to the area in which operations are being conducted.

(3) Direct support is defined as services being supplied to participating forces in the AOE by ground units, ships, and aircraft, provided it involves actually entering the designated AOE. This includes units, ships, and aircraft providing logistics, patrol, guard, reconnaissance, or other military support within the AOE.

f. Limitations

(1) The AFSM shall be awarded only for operations for which no other U.S. campaign or service medal is approved.

(2) For operations in which personnel of only one Military Service participate, the AFSM shall be awarded only if there is no other suitable award available to that Service.

(3) The military service of the individual to whom the AFSM is being awarded shall have been honorable.

(4) Award of the AFSM is not authorized for participation in national or international exercises.

(5) The AFSM shall not be awarded for NATO or UN operations not involving significant, concurrent U.S. military support operations.

g. Designation of Areas of Eligibility. The Joint Chiefs of Staff (JCS) designate U.S. military operations that qualify for the AFSM subsequent to 1 June 1992. The following operations have been designated as qualifying:

(1) Bosnia   01 Jul 92 to TBD
     Total land area and airspace of the former
     Republic of Yugoslavia and total land area and
     airspace of the country of Italy, including
     Sicily.
(2) DENY FLIGHT   12 Apr 93 to 02 Dec 95
(3) PROVIDE PROMISE   02 Jun 92 to 15 Feb 96
(4) SHARP GUARD   15 Jun 93 to 20 Sep 96
(5) JOINT ENDEAVOR   20 Nov 95 to 19 Dec 96
(6) PROVIDE COMFORT   01 Dec 95 to 31 Dec 96
(7) JOINT GUARD   20 Dec 96 to 20 Jun 98
(8) UPHOLD DEMOCRACY (Haiti) 01 Apr 95 to 31 Jan 00
    (Total land area and airspace defined by the
    following coordinates: 16-30N/71-40W; 18-00N/
    71-45W; along the Haitian-Dominican Republic border
    to 20N/71-44W; 21N/71W; 21-25N/73W; 21-25N/74W;
    20N/74W; 19-45N/75W; 19N/76W; 16-30N/76W to
    16-30N/71-40W.)
(9) JOINT FORGE   21 Jun 98 to TBD

4-37

Service members may be awarded the Armed Forces
Expeditionary Medal (AFEM) or AFSM, but not both.
The AFEM may be awarded for service in Bosnia-
Herzegovina, Croatia, the Adriatic Sea, and the
respective air space. The AFSM may be awarded for
service elsewhere in the former Republic of
Yugoslavia, Hungary, and the respective air space.

    (10) Hurricanes Katrina/Rita   27 Aug 05 to 27 Feb 06

18. Humanitarian Service Medal

    a. Authorization. E.O. 11965 of 19 January 1977.

    b. Eligibility Requirements

        (1) The Humanitarian Service Medal (HSM) is awarded to
members of the Armed Forces of the United States who, subsequent
to 1 April 1975, distinguish themselves as individuals or as
members of U.S. military units by meritorious, direct, non-
routine participation in a significant military act or operation
of a humanitarian nature.

        (2) In general, an act or operation must be a direct
humanitarian performance by the individuals or unit, at the
designated location. The following types of military acts or
operations may qualify for award of the HSM:

        (a) Significant assistance in the event of national
or international disasters, natural or man-made, such as (but
not limited to) earthquakes, floods, hurricanes, typhoons, or
conflagrations.

        (b) Relief to a starvation area.

        (c) Evacuation of personnel from an area threatened
by a hostile force.

        (d) Support or resettlement of refugees or evacuees.

        (e) Acts or operations of a similar nature, as
determined by the awarding authority.

        (f) Other significant military activities directly
related to humanitarian service, as designated in military

regulations. These must be above and beyond routine actions.

(3) Services rendered in the act or operation being considered must meet each of the following criteria:

(a) Be above and beyond normal duties, and of major significance.

(b) Provide immediate relief, relieve human suffering, and should save lives; property may be a factor.

(c) Must affect the outcome of the situation (inaction would have produced definite negative consequences).

(d) Specific dates must be defined, and must be restricted to the period of "immediate relief." Periods beyond immediate relief are considered to be established, ongoing operations beyond the initial emergency conditions, and these periods are no longer eligible for the HSM, but may be considered for award of the AFSM.

(4) The emergency assistance must be either:

(a) Requested by the President of the United States for assistance within the United States (such as Presidential Emergency Declaration or established contingency plans issued under Presidential authority); or

(b) Requested by the Department of State for overseas areas.

c. Definitions

(1) Direct participation is defined as being physically present at the designated location, and <u>directly influencing and contributing to the action</u>.

(2) Designated location is the immediate site(s) of the humanitarian operations, as defined by the Presidential or Department of State request for assistance. When appropriate, the local commander may recommend specific clarification of designated boundaries based on the intent of the Presidential or Department of State request.

d. Limitations

(1) Service members or elements who remain at geographically separate locations, or who were assigned to the designated location, but did directly influence or contribute to the action, are ineligible for the HSM.

(2) The HSM shall not be awarded for services rendered in domestic disturbances involving law enforcement, demonstrations, or protection of property.

(3) The HSM shall not be awarded for military acts or operations of a routine, day-to-day nature. For example, normal Search and Rescue (SAR) operations conducted by specially trained SAR units are not eligible for the HSM. Other routine operations such as helicopter or destroyer plane guard duty, or emergency transportation of civilian or military medical patients are also ineligible. Similarly, in accordance with the laws and traditions of the seas, the rescue of stricken vessels by naval units would not normally be an eligible action unless there was extreme danger to those being rescued and those performing the rescue.

(4) No service member shall be entitled to more than one award of the HSM for participation in the same military act or operation.

(5) Except for the AFSM, as discussed in the previous article, award of the HSM does not preclude receipt of other awards based on unit achievement or individual valor, achievement, or meritorious service.

e. Awarding Authorities. The Chairman, Joint Chiefs of Staff is the awarding authority for all operations under the auspices of a Combatant Commander. Effective 14 June 1993, SECNAV was delegated awarding authority for other operations involving Naval personnel.

f. Preparation of Recommendations. Recommendations must be entered administratively into command channels within two years of the act or operation to be recognized. Recommendation packages must include the following:

(1) A written justification specifically addressing the eligibility requirements, and fully explaining and attesting to

the humanitarian aspects of the services rendered by personnel in the act or operation being recommended. It should be noted the HSM is an _individual_ award.

(2) A listing of ships or units that participated directly in the act or operation, including dates of involvement and locations. This is to facilitate the processing and documentation of awards only, and _does not imply unit-wide approval_ of the HSM.

(3) For Navy units, an electronic alphabetical listing of service members (preferably in Excel), detailing full name, rank/rate, social security number, branch of Service, and permanent unit at the time of the act or operation. This listing shall be marked "Privacy Sensitive" and include only those service members who meet the eligibility criteria and guidelines in this section. Listings of eligible of Marine Corps personnel shall be submitted using the format delineated at http://awards.manpower.usmc.mil.

(4) Concurrence by the Military Departments concerned when multi-Service participation is involved. The originating activity shall, prior to submission of the recommendation to SECNAV, obtain the concurrence of the Services concerned, including the Commandant, U.S. Coast Guard when members of the U.S. Coast Guard are involved. Such concurrence shall include verification of their service members' participation, and a specific recommendation for approval or disapproval.

(5) Forwarding endorsements that make specific recommendations for approval or disapproval to the Chairman, Joint Chiefs of Staff or SECNAV, as appropriate.

(6) Endorsement of the Combatant Commander who has authority and/or responsibility for the affected area outside the Continental United States.

(7) Documentation of the Presidential or the Department of State request for assistance.

19. _Military Outstanding Volunteer Service Medal_

    a. _Authorization_. E.O. 12830 of 9 January 1993.

    b. _Eligibility Requirements_. The Military Outstanding

Volunteer Service Medal (MOVSM) may be awarded to members of the Armed Forces of the United States who, after 31 December 1992, perform outstanding volunteer community service of a sustained, direct and consequential nature. To be eligible, an individual's service must:

(1) Be to the civilian community, including the military family community;

(2) Be significant in nature and produce tangible results;

(3) Reflect favorably on the Military Service and the Department of Defense; and

(4) Be of a sustained and direct nature.

c. Guidelines

(1) While there is no specific time period to qualify for the MOVSM, approval authorities shall ensure the service to be honored merits the special recognition afforded by the medal. DON views the sustained time period to be three years. The MOVSM is intended to recognize exceptional community support over time, not a single act or achievement. Further, it is intended to honor direct support of community activities. For the purpose of this award, attending membership meetings or social events of a community service group is not considered qualifying service; however, manning a community crisis action telephone line for a sustained period of time is considered qualifying service. The overall level of volunteer participation and impact of an individual's community service is the key to determining whether award of the MOVSM is justified.

(2) The MOVSM recognizes service provided to a community over time; therefore multiple awards of the MOVSM during a single tour of duty are not authorized. However, approval authorities may consider a sustained record of significant community service performed during successive tours when adjudicating recommendations for award of the MOVSM.

(3) Service recognized by award of the MOVSM shall be of a voluntary nature, not detailed or tasked, nor performed as part of a military mission (for example, a unit project).

(4) Volunteering with the following types of organizations are examples of qualifying service: youth programs such as Boy/Girl Scouts; YMCA or YWCA; 4H; Big Brothers/Sisters; sports programs such as Little League and Special Olympics; abuse/rape/suicide hot line volunteers; hospital/blood drive volunteers; education programs such as volunteer teachers, D.A.R.E., and literacy programs; CFC organizations such as March of Dimes, Make-a-Wish Foundation, Salvation Army; volunteer fire department/rescue squad; community centers; neighborhood watch; Meals-on-Wheels; homeless shelters; senior citizens' programs; working with the hearing impaired; fund drives and telethon support; public library story hour; museum guide; local beautification projects such as Adopt-a-Park and Adopt-a-Highway; military affiliates such as USO, Navy and Marine Corps Relief Society, and Navy League Sea Cadet programs.

(5) A MOVSM recommendation may be submitted by anyone senior to the individual being recommended, on the appropriate personal award recommendation form, to the individual's commanding officer. The commanding officer shall certify that the eligibility requirements have been met, and that the member's service has been honorable throughout the award period.

d. Awarding Authority. Authority to award the MOVSM is delegated to officers who have authority to award the Navy and Marine Corps Achievement Medal or Joint Service Achievement Medal and above. The awarding authority shall issue a letter of authorization which includes the period recognized and the organization(s) for whom the qualifying service was performed, as well as any commendatory remarks desired by the awarding authority. For Navy personnel, copies of the approved OPNAV 1650/3 will be forwarded to NPC (PERS-312). For Marine Corps personnel, a copy of the approved Award Processing System award recommendation will automatically be forwarded to MMSB for inclusion in the Marine's official military record. No citation or certificate will be issued.

20. Sea Service Deployment Ribbon

a. Authorization. SECNAVINST 1650.35 of 26 January 1981.

b. Eligibility Requirements. Awarded to officer and enlisted personnel of the United States Navy and Marine Corps. Each Service has distinct eligibility criteria; Navy personnel assigned to Marine Corps units follow Marine Corps policy, and vice versa.

(1) Personnel assigned to U.S. (including Alaska and Hawaii) homeported ships, deploying units, or units of the Marine Corps operating forces are eligible for the Sea Service Deployment Ribbon (SSDR) upon completion of 12 months of accumulated sea duty, which includes at least one deployment of 90 consecutive days.

(a) Changes in deployment patterns to meet operational commitments have resulted in the reduction of some service force ships' deployment lengths to less than 90 days, with an increase in the frequency of deployments. Consequently, effective 18 October 1991, award of the SSDR to members of Navy units that complete two deployments of at least 80 days each within a given 12-month period is authorized.

(b) As an exception to policy, the 12-month accumulated sea duty requirement was waived for personnel who were called to sea duty or deployed for Operations DESERT SHIELD or DESERT STORM (2 August 1990 to 31 December 1991), ENDURING FREEDOM (11 September 2001 to TBD), or IRAQI FREEDOM (19 March 2003 to TBD) to qualify for the initial award only. This waiver does not affect second and subsequent awards of this ribbon.

(2) Personnel assigned to overseas homeported ships, deploying units, or units of the Marine Corps operating forces outside CONUS are eligible upon completion of 12 months of accumulated sea duty or a tour of duty with the Marine Corps operating forces. For personnel assigned overseas, deployments are not a factor and do not provide credit for additional awards of the SSDR. Second and subsequent awards will be earned for each additional 12-month period of qualifying service. For Navy personnel only, after 1 October 1999, SSDR qualification does not preclude also qualifying for the Overseas Service Ribbon.

(3) The SSDR may be awarded retroactively to 15 August 1974. However, only one award may be earned for the period 15 August 1974 to 1 January 1979, regardless of the number of years of sea duty or number of deployments made.

(4) No subsequent changes to the SSDR requirements are retroactive to meet individual eligibility.

c. Waivers

(1) For Navy personnel, a 14-day waiver of the 12-month accumulated sea duty requirement is authorized as long as the 90-day or two 80-day deployment requirement is met.

(2) For Marine Corps personnel, Squadron and Battalion commanding officers have the authority to waive the 90-day deployment criteria for members of the operating forces in CONUS and the 12-month criteria for members of the operating forces outside CONUS, on a case-by-case basis. The intent of this waiver is to allow personnel to earn the SSDR when, through no fault of their own, their 12-month tour or their 90-day deployment is cut short. All approved waivers must be processed via the Award Processing System (APS). Administrative instructions are outlined in MarAdmin 582/03 and will be published in the next revision of MCO 1650.19.

d. Definitions

(1) Sea Duty. Duty performed in commissioned vessels or units that operate away from their homeport or homebase for extended periods.

(2) Deployable Units. A ship (USN, USNS), aircraft squadron, detachment, battalion, or other unit that operates away from its assigned homeport or homebase for a period of either 90 consecutive days or two periods of at least 80 days each within a given 12-month period.

(3) Deployment. A period of either 90 consecutive days or two periods of at least 80 days each with a deployed unit, within a given 12-month period.

e. The following are examples of qualifying service. Situations not covered in this manual shall be addressed to CNO (DNS-35) or CMC (MMMA) as appropriate.

(1) A person who reports to a ship homeported in Norfolk on 1 July 1978 and completes a 90 consecutive day deployment on 1 December 1978 is eligible for the SSDR on 1 July 1979.

(2) A person who served on a ship or deployed unit homeported overseas from 30 June 1977 to 30 June 1980 will be eligible for two awards; i.e., the initial award for the period

ending 1 January 1979 and a second award for service ending
1 January 1980.

(3) A person attached to a U.S. homebased Marine Corps
unit that goes on one rotational deployment for six months and
remains with that unit for two years will earn only one award
because of the single deployment.

(4) A person attached to a U.S. homeported ship for one
year subsequent to 1 January 1979 but does not deploy for 90
consecutive days is not eligible. The same person is then given
Permanent Change of Station (PCS) orders to another U.S.
homeported ship and immediately goes on a deployment. This
person will be eligible upon completion of the 90-day
deployment.

(5) A person assigned on PCS orders to Naval Air
Station, Guam, serving on shore duty that counts as sea duty
will not be eligible for the SSDR regardless of the length of
time assigned. The Overseas Service Ribbon is applicable.

(6) A person assigned to Marine Corps Base (MCB), Camp
Lejeune, goes TAD to Marine Division for five months, completes
a 90-consecutive day deployment and returns to MCB Camp Lejeune
upon completion of the deployment is not eligible because one
year was not spent with a unit of the Marine Corps operating
forces. However, upon completion of an additional seven months
duty with the Marine Corps operating forces, the person will be
eligible for the award.

(7) A person assigned to MCB Camp Butler, Okinawa, will
not be eligible since it is not a unit of the Marine Corps
operating forces.

(8) A Marine attached to a Marine Detachment aboard a
ship homeported overseas will be eligible upon completion of 12
months sea duty.

(9) A person completing a 36-month accompanied tour
overseas with a unit of the Marine Corps operating forces will
be eligible for three awards.

(10) A Marine whose 12-month overseas tour with the
Marine Corps operating forces is terminated early but who
receives full credit for his/her tour in accordance with Marine

Corps Order P1070.12K is eligible for the award.

    f. Awarding Authority. Commanding officers determine
eligibility from service records, affidavits, or upon completion
of eligibility requirements at the current command, and make
appropriate service record entries for enlisted personnel and
issue letters of eligibility for officers. No citation or
certificate will be issued.

21. Navy Arctic Service Ribbon

    a. Authorization. OPNAVNOTE 1650 of 3 June 1987.

    b. Eligibility Requirements. Awarded to officers and
enlisted personnel of the Navy and Marine Corps, or civilian
citizens, national or resident aliens of the United States who
complete 28 days, consecutive or non-consecutive, above the
Arctic Circle after 1 January 1982. For personnel working at
remote ice camps and divers working under the ice, each day of
duty counts as two days when determining award eligibility. No
more than one day's credit is allowed for flights in or out
during any 24-hour period. Marine Corps personnel undergoing
annual cold weather training above the Arctic Circle do not
qualify for the 2-for-1 credit.

    c. Subsequent Awards. There is no subsequent award.

    d. Awarding Authority. Commanding officers of ships or units
whose operations are above the Arctic Circle. Certification
data, to include dates of eligibility, will be forwarded to CNO
(DNS-35) for Navy personnel. Appropriate entries shall be made
in the official military records of Marines eligible to receive
this award.

    e. Retroactive Awards. Type commanders and commanding
officers of Navy Laboratories will determine and certify
retroactive eligibility to 1 January 1982.

22. Naval Reserve Sea Service Ribbon

    a. Authorization. SECNAV Note 5420 of 28 May 1986,
OPNAVNOTE 1650 of 3 June 1987.

    b. Eligibility Requirements. Awarded to officer and
enlisted personnel of the Navy and Navy Reserve who, after 15

August 1974, complete a cumulative total of 24 months of any combination of active or Selected Reserve service aboard a Navy Reserve ship or its reserve unit or an embarked active or reserve staff.

(1) To be creditable for the ribbon, periods of Selected Reserve service must have been satisfactory service as defined in BUPERSINST 1001.39(series); specifically, 90 percent attendance at scheduled drills prior to 1 October 1997 and 85 percent thereafter, with annual active duty for training (ACDUTRA) performed for each period of 12 months of Selected Reserve duty.

(2) Qualifying ship duty includes duty in a self-propelled Navy Reserve ship, boat, or craft operated under the operational control of fleet or type commanders. Selected Reserve duty with staffs that regularly embark in such Navy Reserve ships, craft, or boats, is also qualifying provided at least 50 percent of the drills performed for each creditable period have been underway drills. The individual's certification that such underway drills were performed is considered acceptable verification.

(3) Qualifying service performed between 15 August 1974 and 1 January 1979 will be credited only toward the initial award of the ribbon. Subsequent to 1 January 1979, one award is earned for each qualifying period.

(4) CNO may waive the requirements in posthumous cases, on a case-by-case basis. An individual cannot receive both the Sea Service Deployment Ribbon and the Naval Reserve Sea Service Ribbon for the same service.

c. Awarding Authority. Commanding officers. All questions regarding eligibility must be addressed via Commander, Navy Reserve Force to CNO (DNS-35).

23. Navy and Marine Corps Overseas Service Ribbon

a. Authorization. SECNAV letter 1650 Ser NDBDM/886 of 17 September 1986.

b. Eligibility Requirements. Awarded to officers and enlisted personnel of the United States Navy, Navy Reserve, Marine Corps, and Marine Corps Reserve. Each service has distinct criteria that delineate eligibility; Navy personnel assigned to Marine Corps units follow Marine Corps policy, and vice versa.

(1) Active Duty Personnel: 12 months of consecutive or accumulated duty at an overseas shore based duty station.

(2) Reserve Personnel: 30 consecutive days or 45 cumulative days of service at overseas duty stations, including deployed units and units homeported overseas, regardless of the type of orders the member is serving under. For eligibility purposes, two Inactive Duty for Training (IDT) periods equal one day of qualifying service. Travel time does not count.

(a) Navy Reserve Personnel

1. Effective 11 September 2001, Navy Reservists may earn their initial award of the Overseas Service Ribbon (OSR) under the Reserve service requirements, but must fulfill the active duty service requirements for any subsequent award. See paragraph (b) below regarding service with the Marine Corps operating forces.

2. For overseas domiciled Reservists, qualifying service must be completed in a billet with an established Navy Reserve Unit.

(b) Personnel Serving with the Marine Corps Reserve. Since personnel serving with the Marine Corps operating forces, active or reserve, are not eligible for this award, Marine Corps personnel or Navy personnel serving with the Marine Corps operating forces, mobilized in support of a specific operation or contingency are also not eligible for the OSR.

(3) Overseas is defined as duty outside the United States at shore based commands. Mainland Alaska and Hawaii are not eligible duty stations; however, service in Adak, Alaska, does qualify. For active duty personnel, duty on board CONUS-based, deploying ships, squadrons, units, or with the Marine Corps operating forces does not qualify.

(4) Restrictions and Waivers

(a) An individual may not receive the Sea Service Deployment Ribbon and the OSR for the same period if assigned to a Marine Corps unit. After 1 October 1999, personnel assigned to overseas Navy commands may receive both awards if all eligibility requirements are met. However, the same period of time cannot be used to earn eligibility for both the Naval Reserve Sea Service Ribbon and the OSR.

(b) For active duty personnel, not more than 14 days of service time may be waived. There is no waiver for inactive reservists. For posthumous awards, the time requirements may be waived by CNO/CMC, on a case-by-case basis.

(c) Personnel serving with the Marine Corps operating forces, active or reserve, are <u>not</u> eligible for this award.

c. <u>Initial and Subsequent Awards</u>. Qualifying service performed between 15 August 1974 and 1 January 1979 will be credited only toward the initial award of the ribbon. Subsequent to 1 January 1979, one award is earned for each qualifying period.

d. <u>Awarding Authority</u>. Commanding officers.

24. <u>Navy Recruiting Service Ribbon</u>

a. <u>Authorization</u>. Established by SECNAV on 2 February 1989. SECNAV letter NDBDM/0087 of 21 February 1997 made the award retroactive to 1 July 1973.

b. <u>Eligibility Requirements</u>

(1) Awarded to officer and enlisted personnel of the United States Navy and Navy Reserve, including Active Duty for Special Work (ADSW) personnel (formerly TEMAC), in support of recruiting, assigned to the activities listed below.

Navy Recruiting Command, Millington, TN
Navy Recruiting Regions
Navy Recruiting Districts
Navy Recruiting Orientation Unit, Pensacola, FL
National Training Team
Navy Recruiting Quality Assurance Team, Great Lakes, IL
Reserve Recruiting Support Units
Navy Recruiting Command Liaison Team, Federal Records
    Center, St. Louis, MO

Navy Recruiting Youth Program Field Representatives
Navy Flight Demonstration Squadron (Blue Angels)
Navy Parachute Team (Leap Frogs)
Director, Candidate Guidance Office, U.S. Naval Academy
    Information Officer Program

NOTE: Prior to February 1989, most eligible Navy Reserve
Recruiting personnel were assigned to Unit Identification Codes
of Naval Reserve Readiness Commands, Naval Air Stations, Reserve
Centers, and Naval Air Reserve activities. Eligibility is
maintained if personnel were assigned to billets specifically
involving recruiting or recruiting support.

    (2) Awarded to Career Force Recruiters (CRF) and
Canvasser Recruiters (CANREC) at the recommendation of their
commanding officer or officer in charge, upon completion of a
successful tour of duty in recruiting. CRF personnel, Campus
Liaison Officers, and Recruiting District Assistance Council
members are eligible for the ribbon upon completion of three
consecutive years of recruiting duty. Reserve CANRECs and ADSW
recruiting personnel are eligible for the ribbon after
completion of three consecutive years of combined recruiting
duty, provided no break in service of more than 60 days occurs
during the period.

    c. Definitions. The following definitions apply for
determining eligibility:

    (1) Recruiting Duty. Duty performed at any one of, or a
combination of, the Navy recruiting activities listed above.

    (2) Prescribed Tour of Duty. The member's projected
rotation date from recruiting, as established by the Chief of
Naval Personnel, is considered the end of a qualifying tour of
duty. Personnel who complete a minimum of 18 months on
recruiting duty, but were transferred prior to their original
projected rotation date to a non-recruiting activity, may submit
a waiver request to Commander, Navy Recruiting Command. In the
case of Navy Reserve recruiting personnel who have at least two
consecutive years of recruiting duty, and are recalled USN or
Full Time Support (FTS) prior to completing three years of
recruiting duty, a waiver request may be submitted, via the
recruiting chain of command at the time of service, to
Commander, Navy Recruiting Command. Recruiters who are fault
transferred from recruiting duty or who are not recommended for

continuation and are subsequently terminated are not eligible for the Navy Recruiting Service Ribbon. Waivers will not be considered.

(3) Successful Tour. For the purpose of this award, a successful tour is defined as completing the prescribed tour of duty as outlined above, with the exception that Navy Reserve CANREC and ADSW personnel may combine consecutive recruiting periods of either recruiting program, provided no break in service exceeding 60 days occurs during the three-year period.

d. Awarding Authority. Commanding officers determine eligibility from service records, affidavits, or upon completion of eligibility requirements at current command and make appropriate service record entries for enlisted personnel and issue letters of eligibility for officers. No citation or certificate will be issued. Situations not covered in this article should be addressed to the Commander, Navy Recruiting Command.

e. Subsequent Awards. Personnel receiving "Gold Wreath" awards for superior productivity shall wear a bronze 5/16 inch Arabic numeral on the Recruiting Service Ribbon indicating the total number of awards received after 1 January 1980. Personnel receiving Individual Awards of the Recruiting Service Ribbon shall wear a 3/16 inch bronze star for second and subsequent awards.

25. Marine Corps Recruiting Ribbon

a. Authorization. SECNAV letter 1650 Ser NDBDM/0491 of 7 June 1995.

b. Eligibility Requirements. Marines possessing Military Occupational Specialty (MOS) 8411 or 8412, who have served in a MOS 8411 or 8412 billet, are eligible to receive the Marine Corps Recruiting Ribbon (MCRR). Eligible members must meet the following criteria:

(1) Recruiters. Marines assigned to recruiting duty (MOS 8411) are eligible to receive the ribbon upon completion of a successful tour of duty. A Marine who extends beyond the basic tour of duty is eligible upon completion of the extension period. Marines returning for subsequent tours are eligible for subsequent awards upon completion of each tour. A recruiter who

becomes a career recruiter is eligible to receive the ribbon upon assignment of the MOS 8412.

(2) Extended Active Duty (EAD) Recruiters. EAD recruiters (MOS 8411) are eligible to receive the ribbon upon completion of 36 months of consecutive service in an 8411 billet. Subsequent awards will be issued for each successful 36-month period.

(3) Career Recruiters. A new award period for career recruiters will begin on the date they receive the 8412 MOS. They will be eligible to receive subsequent awards upon the completion of each 36-month period following that date.

(4) Command recruiters and recruiter aides are not eligible for this award.

c. Definitions. The following definitions apply for determining eligibility:

(1) Recruiting Duty. Duty performed in an 8411 or 8412 billet as set forth in the table of organization. Duty performed at the recruiting station level in the billets of commanding officer (CO), executive officer (XO), operations officer (OPSO), officer selection officer (OSO), or sergeant major (SGTMAJ).

(2) Marine Corps District. Duty performed at the district level in the billets of CO, Deputy for Recruiting Operations, Assistant for Officer Procurement, Assistant for Aviation Officer Procurement, Assistant for Enlisted Recruiting, or SGTMAJ.

(3) Prescribed Tour of Duty. A Marine's date of detachment from recruiting duty is considered the end of a qualifying tour of duty. Personnel who are transferred prior to their original projected rotation date are authorized to receive this award if they complete a minimum of 30 months on recruiting duty. Personnel who are transferred due to Relief for Cause or Relief for the Good of the Service are not eligible for this award. Requests for waivers of the 30-month requirement should be sent to the appropriate CG, Recruit Depot/Marine Corps Recruiting Region for decision.

(4) Successful Tour. Completion of the prescribed tour

of duty as outlined in above.

d. Retroactive Awards. The MCRR may be awarded retroactively to 1 January 1973, reflecting the establishment of the all-volunteer force.

e. Awarding Authority. Authority to award the MCRR is delegated to commanding officers. Issuance of the award is recorded in the Marine's Service Record Book/Officer Qualification Record. The award consists of a ribbon bar only. No citation or certificate will be issued.

26. Marine Corps Drill Instructor Ribbon

a. Authorization. SECNAV letter 1650 Ser NDBDM/482 of 15 July 1997.

b. Eligibility Requirements

(1) Personnel. Marines possessing the 8511 MOS, who have served in an 8511 billet, are eligible to receive the Marine Corps Drill Instructor Ribbon (MCDIR). In addition, Marines in the following billets are eligible to receive the award:

(a) Recruit Training Regiment - CO, XO, Operations Officer (S-3), SGTMAJ, Series Commander.

(b) Recruiting Training Battalion - CO, XO, S-3, SGTMAJ.

(c) Recruit Training Regiment Support Battalion - CO, XO, S-3, SGTMAJ, Company Commanding Officers.

(d) Drill Instructor School - Director and Assistant Director.

(e) Officer Candidate Company - CO, XO, 1STSGT, Company Gunnery Sergeant, and Platoon Commanders.

(2) Period of Service

(a) Drill Instructors. Marines assigned to drill instructor duty (MOS 8511) are eligible to receive the ribbon upon completion of a successful tour of duty. A Marine who extends beyond the basic tour of duty is eligible upon completion of the extension period. Marines returning for subsequent tours as drill instructors are eligible for subsequent awards upon the completion of each tour.

(b) Additional Billets. Marines assigned in those billets listed in subparagraphs (a) through (e) above are eligible to receive the ribbon upon completion of a successful assignment. Marines assigned as Assistant Marine Officer Instructors are not eligible for this award.

(c) Posthumous Awards. On a case-by-case basis, the MCDIR may be awarded posthumously without regard to period of service.

c. Definitions. For the purpose of determining eligibility for this award, the following definitions apply:

(1) Drill Instructor. Duty performed in an 8511 MOS billet as set forth in the Table of Organization.

(2) Prescribed Tour of Duty

(a) Drill Instructor. The Marine's projected detachment date from drill instructor duty is considered the end of a qualifying tour of duty. Personnel who transfer prior to their original projected rotation date are authorized to receive this award if they complete a minimum of 20 months (for those who received their 8511 MOS before December 1996) or 30 months (for those who receive their 8511 MOS on or after 1 December 1996) of drill instructor duty. Personnel who were transferred due to Relief for Cause or Relief for the Good of the Service are not eligible for this award.

(b) Marines serving in the additional billets outlined in subparagraphs b.(1)(a) through (e) above are required to serve a total of 18 cumulative months in those billets in order to be eligible for the ribbon.

(3) Successful Tour. A successful tour is defined as completing the prescribed tour of duty as outlined above.

d. Waivers. Requests for waiver of eligibility criteria, or questions regarding a successful tour of duty, should be sent to the Commanding General of the respective Marine Corps Recruit

Depot, or in the case of Officer Candidate School, to the Commanding General, Training Command, for decision.

e. Award Elements. The award consists of a ribbon bar only. No citation or certificate will be issued.

f. Retroactive Awards. The MCDIR may be awarded retroactively to 6 October 1952.

g. Awarding Authority. Authority to award the MCDIR is delegated to commanding officers.

27. Marine Corps Security Guard Ribbon

a. Authorization. SECNAV letter 1650 Ser NDBDM/482 of 15 July 1997.

b. Eligibility Requirements

(1) Personnel. Marines possessing MOS 8151 who are serving with the Marine Security Guard Battalion (MSGBN), or previously served with the MSGBN in MOS 8151 billets at embassies, are eligible to receive the Marine Corps Security Guard Ribbon (MCSGR). MSGBN personnel are also eligible to receive the ribbon; however, personnel serving at Headquarters, MSGBN are not eligible. In addition, the following personnel are eligible to receive the MCSGR:

(a) Training Personnel: Director of Marine Security Guard (MSG) School/Battalion Commander; Officer in Charge (OIC) of MSG School; Operations Officer MSGBN; Assistant OPS Officer MSGBN; and SGTMAJ of MSGBN.

(b) Command Personnel: Lettered Company Commander /Executive Officer (XO)/Operations (OPS) Inspecting Officers/First Sergeant (1STSGT) and MSGBN XO.

(2) Period of Service

(a) Marines assigned to Marine Security Guard duty (MOS 8151) are eligible to receive the ribbon upon completion of 24 months of service at a foreign establishment. Subsequent awards will be made for every 24 months served, either consecutively or cumulatively.

(b) Marines who served successful tours at a lettered MSGBN company headquarters or at HQ MSGBN, Quantico are not eligible to receive this award.

(c) Posthumous Awards. On a case-by-case basis, the MCSGR may be awarded posthumously without regard to period of service.

(d) Personnel transferred early for the Good of the Service must have served a minimum of 12 months in the program to be eligible for this award. Personnel transferred due to Relief for Cause are not eligible for the ribbon.

c. Definition of Marine Security Guard Duty. For the purpose of determining eligibility for this award, duty performed at a Department of State overseas post in an 8151 MOS billet after graduation from the Marine Security Guard School at MSGBN Headquarters is qualifying duty. This includes Company D located in Fort Lauderdale, Florida.

d. Award Elements. The award consists of a ribbon bar only. No citation or certificate will be issued.

e. Retroactive Awards. The MCSGR may be awarded retroactively to 28 January 1949, the date the first MSGs departed Washington, DC, for their overseas assignments. One award is authorized for the period 28 January 1949 to 15 August 1974, regardless of the number of qualifying periods.

f. Awarding Authority. Authority to award the MCSGR is delegated to commanding officers. An entry will be recorded in the Marine's service record denoting issuance of the award.

g. Waivers. Requests for waiver shall be submitted to Commanding Officer, MSGBN, 2007 Elliot Road, Quantico, VA 22134-5112.

28. Navy Recruit Training Service Ribbon

a. Authorization. Established by SECNAV 13 March 1998.

b. Eligibility Requirements. Awarded to enlisted personnel of the U.S. Navy assigned to Recruit Training Command (RTC), Naval Training Center, Great Lakes, serving as Recruit Division Commander (RDC) upon completion of a successful tour of duty.

c. Definitions. For the purpose of determining eligibility for this award, the following definitions apply:

(1) Recruit Training Service Duty. Personnel assigned as RDC. Support personnel, company assistants, echelon supervisors, liaison officers, instructors, or other personnel attached to RTC are not eligible for this award.

(2) Successful Tour of Duty. The RDC must have completed a minimum of five divisions trained over a minimum tour length of three years.

(3) Personal Standards. The RDC must have maintained outstanding personal standards without disciplinary incidents throughout the tour.

(4) Establishment Date. Tour completion must be as of 1 October 1995 or later. No retroactive awards are authorized under any circumstances.

d. Examples of Qualifying Service

(1) An RDC successfully completes a four-year tour that started on 1 October 1992. If all other parameters are met, the RDC is eligible since the tour completion date is after 1 October 1995.

(2) An RDC trains 14 divisions from 30 September 1994 to 20 August 1997, and is medically released from duty. Not eligible due to tour length of less than three years.

(3) An RDC trains six divisions from October 1991 to October 1993, moves to Recruit Liaison from October 1993 to October 1995, and moves back to RDC for three more divisions from October 1995 to October 1996. Eligible: tour length of more than three years and more than five divisions trained.

(4) An RDC completes nine divisions in three years after 1 October 1995, but sporadically did not meet Physical Readiness standards. Eligibility is determined by CO, RTC. Fulfillment of the outstanding personal standards requirement is determined by the awarding authority.

e. Award Elements. The award consists of a ribbon bar

only. No citation or certificate will be issued.

f. Awarding Authority. The Commanding Officer of RTC is the awarding authority.

29. Navy Ceremonial Guard Ribbon

a. Authorization. SECNAV letter Ser NDBDM 0750 of 12 December 2003.

b. Eligibility Requirements

(1) Military personnel assigned to the Navy Ceremonial Guard in Washington, DC, on 1 May 2001 or later.

(2) Personnel must complete a successful tour of at least two years duration including a minimum of eighteen months (consecutive or non-consecutive) in a drilling status.

(a) Drilling status is defined as actual participation in ceremonies and funerals as casket bearers, firing party, color guard, ceremonial drill team, and marching platoons (to include commanders of troops, platoon petty officers, and petty officers-in-charge).

(b) Successful tour of duty is defined as service in a drilling status for a minimum of eighteen months and completion of standard honors qualification or higher. The awarding authority may waive the eighteen-month minimum requirement only for those personnel receiving full honors qualification.

(c) Successful tour of duty also includes maintaining outstanding personal standards without disciplinary incidents (no NJP, indebtedness issues, failure to meet PRT standards, or other actions bringing discredit upon the Ceremonial Guard or the Navy) throughout the tour.

c. Awarding Authority. The Commanding Officer, U.S. Navy Ceremonial Guard is designated as the awarding authority. Only one award per tour will be authorized, regardless of tour length. No citation or certificate will be issued.

d. Retroactive Awards. This award is approved for all personnel meeting the above criteria who have completed a successful tour of duty since the formal establishment of the unit in May 2001.

30. Armed Forces Reserve Medal

    a. Authorization. E.O. 10163 of 25 September 1950, as amended by E.O. 10439 of 19 March 1953.

    b. Eligibility Requirements. Issued to any officer or enlisted member of the Reserve Components of the Armed Forces of the United States who completes a total of 10 years of honorable satisfactory service, under the following conditions:

    (1) The required 10 years must have been performed within a period of 12 consecutive years.

    (2) Such service shall not include service in a Regular component of the Armed Forces; however, any period of time during which Reserve service is interrupted by service in a Regular component of the Armed Forces (including Naval Academy Midshipman service) shall not be considered a break in the said period of 12 consecutive years, but will not count as qualifying service.

    (3) Any period during which Reserve service is interrupted by one or more of the following will be excluded in computing qualification time, but will not be considered as a break in the period of 12 years:

        (a) During tenure in office as any state official chosen by the voters of the entire state, territory, or possession.

        (b) During tenure in office as a member of the legislative body of the United States or of any state, territory, or possession.

        (c) While serving as judge of a court of record of the United States, or of any state, territory, possession, or the District of Columbia.

    (4) Service in the Retired Reserve (with or without pay) or on the Inactive Status List shall not count toward eligibility.

(5) In order to achieve one year of honorable satisfactory service, a Reservist must accumulate a total of at least 50 retirement points during each anniversary year of service subsequent to 30 June 1949. All honorable service prior to 1 July 1949, active or inactive, as a member of a Reserve component of the Armed Forces, is qualifying service. The 50 required points may be accumulated by any combination of the authorized methods, such as drills, active duty, or correspondence courses. Membership points are also qualifying.

(6) After 1 July 1950, U.S. Navy Reserve Midshipmen are not eligible since they are not in a position to earn 50 points per anniversary year.

(7) Reserve Aviation Cadet time is considered to fulfill the requirements for this medal subsequent to 1 July 1950, since such Reservists are on active duty and thus earning the yearly 50 points.

(8) Navy Reserve personnel who, prior to 12 September 1958, were eligible to receive the Naval Reserve Medal, may at their election be awarded in lieu thereof the Armed Forces Reserve Medal (AFRM), provided they have met the foregoing requirements; however, both medals shall not be awarded for the same period of service.

(9) Marine Corps Reserve personnel who, prior to 17 December 1965, were eligible to receive the Marine Corps Reserve Ribbon, may at their election be awarded in lieu thereof the AFRM, provided they have met the foregoing requirements; however, both awards shall not be issued for the same period of service.

(10) Marine Corps Reserve personnel serving in an Active Reserve (AR) billet may continue to count service for the award for which they were qualifying upon entering the AR, but may not commence a new period of qualifying service.

c. Hour Glass and M Devices

(1) Upon completion of the first 10-year period, a bronze hourglass shall be awarded for the AFRM. Upon completion of the second 10-year period, a silver hourglass shall be awarded. Upon completion of the third 10-year period, a gold hourglass shall be awarded. Upon completion of the fourth 10-

year period, a gold hourglass followed by a bronze shall be awarded.

(2) Executive Order 13013 authorizes the "M" device for the AFRM for participation in designated contingency operations. Members must have been mobilized (as a unit or individual) and performed active duty on or after 1 August 1990 as follows:

(a) The member was called to active service under §12301(A), 12302, 12304, 12406 of Title 10 U.S.C. (formerly §672(A), 673, 673(B), 3500, and 8500) or Chapter 15 of Title 10 U.S.C.

(b) The member volunteered and served on active duty in support of the designated operations. Designated operations include:

> DESERT SHIELD/DESERT STORM (Persian Gulf War)
> RESTORE HOPE (Somalia)
> UPHOLD DEMOCRACY (Haiti)
> JOINT ENDEAVOR (Bosnia and surrounding areas)
> DESERT FOX (Iraq)
> JOINT FORGE (Bosnia and surrounding areas)
> JOINT GUARD (Bosnia and surrounding areas)
> ALLIED FORCE (Kosovo)
> NOBLE EAGLE (U.S. Homeland Defense)
> ENDURING FREEDOM (Afghanistan)
> IRAQI FREEDOM (Iraq)

(c) Active Guard and Reserve members who receive orders changing their current duty status (legal authority under which they perform duty) or their duty location or assignment to support a designated contingency operation are eligible for the award of the "M" device. All components of the Navy Reserve (i.e., Full Time Support (FTS), Active Duty for Special Work (ADSW), One-Year Recall (OYR), and Canvasser Recruiter (CANREC)) are eligible for the "M" device, provided all other eligibility requirements are met.

(d) Upon qualification, a bronze "M" shall be awarded for wear on the AFRM. A bronze numeral indicating the number of the award shall be included after the initial award. Multiple periods of service during a specific contingency/operation shall count as only one "M" device qualifying period (no additional numerals). In addition, only one "M" device shall be earned for each mobilization (set of orders) even if more than one operation is supported. The ribbon is authorized upon award of the "M" device, despite having served less than 10 years.

d. Appropriate Wear of the Ribbon

(1) Only one AFRM is authorized for wear.

(2) Not entitled to "M" device, entitled to AFRM: AFRM with appropriate bronze/silver/gold hourglass centered on the ribbon bar and suspension ribbon.

(3) Not otherwise entitled to AFRM, entitled to the "M" device: AFRM worn with "M" centered on the ribbon bar and suspension ribbon.

(4) Entitled to "M" device and AFRM: "M" device is centered and appropriate hourglass is to wearer's right on the ribbon bar and suspension ribbon.

(5) Entitled to numerous "M" devices and AFRM: "M" is centered, appropriate hour glass to wearer's right, and bronze Arabic numeral to the wearer's left on the ribbon bar and suspension ribbon. Numerals begin with the second award.

e. Awarding Authority. Commanding officers determine eligibility from service records, affidavits or upon completion of eligibility requirements at the current command, and make appropriate service record entries for enlisted personnel and issue letters of eligibility for officers. Questions regarding eligibility shall be addressed via the chain of command to CNO (DNS-35) or CMC (MMMA), as appropriate.

31. Marksmanship Awards

a. Eligibility Requirements

(1) A marksmanship award is bestowed upon an individual for proficiency in a particular type of small arms. A marksman, sharpshooter, or expert is a member in any rank, rate, or rating who qualifies by firing the prescribed pistol or rifle over one of the Service prescribed courses and has attained the minimum qualifying score.

(2) Qualification requirements and administrative procedures are set forth in OPNAVINST 3590.7(series) for Navy personnel and in Marine Corps Order P3590.13A for Marine Corps personnel.

b. <u>Precedence</u>. Marksmanship awards take precedence after all other awards earned. The precedence of Navy and Marine Corps Marksmanship awards is listed in Appendix B to Chapter 1. For a full listing of the precedence of all Marksmanship awards and badges, consult the respective Navy and Marine Corps Uniform Regulations.

c. <u>Procurement</u>. CNO (DNS-35) is responsible for providing marksmanship medals to the coordinator of the Navy's Marksmanship Program.

ARMED FORCES EXPEDITIONARY MEDAL ELIGIBILITY PERIODS

The Joint Chiefs of Staff (JCS) have designated the following operations as eligible for award of the Armed Forces Expeditionary Medal (AFEM):

1. U.S. Military Operations

    a. Lebanon: 1 Jul to 1 Nov 58. The area is composed of the adjacent water area defined as that portion of the Mediterranean Sea east of 31E longitude.

    b. Quemoy and Matsu Islands: 23 Aug 58 to 1 Jun 63. The area is composed of the water area 21N to 26N and 116E to 121E.

    c. Taiwan Straits: 23 Aug 58 to 1 Jan 59. The area is composed of the water area from 19N to 28N between 117E and 123E.

    d. Berlin: 14 Aug 61 to 1 Jun 63, including the city of West Berlin.

    e. Cuba: 24 Oct 62 to 1 Jun 63. Although JCS established the terminal date of Cuban operations as 1 Jun 63, no Navy/Marine Corps units are considered eligible after 31 Dec 62. The area of eligibility includes the water area between 12N and 28N latitudes and 66W and 84W longitudes.

    f. Congo: 23 to 27 Nov 64. The area is composed of the land and water area of the Congo.

    g. Dominican Republic: 28 Apr 65 to 21 Sep 66. The area is composed of the contiguous water and airspace within the following boundaries: from the point 17N, 75W eastward to 17N, 67-45W; thence northward to 20-25N, 73-35W; thence southwestward to 18-40N, 75W; thence south to the initial point at 17N, 75W.

    h. Korea: 1 Oct 66 to 30 Jun 74. This area includes the entire land mass of the Republic of Korea and the waters and air space enclosed by the following boundaries: from a point located at 32N on the coast of China, east to 32N by 129-20E; thence northeastward to 36N by 134E; thence north to the coast of the former Union of Soviet Socialist Republics (USSR); thence along the coastline of the USSR, Korea, and China to the initial point.

i.   Cambodia Evacuation (Operation EAGLE PULL):
11 to 13 Apr 75.

j.   Vietnam Evacuation (Operation FREQUENT WIND):
29 to 30 Apr 75.

k.   Mayaguez Operation: 15 May 75.

l.   Grenada Operation: 23 Oct to 21 Nov 83. The area
includes the island nation of Grenada, including Grenada,
Carriacou, Green, Hog, Calivigny, other outlying islands and the
territorial seas of Grenada; waters adjacent to Grenada in which
Atlantic Fleet ships operated in direct support of operations in
Grenada; the airspace above Grenada and the adjacent sea areas
where the operations were conducted; and the Grantley Adams
International Airport, Barbados.

m.   Libya (Operation ELDORADO CANYON): 12 to 17 Apr 86.
The area bounded by the following coordinates: 37N, 11E to 37N,
21E to 34N, 25E to 23N, 25E to 23N, 11E to 37N, 11E.

n.   Panama (Operation JUST CAUSE): 20 Dec 89 to 31 Jan
90. The total land area of Panama, including internal waters,
territorial seas, and airspace thereover.

o.   Haiti (Operation UPHOLD DEMOCRACY): 16 Sep 94 to 31
Mar 95. The area of operations consists of the total land area,
sea, and air space defined by the following coordinates:
16-30N, 71-40W; 18-00N, 71-45W; along the Haitian-Dominican
Republic Border to 20-00N, 71-44W; 21-00N, 71-40W; 21-25N/73-
00W; 21-25N, 74-00W; 20-00N, 74-00W; 19-45N, 75-00W; 19-00N, 76-
00W; 16-30N, 76-00W; to 16-30N, 71-40W.

p.   Haiti (Operation SECURE TOMORROW): 27 Feb to 15 Jun 04

2.   U.S. Operations in direct support of the United Nations

a.   Congo: 14 Jul 60 to 1 Sep 62. Water area from 3S to
9S between 9E and the mainland of Africa.

b.   Somalia (Operations RESTORE HOPE and UNITED SHIELD):
5 Dec 92 to 31 Mar 95. The area of operations is from 20N
northward to 30-30E and from 46-36E eastward to 63E.

3.   U.S. Operations assisting friendly foreign nations

a. Vietnam: 1 Jul 58 to 3 Jul 65. Water areas from a point on the east coast of Vietnam at the border of Vietnam with China southeastward to 21N, 108-15E; thence southward to 18N, 108-15E; thence southeastward to 17-30N, 111E; thence southward to 11N, 111E; thence southwestward to 7N, 105E; thence westward to 7N, 103E; thence northward to 9-30N, 103E; thence northeastward to 10-15N, 104-27E; thence northward to a point on the west coast of Vietnam at the border of Vietnam with Cambodia. In addition, the land area of Thailand is included.

b. Laos: 19 Apr 61 to 7 Oct 62.

c. Cambodia (land only): 29 Mar to 15 Aug 73.

d. Thailand: 29 Mar to 15 Aug 73 (only those in direct support of Cambodia operations).

e. El Salvador: 1 Jan 81 to 1 Feb 92. The total land area of El Salvador, as approved by Section 525 of the FY96 Defense Appropriations Act.

f. Lebanon: 1 Jun 83 to 1 Dec 87. JCS established the terminal date of Lebanon operations as 1 Dec 87; however, no Navy ships/units are considered to be eligible after 1 Aug 84. Marine Security Guard personnel or other personnel serving in Lebanon may be awarded medal for the entire period.

g. Operation ERNEST WILL (Persian Gulf): 24 Jul 87 to 1 Aug 90.

h. Operation JOINT ENDEAVOR (Serbia, Montenegro, Croatia, Bosnia-Herzegovina, Italy, Hungary, and the waters of the Adriatic Sea north of 60 degrees north latitude): 20 Nov 95 to 16 Dec 96.

i. Operations SOUTHERN WATCH - 1 Dec 95 to 18 Mar 03; MARITIME INTERCEPT - 1 Dec 95 to 18 Mar 03; VIGILANT SENTINEL - 1 Dec 95 to 15 Feb 97; DESERT THUNDER - 11 Nov to 22 Dec 98; DESERT FOX - 16 to 22 Dec 98; DESERT SPRING - 31 Dec 98 to 18 Mar 03; and NORTHERN WATCH - 1 Jan 97 to 18 Mar 03 (Persian Gulf/Iraq). Only one AFEM may be earned for participation in one or all of these operations. The area consists of the land area and airspace of Saudi Arabia, Kuwait, and Iraq and the waters of and airspace above the Arabian Gulf west of 56E longitude. Individuals serving aboard vessels in the Red Sea in direct support of Operation SOUTHERN WATCH are also eligible for the AFEM. Service members who earned the Southwest Asia Service Medal (SWASM) and then became eligible for the AFEM in a subsequent tour are eligible for both medals. For example, an individual who earned the SWASM in 1991 and subsequently returned to the area after 1 Dec 95 may earn both awards. However, an individual who serves a single tour that spanned the transition date of 1 Dec 95 may not earn both awards. In this case, the individual may elect the AFEM or the SWASM, but may not earn both awards for a single tour. Also see paragraph m. below regarding the transition from Operation SOUTHERN WATCH to IRAQI FREEDOM.

j. Operation JOINT GUARD (Serbia, Montenegro, Croatia, Bosnia-Herzegovina, Hungary, and the airspace above the Adriatic Sea north of 40 degrees north latitude): 20 Dec 96 to 20 Jun 98.

k. Operation JOINT FORGE (Bosnia-Herzegovina): 21 Jun 98 to TBD. For service in the Federation of Bosnia and Herzegovina, Croatia, the Adriatic Sea, and all related air space.

l. Operation IRAQI FREEDOM: 19 Mar 03 to 30 Apr 05. Personnel who deployed in support of Operation SOUTHERN WATCH and subsequently transitioned into IRAQI FREEDOM on or after 19 March 2003 must elect to receive either the AFEM, the Global War on Terrorism Expeditionary Medal (GWOTEM), or the Iraq Campaign Medal (ICM). Personnel who earned the AFEM for service in support of SOUTHERN WATCH on a previous tour and then became eligible for the GWOTEM or ICM in a subsequent tour may retain the AFEM and are eligible for the GWOTEM or ICM. However, an individual who served a single tour that spanned the transition date of 19 Mar 03 may not earn both the AFEM and the GWOTEM or ICM. In this case, the individual may elect the AFEM, GWOTEM, or ICM, but may not earn more than one award for a single tour.

GLOBAL WAR ON TERRORISM EXPEDITIONARY MEDAL ELIGIBILITY AREAS

The geographic locations listed below are currently approved as eligible for award of the GWOTEM. The eligibility area includes all airspace above and water areas adjacent to the landmasses. Updated lists will be posted at https://awards.navy.mil and http://awards.manpower.usmc.mil.

Afghanistan
Algeria
Bahrain
Bosnia-Herzegovina
Bulgaria (Bourgas)
Chad
Crete
Cyprus
Diego Garcia
Djibouti
Egypt
Eritrea
Ethiopia
Georgia
Hungary
Iran
Iraq
Israel
Jordan
Kazakhstan
Kenya
Kosovo (only specified GWOT operations not associated with
      operations qualifying for the Kosovo Campaign Medal)
Kuwait
Kyrgyzstan
Lebanon
Mali
Mauritania
Niger
Oman
Pakistan
Philippines
Qatar
Romania (Constanta)
Saudi Arabia

Somalia
Syria
Tajikistan
Turkey
Turkmenistan
Uganda
United Arab Emirates
United States Central Command (less the lower Horn of
    Africa)
Uzbekistan
Yemen

In addition, the following bodies of water are approved
qualifying areas:

Arabian Sea (north of 10 degrees north latitude and west of
    68 degrees longitude)
Bab el Mandeb
Gulf of Aden
Gulf of Aqaba
Gulf of Oman
Gulf of Suez
Mediterranean Sea (east of 28 degrees east longitude)
Mediterranean Sea (for maritime interception operations,
    boarding and searching vessels, in support of the GWOT)
Persian Gulf
Red Sea
Strait of Hormuz
Suez Canal

CHAPTER 5
U.S. NON-MILITARY DECORATIONS

SECTION 1 - GENERAL

510. DEFINITION. A U.S. non-military decoration is any U.S. decoration not classified as a military decoration.

511. POLICY CONSIDERATIONS

1. The military awards system is designed to recognize military personnel for exceptional performance. Like the military, many federal agencies have developed awards that mirror non-combat military awards (e.g., achievement, commendation, and meritorious service medals). These awards are designed primarily to recognize superior performance of civilian personnel employed by the respective federal agency.

2. The most appropriate means for recognizing Naval personnel serving with a federal agency remains the military awards system. Naval personnel deserving of special recognition, while assigned to a non-military federal agency, should be recommended for an appropriate Service or Joint personal decoration. Personnel should be recommended for non-military decorations only in rare instances when a military decoration is considered inappropriate.

512. PROCEDURES

1. Approval. When non-military federal agencies desire to present agency-specific medals to Naval personnel, those Naval personnel must request approval from CNO (DNS-35) or CMC (MMMA), as appropriate, to accept, retain, or wear the award. In the case of those decorations specifically authorized for presentation to military personnel by their establishing orders or other applicable regulations, e.g., the Presidential Medal of Freedom, the National Security Medal, and certain National Intelligence Agency and NASA Medals, concurrence will be granted. CNO or CMC may authorize other decorations, on a case-by-case basis, to be accepted, retained, or worn. Note that, in accordance with Article 113, paragraph 2, Naval personnel may only receive one award for the same act, achievement, or period of meritorious service.

2. <u>Appropriate Wear</u>. At least one U.S. military decoration must be worn in order to wear a non-military decoration.

3. <u>Precedence</u>. U.S. non-military decorations take precedence immediately after all U.S. military unit awards, in the order earned, except when more than one decoration is from the same agency, in which case the precedence is as established by the awarding agency.

4. <u>Non-military Awards Earned as a Civilian</u>. U.S. non-military awards earned by personnel prior to entrance into the Naval Service or by Reserve personnel while in a civilian status may not be worn on the military uniform.

5. <u>Issue And Replacement</u>. Regulations for issue and replacement of U.S. non-military decorations are as authorized by the awarding agency.

CHAPTER 6
U.S. AWARDS TO FOREIGN MILITARY PERSONNEL

SECTION 1 - GENERAL

610. POLICY CONSIDERATIONS

1. Recognition of Foreign Military Personnel. It is DoD policy to recognize individual acts of heroism, extraordinary achievement, or meritorious achievement on the part of Service members of friendly foreign nations when such acts have been of significant benefit to the United States or materially contributed to the successful prosecution of a military campaign by the Armed Forces of the United States.

2. Comparable Acts or Services. The awarding of any DON personal or unit decoration to member(s) of the armed forces of a friendly foreign nation shall be based upon an act or service that would satisfy the criteria governing the award of that decoration to member(s) of the U.S. Armed Forces.

3. Processing Requirements. The required elements of award recommendation packages for foreign military personnel, and the chain of command through which they are submitted to the final awarding authority, shall be the same as specified for awards to U.S. personnel and units.

4. Joint Awards. Foreign military personnel are ineligible to receive Joint or DoD awards. When recognition is appropriate for foreign military personnel serving at a Defense Agency or Joint activity, the appropriate U.S. Service Chief shall process the award. Therefore, CNO and CMC, respectively, shall process awards for foreign Navy and Marine Corps personnel serving in Joint activities and Defense Agency billets.

5. Unit Awards. The Presidential Unit Citation, Navy Unit Commendation, and Meritorious Unit Commendation may be awarded to units of the armed forces of friendly foreign nations, serving with the Armed Forces of the United States, for outstanding performance, in accordance with the same criteria applicable for such awards to U.S. units. See Chapter 3 for further information on unit awards.

6. <u>Campaign and Service Medals</u>. Except for the Antarctica Service Medal, it is DoD policy not to award campaign or service medals to foreign military personnel. This policy has been in effect since World War I, when the United States and its allies first agreed not to exchange campaign or service medals.

611. <u>PERSONAL AWARDS FOR FOREIGN MILITARY PERSONNEL</u>

1. <u>DON Awards</u>. SECNAV, or his designee, may award the following DON decorations to foreign military personnel, in grades comparable to O-6 and below at the time the act was performed, and at the time the decoration is presented. These decorations may not be awarded to foreign general or flag officers without the approval of SECDEF. Note: Delegated authority to award DON personal awards to foreign military personnel is always in writing and is <u>not</u> commensurate with a commander's delegated awarding authority for awards to U.S. personnel.

a. For heroic acts in actual combat in direct support of operations: Silver Star Medal, Distinguished Flying Cross, Bronze Star Medal, or Air Medal. The Bronze Star Medal may also be awarded for meritorious service in direct support of combat operations.

b. The Legion of Merit may be awarded to personnel assigned under U.S. command for exceptionally meritorious conduct in performing outstanding service.

c. The Navy and Marine Corps Medal may be awarded for heroic acts in direct support of operations not involving actual combat.

d. As authorized by E.O. 11448, commencing 1 June 1962, the Meritorious Service Medal, Navy and Marine Corps Commendation Medal, and Navy and Marine Corps Achievement Medal may be awarded to members of the armed forces of friendly foreign nations, who distinguish themselves by extraordinary achievement or meritorious service that has been of mutual benefit to a friendly nation and the United States.

2. <u>Awards Exclusively for Foreign Military Personnel</u>. E.O. 9260 authorized the Legion of Merit, in four degrees, for

award to foreign military personnel, beginning 8 September 1939. The Legion of Merit, in the degrees identified below, may be awarded to individuals who distinguish themselves by exceptionally meritorious conduct in performing outstanding service to the United States. The second or any subsequent award of this decoration must be in the same or a higher degree than the previous award.

a. <u>Degree of Chief Commander</u>. Awarded by the President of the United States, upon the recommendation of SECDEF, after concurrence by the Secretary of State, to foreign chiefs of state or heads of government.

b. <u>Degree of Commander</u>. Awarded by SECDEF, after concurrence by the Secretary of State, to individuals holding a grade equivalent to a U.S. Military Service Chief or higher position, but not to chiefs of state.

c. <u>Degree of Officer</u>. Awarded by SECDEF, after concurrence by the Secretary of State, to individuals of the following grades or positions:

(1) Officers of general or flag grade serving in positions below the equivalent of a U.S. Military Service Chief.

(2) Officers in grades equivalent to O-6 for service in positions comparable to those normally held by general or flag officers in the U.S. Armed Forces.

(3) Foreign military attaches.

d. <u>Degree of Legionnaire</u>. Awarded by SECDEF, after concurrence by the Secretary of State, to personnel of other grades.

SECTION 2 - PROCESSING REQUIREMENTS AND PROCEDURES

620. <u>RESPONSIBILITIES OF AWARD ORIGINATORS</u>

1. The processing of awards to foreign military personnel may require coordination with various offices, including the Department of State and numerous DoD agencies. In addition to ensuring the recommendation package is properly prepared, award

originators are responsible for obtaining the appropriate additional background checks and concurrences, as listed below, to ensure the award is consistent with the overall interests of the United States.

    2. The following general processing guidelines apply:

      a. Sufficient processing time must be allowed in order for an award recommendation to reach SECNAV no later than 90 days following the completion of the period of service for which the award is being recommended. (Note: This is in addition to Service processing time, which generally requires an additional 60-90 days.) In particular, any award requiring SECDEF approval (i.e., the four degrees of the Legion of Merit) that does not meet this timeline may be returned to the originator for amplifying justification (see paragraph 4.g. below).

      b. Premature disclosure must be avoided, including the scheduling of ceremonies and any public announcement of the award.

    3. Background Record Checks

      a. The award originator shall request the Naval Criminal Investigative Service (NCIS) conduct a counterintelligence check. Requests may be forwarded to the following address:

            NCIS (Code 22A2)
            Washington Navy Yard, Building 111
            Washington, DC 20388

      b. The award originator shall request the Defense Intelligence Agency (DIA) conduct record checks to ensure the nominee has committed no act or engaged in any activity wherein the award of the decoration would cause embarrassment to the United States. DIA will provide the award originator a statement of concurrence or non-concurrence regarding the recommended award and biographic information, including date and country of birth, of the proposed awardee. Requests may be sent to DIA Joint Military Awards via email at sea0102@dia.mil.

c. Award originators shall also coordinate with the appropriate U.S. Embassy personnel. The concurrence of the U.S. Chief of Mission and the U.S. Defense Attaché, when assigned, to the country of the recipient individual or unit will be obtained prior to forwarding the recommendation to the final awarding authority.

d. End of tour awards for foreign military personnel permanently assigned to a Navy or Marine Corps command do not require the above background checks, as they were completed at the time of the member's assignment. Award recipients are responsible for notifying their respective countries of receipt of the award.

4. In addition to the above requirements, award recommendations for any of the four Degrees of the Legion of Merit, which require SECDEF's signature, shall include the following:

a. Memorandum for SECDEF recommending approval and, when appropriate, a proposed memorandum from SECDEF to the President recommending approval.

b. Approved citation and certificate.

c. Biographic sketch of the proposed award recipient including the date and place of birth, current duty station, address, and military affiliation of the nominee.

d. Statement of concurrence from the U.S. Chief of Mission and the U.S. Defense Attaché, when assigned, to the country of the award recipient.

e. Statement of concurrence from the DIA.

f. Additional documentation supporting the recommendation, to include at a minimum, a narrative that addresses why the recommended award is in the overall interests of the United States and what specific actions by the individual justify the award. This narrative shall be similar in nature to the Summary of Action used for DON U.S. personal awards.

g. If the recommendation is not being submitted within six months of the completion of the period of service being recognized, a concise yet thorough narrative explaining the delay, a maximum of one page in length, must also be included.

h.   SECNAV will forward the completed recommendation package to the Under Secretary of Defense for Policy (USD(P)), who will obtain a statement of concurrence from the Department of State. If deemed appropriate, USD(P) will also request the Department of State to obtain the foreign country's clearance for the award.

621.   CITATIONS AND CERTIFICATES

1.   Four Degrees of the Legion of Merit. When in the Degree of Chief Commander, the certificate is signed jointly by the President and the Secretary of Defense. When awarded in other Degrees, the certificate is signed jointly by SECDEF and SECNAV. All citations have the DoD seal affixed.

2.   DON Personal Awards. SECNAV or his designee signs the citation and certificate.

3.   Unit Awards. The original citation, with copies and ribbon bars for personnel of the unit, are provided by CNO or CMC, as appropriate.

622.   PRESENTATION OF AWARDS. If the recipient is in the Washington, DC, area, presentation will be made in the name of the President by SECNAV, CNO, CMC, or their personal representatives. Otherwise, it will be made in the name of the President by the Ambassador to the country concerned, or such other official as he or she may designate. The recipient is presented with the citation, certificate, and medal set for each award. In instances when the recipient is receiving a second or subsequent award of the same decoration, the appropriate distinguishing device will be attached to the suspension ribbon of the medal. End of tour awards to members permanently assigned to a Navy or Marine Corps command may be made at the command level following approval of the award.

CHAPTER 7 - FOREIGN AWARDS AND SERVICE
DECORATIONS TO U.S. PERSONNEL

SECTION 1 - GENERAL

710. <u>PURPOSE</u>. The purpose of this chapter is to provide
guidance governing the acceptance and retention of awards and
service decorations from foreign governments.

711. <u>POLICY</u>

1. Article I, Section 9, Clause 8, of the Constitution
provides that "no Person holding any Office of Profit or Trust
under [the United States] shall, without the Consent of the
Congress, accept of any present, Emolument, Office, or Title, of
any kind whatever, from any King, Prince or foreign State."
Congress, in 5 U.S.C. §7342, as amended, has sanctioned
acceptance of such items under limited circumstances, subject to
approval of the recipient's employing agency.

2. No service member shall request or otherwise encourage
the offer of a decoration from a foreign government.

712. <u>ISSUE AND WEAR OF FOREIGN AWARDS</u>. Issue of foreign awards
is the responsibility of the country concerned. Authorized
recipients may purchase medals and ribbons from commercial
sources. When authorized for wear, foreign awards shall be worn
as prescribed in the applicable Navy or Marine Corps Uniform
Regulations.

SECTION 2 - FOREIGN DECORATIONS

720. <u>FOREIGN PERSONAL AWARDS</u>

1. Foreign personal awards may be accepted and retained
only upon the approval of CNO (DNS-35) or CMC (MMMA), as
appropriate. In the absence of such approval, the decoration
becomes the property of the United States and shall be deposited
with the Navy or Marine Corps for use or disposal as delineated
in Chapter 9. Approval by CNO or CMC shall be contingent upon a
determination that the decoration has been tendered in
recognition of active field service in connection with combat
operations or for outstanding or unusually meritorious

performance. Paragraph 4 below provides information regarding the wear of foreign personal awards.

2. In the event an individual is advised that a foreign nation has tendered an award and his/her presence is desired at a formal presentation ceremony, the individual may participate in the ceremony and receive the award. The receipt of a foreign award, under such circumstances, shall not constitute an acceptance of the award by the recipient.

3. Immediately upon such presentation, or once an award has been tendered, the recipient shall submit a request for approval to accept and retain the award to CNO (DNS-35) or CMC (MMMA), as appropriate. The request shall be marked "For Official Use Only - Privacy Sensitive" and contain, at a minimum, the following information:

a. Proposed recipient's full name, grade, social security number, current unit, and a brief description of the duty assignment during the period being recognized.

b. Title of the decoration, the country offering it, name and title of person making the presentation, and the date and place of presentation.

c. A statement of the service for which the decoration is being offered. Enclose a copy of the citation, with an English translation. If no citation was issued, indicate this in the request. Additionally, Marine Corps personnel shall submit a color photograph of the award on a neutral background next to a Naval Service award, for scale.

4. Personnel are prohibited from wearing any foreign personal awards unless attending a public function of the country, or in the house of, or in honor of a public official or other distinguished citizen of that foreign country. When personnel attend an event where dignitaries from various countries are present, foreign personal decorations from multiple countries may be worn. In such situations when foreign personal awards are authorized for wear, they shall be worn in the manner prescribed in the applicable Navy or Marine Corps Uniform Regulations.

721. FOREIGN UNIT AWARDS. Unit awards tendered by friendly foreign nations to units of the Naval service will be forwarded

to SECNAV via the chain of command for approval of acceptance. The foreign unit awards listed below have been authorized for acceptance as indicated and shall be worn in the manner prescribed in the applicable Navy or Marine Corps Uniform Regulations.

1. Philippine Republic Presidential Unit Citation

    a. World War II

        (1) Authorization. Headquarters Philippine National Defense Force G.O. No. 500 of 29 October 1948 and No. 152 of 7 March 1951.

        (2) Eligibility Requirements. Approved by SECNAV for wear by members of the Naval Service serving in units engaged in the defense of the Philippines between 7 December 1941 and 5 May 1942; serving in units which participated in the liberation campaigns during 1944 and 1945; or serving in certain submarines which had maintained physical contact with guerrilla forces during the Japanese occupation of the Philippine Islands. All ships and units that earned any of the Philippine engagement stars are eligible for this award.

    b. Disaster Relief Operations

        (1) Authorization

            (a) SECNAV letter Ser 0182 of 29 April 1971 approved acceptance of the award for the following units:

Navy Disaster Task Force	01 Sep 70 to 14 Dec 70
Navy and Marine Corps Units of Joint U.S. Military Advisory Group, Philippines	01 Aug 70 to 15 Dec 70
Amphibious Ready Group Alpha	21 Oct 70 to 26 Oct 70

            (b) SECNAV letter Ser 1582 of 9 January 1973 approved acceptance of the award for Commander in Chief, Pacific Representative Philippine Disaster Task Force and U.S. Disaster Task Force Manila for the period 21 July to 15 August 1972.

            (c) SECNAV letter Ser 1650 NDBDM/1665 of 16 December 1987 approved acceptance of the award for Task Element

73.7.1.1 (Operation MERCY MISSION) for the period 20 March to 28 May 1987.

(d) SECNAV letter Ser 1650 NDBDM/1959 of 18 August 1992 approved acceptance of the award for U.S. Naval Hospital, Subic Bay for the period 1 August 1987 to 30 November 1991 and for USS STERETT (CG 31) for the period May 1989 to June 1991.

(2) Eligibility Requirements. Approved by SECNAV for wear by Navy and Marine Corps personnel attached to the units listed above or any of the authorized supporting units. Lists of eligible units are maintained by CNO and CMC.

(3) Subsequent Awards. Personnel who qualify for more than one award of the Philippine Republic Presidential Unit Citation are authorized to wear a 3/16 inch bronze star for each subsequent award.

2. Republic of Korea Presidential Unit Citation

a. Authorization. Awarded by the President of the Republic of Korea, and approved by SECNAV for wear by eligible Naval service personnel.

b. Eligibility Requirements. Authorized for wear by personnel who served with certain commands or with units of those commands that were individually cited by the President of the Republic of Korea for service in Korea. Lists of eligible units are maintained by CNO and CMC.

c. Eligible Operations. The following operations have been designated as eligible for the Republic of Korea Presidential Unit Citation. Note: Service stars are not authorized for wear on this award.

Task Force 90	01 Jul 50 to 31 Mar 51
1st Provisional Marine Brigade	02 Aug 50 to 06 Sep 50
1st Marine Aircraft Wing	03 Aug 50 to 26 Feb 51
Task Force 95	12 Sep 50 to 03 Aug 51
1st Marine Division	15 Sep 50 to 27 Sep 50
1st Marine Division	26 Oct 50 to 27 Jul 53
1st Marine Aircraft Wing	27 Feb 51 to 11 Jun 53
1st Korea Regimental Combat Team & USMC Advisory Group	30 Oct 52 to 01 Nov 52

USMC Advisory Component of the
U.S. Navy Advisory Group Korea 01 Feb 53 to 27 Jul 54
Commander, U.S. Marine Corps
Forces Korea   09 Dec 99 to 24 Apr 02

3. Vietnam Presidential Unit Citation

a. Authorization. Awarded by the President of the Republic of Vietnam, and approved by SECNAV for wear by eligible U.S. Navy personnel; no Marine Corps personnel are eligible for this award.

b. Eligibility Requirements. Authorized for wear by personnel who served with certain units cited by the President of the Republic of Vietnam for humanitarian assistance during August and September 1954 in the evacuation of civilians from North and Central Vietnam. A list of eligible units is maintained by CNO.

4. Republic of Vietnam Meritorious Unit Citation

a. Authorization. Awarded by the Chief of the Joint General Staff, Republic of Vietnam Armed Forces in two colors: Gallantry Cross Color with Palm and Frame (8 February 1962 to 28 March 1973) and Civil Actions First Class Color with Palm and Frame (1 January 1965 to 28 March 1973). SECNAV has specifically authorized certain units of the Naval service to accept and wear these awards. Such authorization is required in all cases for participation.

b. Eligibility Requirements. The ribbon bar with palm and frame are authorized for wear by personnel who served with certain cited units in Southeast Asia during the approved periods. Lists of eligible units are maintained by CNO and CMC.

c. In addition to those specific ships/units cited, all Navy and Marine Corps personnel who served "in country" Vietnam during the eligibility periods are eligible for both awards.

722. MULTILATERAL SERVICE AWARDS. All multilateral organization offers of medals and ribbons not listed below to individual members of the Naval service, including the Coast Guard when operating under control of the Navy, shall be forwarded to CNO (DNS-35) or CMC (MMMA), as appropriate, with

the following information: title of award and when, where, and by whom it was offered. Requests by multilateral organizations, other than the United Nations, for inclusion of a specific service medal on the approved list will be forwarded by SECNAV to SECDEF for a determination of acceptance under Executive Order 11446. Subsequent to the approval of each multilateral award, conditions and qualifications for acceptance will be issued. The multilateral service awards listed below have been authorized for acceptance as indicated and shall be worn in the manner prescribed in the applicable Navy or Marine Corps Uniform Regulations.

1. United Nations Service Medal

    a. Authorization. U.N. General Assembly Resolution 438(V) of 12 December 1950.

    b. Eligibility Requirements. Awarded to members of the U.S. Armed Forces who participated in the U.N. action in Korea and who are eligible for the Korean Service Medal.

2. United Nations Medal

    a. Authorization. Established by Secretary General, United Nations Regulations dated 30 July 1959. E.O. 11139 authorized SECDEF to approve acceptance and wear.

    b. Eligibility Requirements. U.S. service members who are or have been in the service of the U.N. in operations designated by SECDEF may accept the United Nations Medal when awarded by the Chief of the U.N. Mission. Following are the qualifying operations:

Truce Supervisory Organization in Palestine (Jun 48 - TBD)
Military Observer Group in India and Pakistan (Jan 49 - TBD)
Observation Group in Lebanon (Jun - Dec 58)
Security Forces, Hollandia (Dates Unknown)
Iraq/Kuwait Observation Group (Apr 91 - TBD)
Mission for the Referendum in Western Sahara (May 91 - TBD)
Advance Mission in Cambodia (Oct 91 - Mar 92)
Transitional Authority in Cambodia (Feb 92 - TBD)
Protection Force in Yugoslavia (Feb 92 - TBD)
Somalia (includes U.S. Quick Reaction Force) (24 Apr 92 - TBD)
Mission in Haiti (23 Sep 94 - TBD)
U.N. Special Service (6 Oct 97 - TBD)

c. The United Nations Medal is awarded by the U.N. to individuals who are actually assigned to U.N. operations. The U.N.'s practice is to use the same medallion for all awards, with a different suspension ribbon for each authorized operation.

d. If approved by SECDEF, U.S. personnel who meet the criteria may accept and wear the first U.N. medal, with unique suspension and service ribbon, for which they are eligible. To recognize subsequent awards for service in a different U.N. mission or action, the member will affix a bronze 3/16 inch service star to the first U.N. suspension and service ribbon awarded.

e. The United Nations Medal will normally be awarded by the Chief of the U.N. Mission to qualifying U.S. service members prior to their departure from service with the U.N. Questions regarding eligibility must be addressed directly to the U.N. Mission.

3. NATO Medal

a. Authorization. Established by the Secretary General, North Atlantic Treaty Organization (NATO). As authorized by E.O. 11446, SECDEF approved acceptance and wear on 25 July 1995.

b. Eligibility Requirements. The NATO Medal is awarded to members of the Armed Forces of the United States who served either 30 days (consecutive or cumulative) in the territory and airspace of the former Republic of Yugoslavia and the Adriatic Sea, or 90 days (consecutive or cumulative) in the area of operations. Two operations were approved for award:

(1) The former Republic of Yugoslavia and Adriatic Sea, between 1 July 1992 and 12 October 1998, including Operations DENY FLIGHT, MARITIME MONITOR, MARITIME GUARD, and SHARP GUARD.

(2) Kosovo Operations from 13 October 1998 to TBD, including ALLIED FORCE, JOINT GUARDIAN, ALLIED HARBOR, SUSTAIN/SHINING HOPE, NOBLE ANVIL, and Kosovo Task Forces.

c. U.S. Armed Forces personnel may qualify for the
NATO Medal under one or more of the following conditions:

(1) Served under NATO command in Headquarters,
Allied Forces Southern Europe; Headquarters, Allied Naval Forces
Southern Europe; Headquarters, Allied Air Forces Southern
Europe; or HQ 5ATAF, and in direct support of NATO operations in
the former Republic of Yugoslavia.

(2) Served under NATO command in other
installations, within the area of operations and in direct
support of NATO operations, as designated by Supreme Allied
Commander Europe (SACEUR).

(3) Served under NATO operational command in the
NATO Airborne Early Warning Force, or in ships assigned to
specified operations.

(4) Served under NATO operational command in
specified operations, or as NATO Liaison Officers.

d. Eligibility Determinations. Assigned units submit
requests through their operational chain of command to
COMUSNAVEUR or MARFOREUR. Include unit name, period of service
in theater, anticipated date of departure from the theater, and
name and grade of all eligible personnel.

e. Appropriate Wear. The NATO Medal presentation set
may include a ribbon clasp denoting the specific operation for
which the award was made. U.S. service members may retain the
ribbon clasp if presented; however, wearing of the ribbon clasp
with the NATO Medal or service ribbon is not authorized; only
the basic medal or service ribbon is worn. A 3/16 inch bronze
star is affixed to the suspension ribbon and service ribbon to
denote subsequent awards.

4. Multinational Force and Observers Medal

a. Authorization. Established by Director General,
Multinational Force and Observers (MFO).

b. Eligibility Requirements. Awarded by the Director
General, MFO, to personnel of the Armed Forces who served with
the MFO for at least 90 cumulative days in the Sinai.
Subsequent awards will be denoted by an appropriate metallic

numeral. Effective date of the award is 3 August 1981. This award is <u>not</u> authorized for service in Lebanon.

    5. <u>Inter-American Defense Board Medal</u>

        a. Authorized by the Ninety-first Session of the Inter-American Defense Board (IADB) on 11 December 1945.

        b. Eligibility Requirements. Awarded to the Chair of the Board, delegates, advisors, officers of the staff, officers of the secretariat, and officers of the IAD College who constitute the Directorate, the Department of Studies, and the Department of Administration, who have served for at least one year.

        c. Subsequent Awards. For each five years of service to the IADB, a gold star will be awarded.

723. <u>FOREIGN SERVICE AWARDS</u>. As a general policy, DoD does not permit U.S. military personnel to accept service medals from foreign governments. However, personnel meeting the eligibility requirements are authorized to accept the following medals. These medals shall be worn in the manner prescribed in the applicable Navy or Marine Corps Uniform Regulations.

    1. <u>Republic of Vietnam Campaign Medal</u>. Established by Republic of Vietnam Armed Forces Order No. 48 of 24 March 1966. The provisions of Public Law 88-257 permit acceptance of this medal to recognize service performed in Vietnam during the period 1 March 1961 to 28 March 1973, inclusive.

        a. Eligibility Requirements. U.S. Armed Forces personnel are eligible for the Republic of Vietnam Campaign Medal under one or more of the following conditions:

        (1) Wounded or injured in hostile action.

        (2) Captured by the opposing force during actions or in the line of duty, but later rescued or released.

        (3) Killed in action or in the line of duty.

        (4) Served a cumulative six months in South Vietnam.

(5) Served a cumulative six months outside the geographical limits of South Vietnam, but contributing direct combat support to the Republic of Vietnam Armed Forces during such period. Only those personnel who meet the criteria established for the Armed Forces Expeditionary Medal (Vietnam) or the Vietnam Service Medal are considered to have contributed direct combat support.

(6) Assigned in Vietnam on 28 January 1973 and served during the entire period from 29 January to 28 March 1973, inclusive.

b. Eligibility Determinations and Record Entries. If eligibility cannot be determined from available records, commanding officers are authorized to accept the individual's affidavit, similar to the following:

Affidavit

I certify that I served on board (name of ship or unit) from (date) to (date). This affidavit is made to confirm my eligibility for the Republic of Vietnam Campaign Medal for service in the Vietnam area.

After eligibility determination, the commanding officer shall make appropriate entries in enlisted service records and address official letters to officers, certifying eligibility for the award, authorizing wear of the ribbon bar with device, and indicating the date of issue. Copies of the letters to officers shall be forwarded to NPC (PERS-312) or CMC (MMSB), as appropriate, for filing in their records.

2. Kuwait Liberation Medal (Saudi Arabia)

a. Authorization. Established by the Government of Saudi Arabia and accepted by Deputy SECDEF on 3 January 1992.

b. Eligibility Requirements. The Kuwait Liberation Medal (Saudi Arabia) is awarded to members of the Armed Forces of the United States who participated in Operation DESERT STORM between 17 January and 28 February 1991 in one or more of the following areas: the Persian Gulf; Red Sea; Gulf of Oman; that portion of the Arabian Sea that lies north of 10 degrees north latitude and west of 68 degrees east longitude; the Gulf of Aden; or the total land areas of Iraq, Kuwait, Saudi Arabia,

Oman, Bahrain, Qatar, and the United Arab Emirates. U.S. Armed Forces personnel are eligible for the Kuwait Liberation Medal (Saudi Arabia) under one or more of the following conditions:

       (1) Attached to or regularly serving for one or more days with an organization participating in ground/shore operations.

       (2) Attached to or regularly serving for one or more days aboard a naval vessel directly supporting military operations.

       (3) Actually participating as a crewmember in one or more aerial flights supporting military operations in the areas designated above.

       (4) Serving on temporary duty for 30 consecutive days during the period 17 January to 28 February 1991 under any of the criteria above. This time limit may be waived for personnel participating in <u>actual combat operations</u>.

       (5) The medal may be awarded posthumously.

       c. Eligibility Determinations and Record Entries. Commanding officers shall determine eligibility upon review of an individual's service record and are authorized to issue the award. Commanding officers shall make appropriate service record entries for enlisted personnel and issue letters of eligibility for officers. Copies of the letters to officers shall be forwarded to NPC (PERS-312) or CMC (MMSB), as appropriate, for filing in their records. No citation or certificate will be issued. The eligibility period and geographic boundaries were specified by the Government of Saudi Arabia and may not be waived.

    3. <u>Kuwait Liberation Medal (Kuwait)</u>

       a. Authorization. Established by the Government of Kuwait and accepted by Deputy SECDEF on 7 August 1995.

       b. Eligibility Requirements. The Kuwait Liberation Medal (Kuwait) is awarded to members of the Armed Forces of the United States who participated in Operations DESERT SHIELD/DESERT STORM between 2 August 1990 and 31 August 1993 in one or more of the following areas: Arabian Gulf; Red Sea; Gulf of Oman; that portion of the Arabian Sea north of 10 degrees north latitude and west of 68 degrees east longitude; the Gulf of Aden; or the total land areas of Iraq, Kuwait, Saudi Arabia, Oman, Bahrain, Qatar, and the United Arab Emirates. U.S. Armed Forces personnel are eligible for the Kuwait Liberation Medal (Kuwait) under one or more of the following conditions:

(1) Attached to or regularly serving for one or more days with an organization participating in ground/shore operations.

(2) Attached to or regularly serving for one or more days aboard a naval vessel directly supporting military operations.

(3) Actually participating as a crewmember in one or more aerial flights supporting military operations in the areas designated above.

(4) Serving on temporary duty for 30 consecutive or 60 nonconsecutive days, during the period 2 August 1990 to 31 August 1993, under any of the criteria above. This time limit may be waived for personnel participating in <u>actual combat operations</u>.

(5) The Kuwait Liberation Medal (Kuwait) may be awarded posthumously to the primary next of kin of service members who lost their lives while, or as a direct result of, participating in Operations DESERT SHIELD/DESERT STORM between 2 August 1990 and 31 August 1993, without regard to length of service, if otherwise eligible.

c. Eligibility Determinations and Record Entries. Commanding officers shall determine eligibility upon review of an individual's service record, and are authorized to issue the award. Commanding officers shall make appropriate service record entries for enlisted personnel and issue letters of eligibility for officers. Copies of the letters to officers shall be forwarded to NPC (PERS-312) or CMC (MMSB), as appropriate, for filing in their records. No citation or certificate will be issued. The eligibility period and geographic boundaries were specified by the Government of Kuwait and may not be waived.

4. <u>Republic of Korea War Service Medal</u>

    a. Authorization. Awarded by the Republic of Korea Minister of Defense and accepted by SECDEF on 20 August 1999.

    b. Eligibility Requirements. Military personnel, workers, and policemen who either served in or through some special duty deployed to and returned from the combat zone during the Korean War from 25 June 1950 to 27 July 1953.

    c. Information on obtaining this medal is available online at <u>https://awards.navy.mil</u>.

CHAPTER 8 - PRIOR SERVICE AND VETERAN AWARDS

SECTION 1 - GENERAL

810. PURPOSE. To provide guidance and regulations concerning award procedures for personnel no longer active in the Naval Service.

811. RESERVE PERSONNEL. Personnel currently serving in the Navy or Marine Corps Reserve shall process any request for an award, including those for prior service, through their current chain of command.

812. POLICY CONSIDERATIONS

1. Campaign and Service Awards. Eligibility for campaign and service awards is a matter of service record verification, and is not subject to time limits. The procedures for verifying eligibility are provided in Article 820 below.

2. Personal and Unit Awards

a. Previously Approved Awards. To obtain information regarding awards previously received, see Article 820 below. Additional information is also available via the Navy Awards website at https://awards.navy.mil under the "Veterans" tab.

b. New Awards. In general, the time limit for submitting a personal or unit award recommendation is three years from the date of the action for which recognition is desired. However, in accordance with 10 U.S.C. §1130, upon the request of a Member of Congress, SECNAV will review any proposal for a new award or upgrade of an existing award, and make a determination, based on the merits of the case, regardless of time limits prescribed by policy or law. All §1130 requests shall be reviewed by CNO or CMC, as appropriate, to both ensure the completeness of the recommendation package and to provide a recommendation regarding the merits of the case. Complete packages shall be submitted to SECNAV, via the Navy Department Board of Decorations and Medals, with the Service Chief's recommendation based solely on the merits of the request, notwithstanding any time limits. Appendix A to this chapter provides information regarding the submission requirements for §1130 cases.

c. <u>Upgrade of Previously Approved Awards</u>.
Reconsideration of a previously approved award requires the presentation of new and relevant material evidence that was not available at the time the original recommendation was considered. Additional details regarding information that was previously provided in the original award recommendation will <u>not</u> meet the "new and relevant" requirement. If, however, new and relevant information is available, and consideration for an award upgrade is desired after the normal time limits have passed, the request may be submitted through a Member of Congress in accordance with 10 U.S.C. §1130, as noted in the previous paragraph. A request for an award upgrade must include the submission of a complete recommendation package in accordance with the requirements delineated in Appendix A to this chapter.

SECTION 2 - ADMINISTRATIVE PROCEDURES

820. <u>AWARD INQUIRIES</u>. To confirm eligibility for campaign and service awards, and to obtain information regarding awards previously received, a service record review is required. Therefore, requests must be submitted to the command currently maintaining the member's service record, as listed below.

1. Navy veterans discharged without further obligated service or transferred to the Fleet Reserve or the Retired List prior to 1 January 1996, and Marine Corps veterans discharged without further obligated service or transferred to the Fleet Marine Corps Reserve or the Retired List prior to 1 January 1999, may submit award inquiries to the following address:

        Navy Personnel Command
        Retired Records Section (PERS-312D2)
        9700 Page Avenue, Room 5409
        St. Louis, MO 63132-5100

2. Navy veterans discharged without further obligated service or transferred to the Fleet Reserve or the Retired List after 1 January 1996, may submit requests to the following address:

Navy Personnel Command
PERS 312
5720 Integrity Drive
Millington, TN 38055-3120

3. Marine Corps veterans discharged without further obligated service or transferred to the Fleet Marine Corps Reserve or the Retired List after 1 January 1999, may submit requests to the following address:

Headquarters, U.S. Marine Corps
Military Awards Branch (MMMA)
3280 Russell Road
Quantico, VA 22134-5103

4. Marine Corps veterans released from active duty with further obligated service, but not in an active drilling status (e.g., Individual Ready Reserve), may submit award inquiries to the following address:

Marine Corps Mobilization Command
15303 Andrews Road
Kansas City, MO 64147-1207

5. Include the following information in all requests, and mark the letter "For Official Use Only - Privacy Act Protected." The SF-180 form, "Request Pertaining to Military Records," may also be used and is available online at https://awards.navy.mil, the Navy Awards website.

a. Full name, grade/rate at time of discharge.

b. Social security number and service number (if service was before 1972).

c. Periods of service - indicate periods of active duty/reserve duty.

d. Date of last discharge.

e. Organization: ship, squadron, unit, battalion, regiment, etc., during period for which inquiry is made.

f. Date and place of birth.

g. Mailing address, phone number, and email address.

h. If the requestor is someone other than the veteran for whom the information is being requested, also include the relationship to the veteran, such as daughter, brother, etc. If the veteran is deceased, include a copy of the death certificate.

821. <u>REPLACEMENT MEDALS</u>. All medals, except the Medal of Honor, which is strictly controlled by CNO and CMC, are now available and authorized for purchase from numerous commercial sources, including the Services' Military Exchange systems. Replacement medals (except the Medal of Honor) may also be available to veterans and next of kin of veterans killed in combat on a one-time basis, if stock is sufficient, by writing to the addresses shown above. However, due to the volume of requests received, the processing time may be lengthy; therefore, procurement from commercial sources is recommended for more timely receipt.

822. <u>ELIGIBILITY OF MERCHANT MARINE PERSONNEL</u>. During the period 1939 through 1952 members of the Merchant Marine with concurrent membership in the Navy Reserve may be eligible for certain DON awards as listed below.

1. Certain Merchant Marine personnel may be eligible for some campaign and service medals, provided <u>all</u> of the following criteria are met:

a. Concurrent Merchant Marine Reserve (MMR)/U.S. Navy Reserve status (USNR).

b. Attended a Merchant Marine Academy and upon graduation were commissioned ensigns in the United States Navy Reserve without a break in service.

c. Meets all the requirements for the specific campaign and/or service medal.

2. If the specific eligibility criteria are met, other members of the Merchant Marine with concurrent membership in the Navy Reserve may be awarded the Naval Reserve Medal or the Armed Forces Reserve Medal.

3. Requests for eligibility determinations should be submitted to CNO (DNS-35), 2000 Navy Pentagon, Washington, DC, 20350-2000 with the following information:

(a) Medals requested.

(b) The period of service as MMR/USNR without a break in service following Merchant Marine Academy graduation.

(c) Theatres, vessels, and accompanying dates for any qualifying period(s).

(d) Official military documentation supporting the above information.

(e) A sealed letter from the appropriate Merchant Marine Academy confirming the period of attendance.

823. <u>SUBMISSION OF REQUESTS UNDER 10 U.S.C. §1130</u>. Appendix A to this chapter provides information regarding submission requirements for §1130 cases. In the event an incomplete recommendation package is submitted, CNO or CMC shall contact the requesting Member of Congress and provide specific guidance regarding the additional information required in order for the case to be considered.

824. <u>INFORMATION RESOURCES</u>. The following offices may be able to assist in obtaining the official military documentation required to substantiate an award recommendation submitted in accordance with 10 U.S.C §1130.

> The National Archives and Records Administration
> 8601 Adelphi Road
> College Park, MD 20740-6001
> http://www.archives.gov/

> The Naval Historical Center
> 805 Kidder Breese SE
> Washington Navy Yard, DC 20374-5060
> http://www.history.navy.mil/

> United States Marine Corps
> Marine Corps Education Command
> Marine Corps University

History Division
3079 Moreell Avenue
Quantico, VA 22134
http://hqinet001.hqmc.usmc.mil/HD/

Copies of documents from individual service and medical records
for members detached from the Navy prior to 1 January 1996, and
from the Marine Corps prior to 1 January 1999, may be obtained
from the National Personnel Records Center (NPRC). It is
important to provide the member's full name, service and/or
social security number, and date of birth in any correspondence
to NPRC. The correspondence shall be marked "For Official Use
Only - Privacy Act Protected."

National Personnel Records Center
Military Personnel Records
9700 Page Avenue
St. Louis, MO 63132-5100
http://www.archives.gov/st-louis/military-personnel/

SECTION 3 - AWARD REQUIREMENTS

830. GENERAL. Eligibility requirements for all personal, unit,
and campaign and service awards listed in Chapters 2, 3, and 4,
respectively, remain in effect for prior service and veteran
awards. The following sections provide supplemental guidance
for certain awards currently authorized for issue, as well as
information regarding certain awards no longer being issued.
Chapter 7 contains guidance regarding foreign awards.

831. SPECIFIC AWARD INFORMATION

1. Purple Heart Medal. The complete eligibility
requirements for the Purple Heart are contained in Chapter 2 of
this manual.

a. Type of Enemy Action. During World War I, World
War II, and the Korean War, an individual must have been wounded
as a direct result of enemy action. After 15 October 1962, an
individual who was wounded, either as a direct or indirect
result of enemy action, is eligible for the Purple Heart.

b. Time Limits. Award of the Purple Heart, unlike
other personal awards, is not subject to time limits and,

therefore, it is not necessary to process eligibility requests through a Member of Congress.

c. Eligibility Determinations. Personnel may apply directly to the appropriate address listed in Article 820 above for an eligibility determination based on <u>documented evidence</u> in personnel and/or medical records. A Personal Award Recommendation Form is not required.

d. If adequate documentation is not available, <u>due to the complete or partial loss of an individual's records</u>, two sworn affidavits from eyewitnesses to the injury, who were present at the time of the injury and have personal knowledge of the circumstances under which the injury occurred, may be submitted for consideration. (Statements from witnesses "after the fact" will <u>not</u> be considered.) The affidavits must be in the eyewitnesses' own words, not on a prepared form, and must be notarized. When all necessary information has been compiled, the complete package may be sent to the appropriate address:

(1) For Navy Veterans:

Chief of Naval Operations
DNS-35
2000 Navy Pentagon
Washington, DC 20350-2000

(2) For Marine Corps Veterans:

Headquarters, U.S. Marine Corps
Military Awards Branch (MMMA)
3280 Russell Road
Quantico, VA 22134-5103

2. <u>Distinguished Flying Cross and Air Medal Based on Strike/Flight Criteria</u>. The complete eligibility requirements for the Distinguished Flying Cross (DX) and Air Medal are contained in Chapter 2 of this manual.

a. Eligibility Determinations. Personnel who believe they may be eligible for a DX or Air Medal based on Strike/Flight criteria during World War II may submit an officially notarized copy of their Aviator's Flight Log Book (NAVAER-4111) to CNO or CMC, as appropriate, at the address listed in the previous paragraph. Copies of award citations for any DX or Air Medal previously awarded must be included with the

request. Requests for Strike/Flight awards for other time
periods shall be processed in accordance with the stated
procedures for §1130 cases; i.e., through a Member of Congress.

b. Eligibility Criteria. The point requirements for
Strike/Flight awards, as well as the definitions of "strike" and
"flight," vary depending on the time period, as outlined below.

(1) World War II: 7 December 1941 to 14 April
1946.

(a) Award of an Air Medal on a Strike/Flight
basis requires five points, and award of a DX requires 20
points.

(b) One strike equals one point, and one flight
equals one point.

(c) Definitions

1. A strike is deemed to have taken place
when an aircraft, ordered on an offensive mission in a combat
area, attacked the enemy, met enemy opposition, or was subjected
to enemy attack.

2. A flight is deemed to have taken place
when the mission was primarily non-offensive (transport, search,
patrol, etc.), and when the aircraft operated in an active
combat area where enemy anti-aircraft fire was expected to be
effective, or where enemy aircraft patrols usually occurred.

(2) Korean Conflict: 27 June 1950 to 6 November
1951.

(a) Award of an Air Medal on a Strike/Flight
basis requires 10 points, and award of a DX requires 35 points.

(b) One strike equals one point, and one flight
equals one point.

(c) Definitions

1. A strike is deemed to have taken place
when an aircraft, ordered on an offensive mission in a combat

area, attacked the enemy, met enemy opposition, or was subjected to enemy attack.

2. A flight is deemed to have taken place when the mission was primarily non-offensive (transport, search, patrol, etc.), and when the aircraft operated in an active combat area where enemy anti-aircraft fire was expected to be effective, or where enemy aircraft patrols usually occurred.

(3) Korean Conflict: 7 November 1951 to 16 November 1952.

(a) Award of an Air Medal on a Strike/Flight basis requires 20 points, and the service must have been meritorious. Personnel cannot qualify for a DX based on Strike/Flight points during this period.

(b) One strike equals one point, and one flight equals one point.

(c) Definitions

1. A strike is deemed to have taken place when an aircraft ordered on an offensive mission in a combat area attacked the enemy, met enemy opposition, or was subjected to enemy attack.

2. A flight is deemed to have taken place when the mission was primarily non-offensive (transport, search, patrol, etc.), and when the aircraft operated in an active combat area where enemy anti-aircraft fire was expected to be effective, or where enemy aircraft patrols usually occurred.

(4) Korean Conflict: 17 November 1952 to 27 July 1953.

(a) Award of an Air Medal on a Strike/Flight basis requires 20 points. Personnel cannot qualify for a DX based on Strike/Flight points during this period.

(b) One strike equals two points, and one flight equals one point.

(c) Definitions

<u>1</u>. A strike is deemed to have taken place when an aircraft on a combat mission attacked the enemy, met enemy opposition, or was subjected to enemy attack.

<u>2</u>. A flight is deemed to have taken place when an aircraft on a combat mission operated in an active combat area where enemy anti-aircraft fire was expected, or where enemy aircraft patrols usually occurred, but did not attack the enemy or meet enemy opposition.

(5) Vietnam Conflict: 4 July 1965 to 29 February 1968.

(a) Award of an Air Medal on a Strike/Flight basis requires 20 points. Personnel cannot qualify for a DX based on Strike/Flight points during this period.

(b) One strike equals two points, and one flight equals one point.

(c) Definitions

<u>1</u>. A strike is deemed to have taken place when an aircraft on a combat mission attacked the enemy, met enemy opposition, or was subjected to enemy attack.

<u>2</u>. A flight is deemed to have taken place when an aircraft on a combat mission operated in an active combat area, where enemy anti-aircraft fire was expected, or where enemy aircraft patrols usually occurred, but did not attack the enemy or meet enemy opposition.

(6) Vietnam Conflict: 1 March 1968 to 31 May 1968.

(a) Award of an Air Medal on a Strike/Flight basis requires 20 points. Personnel cannot qualify for a DX based on Strike/Flight points during this period.

(b) One strike equals two points, one flight equals one point, and one direct combat support mission equals 0.2 points.

(c) The definitions of strike, flight, and direct combat support mission are as indicated in Chapter 2.

(7) All qualifying periods subsequent to 31 May 1968 are as indicated in Chapter 2.

3. <u>Combat Action Ribbon</u>. The complete eligibility requirements for the Combat Action Ribbon (CR) are in Chapter 2 of this manual.

a. In addition to the criteria in Chapter 2, from 7 December 1941 through 24 May 2006 the following criteria also apply:

(1) Personnel in riverine and coastal operations, assaults, patrols, sweeps, ambushes, convoys, amphibious landings, and similar activities who have participated in firefights are eligible.

(2) Personnel assigned to areas subjected to sustained mortar, missile, and artillery attacks who actively participate in retaliatory or offensive actions are eligible.

(3) Personnel aboard a ship are eligible when the safety of the ship and the crew was endangered by enemy attack, such as a ship hit by a mine or a ship engaged by shore, surface, air, or sub-surface elements.

(4) Personnel serving in peacekeeping missions, if not eligible by other criteria, are eligible to receive the award when all of the following criteria are met:

(a) The member was subject to hostile, direct fire;

(b) Based on the mission and the tactical situation, not returning fire was the best course of action; and

(c) The member was in compliance with the rules of engagement and his orders by not returning fire.

b. Eligibility Determinations

(1) Award of the Combat Action Ribbon, unlike other personal awards, is <u>not</u> subject to time limits and, therefore, it is not necessary to process eligibility requests through a Member of Congress.

(2) All personnel should submit the required documentation to the appropriate address listed in Article 820 above, except Navy personnel with service from 7 December 1941

through 28 February 1961, who should submit their request to:

Chief of Naval Operations
DNS-35
2000 Navy Pentagon
Washington, DC 20350-2000

(3) In addition to the information listed above in Article 820, paragraph 5, also include a copy of Form 553 or Form DD-214/215, as applicable, and any other relevant substantiating documentation that provides evidence of personal combat action or assignment to a particular unit during the time that unit earned the Combat Action Ribbon, such as copies of combat awards, performance reports, unit muster sheets, or assignment orders.

4. <u>Navy Fleet Marine Force Ribbon</u>

a. <u>Authorization Period</u>. SECNAVINST 1650.36 of 1 September 1984 authorized this ribbon. However, the Fleet Marine Force (FMF) Officer Warfare Qualification Badge superseded this ribbon for Navy officer personnel as of 1 January 2006. Similarly, the FMF Enlisted Warfare Qualification Badge replaced this ribbon for Navy enlisted personnel as of 1 October 2006. See OPNAVINST 1414.6(series) and OPNAVINST 1414.4(series) for the respective guidelines on officer and enlisted FMF warfare qualification.

b. <u>Eligibility Requirements</u>

(1) General. For personnel serving during the authorized period noted above, qualification for the Navy FMF Ribbon signifies the acquisition of specific professional skills, knowledge and military experience that result in qualifications above those normally required of Navy personnel serving with the Marine Corps operating forces. This qualification must be obtained through a formal qualification program, and successful completion of the written test prescribed below. <u>Officer and enlisted personnel must</u>:

(a) Be assigned to a unit of the Marine Corps operating forces. Only those personnel assigned to Type II and Type IV sea duty are eligible.

(b) Successfully complete the following sections of the Marine Battle Skills Training Handbook (Books 1, 2 and 4):

Section	Tasking
Military Justice and Law of War	1-1-1 to 1-1-19
Marine Corps Organization, History, Customs, and Courtesies	1-2-1 to 1-2-39
Marine Corps Uniform, Clothing and Equipment	1-4-1 to 1-4-69
Marine Corps General Leadership	1-5-1 to 1-5-23
Substance Abuse	1-6-1 to 1-6-15
Troop Information/Training Management	1-7-1 to 1-7-39
Combat Leadership	1-8-1 to 1-8-27
Individual Weapons:	
M16A2 Service Rifle	2-11-1 to 2-11-37
M9 Service Pistol	4-11-1 to 4-11-7
Tactical Measures	2-14-1 to 2-14-87
Hand Grenades, Mines, and Pyrotechnics:	
Locating Mines	2-15-33 to 2-15-36
Movement through Mine Field	2-15-37 to 2-15-38
NBC Defense	2-16-1 to 2-16-100
First Aid and Field Sanitation	2-17-1 to 2-17-65
Land Navigation	2-18-1 to 2-18-29
Communication:	
Operate the SINCGARS RADIO	2-19-13 to 2-19-16
Communicate Using a Radio	2-19-17 to 2-19-22
Maintain Physical Fitness	2-20-1 to 2-20-40

(c) Pass the USMC Physical Fitness Test (PFT). All applicants, regardless of age, must complete this requirement. Individuals over 45 years of age, if found physically qualified by a medical officer, shall take the Marine Corps PFT under the age category 39-45.

(d) Be recommended for the award by the Marine Corps battalion/squadron commanding officer.

(2) Specific

(a) Enlisted active duty members of the Navy must:

1. Serve a minimum of 12 months with Marine Corps operating forces.

2. Graduate from Field Medical Service School (FMSS), or Chaplain and RP Expeditionary Skills Training (CREST) course, and obtain the appropriate Navy Enlisted Classification (NEC) (KM 8404/DT 8707/RP 2401). Navy personnel

assigned to an FMF unit, who have no Navy Enlisted
Classification Code (NEC) producing pipeline school (i.e., YN,
PN, DK, etc.), are also eligible.

<u>3</u>. Have no single performance trait mark
below 3.0, and no promotion recommendation lower than promotable
for the last two periodic evaluations.

(b) Enlisted members in Navy Reserve Marine
Corps operating force units must:

<u>1</u>. Serve a minimum of 24 months in a
Navy Reserve FMF unit with satisfactory drill attendance.

<u>2</u>. Obtain the appropriate NEC (KM 8404/DT
8707/RP 2401) for their billet.

<u>3</u>. Complete a two-week Active Duty
Training period in support of a Marine Corps field training
exercise.

<u>4</u>. Have no single performance trait mark
below 3.0, and no promotion recommendation lower than promotable
for the last two periodic evaluations.

(c) Navy active duty officers must serve a
minimum 12 months of duty with the Marine Corps operating
forces.

(d) Navy Reserve officers must serve a minimum
of 24 months in a Navy Reserve unit of the Marine Corps
operating forces with satisfactory drill attendance.

(3) With the concurrence of CMC and CNO, the
awarding authority may waive the above requirements in cases
when Navy personnel demonstrate exceptional skill, knowledge,
and leadership while providing support to the Marine Corps in a
combat environment.

c. <u>Awarding Authority</u>. Only Marine Corps
battalion/squadron commanding officers may award the Navy FMF
Ribbon. There are no subsequent awards and no citation or
certificate will be issued. Commanding officers shall make
appropriate service record entries for enlisted personnel, and
issue letters of eligibility for officers. Award of the ribbon
shall be noted in the member's next evaluation or fitness
report.

d. Advancement Credit. The award of this ribbon shall entitle enlisted personnel to be designated FMF, and have two points applied on the E4 through E6 advancement exams.

5. Navy Occupation Service Medal

a. Authorization. Navy Department General Order No. 10 of 28 January 1948.

b. Eligibility Requirements. Awarded to personnel in the Naval Service who participated in the occupation of the territories of the enemies of the United States during World War II and subsequent to the surrender of these enemies.

(1) To establish eligibility, the individual shall have been attached to, present, and serving on permanent duty with an organization in the Naval Service of the United States during those periods when such organization has been credited by SECNAV, or a delegated fleet command, with having performed duty in the occupation of enemy or former enemy national territory.

(2) Passenger, observer, visitor, courier, escort, inspector or other similar status, when not permanently attached to an eligible unit, is not creditable toward this award.

(3) Occupation duty in the European-African-Middle Eastern area may be credited to organizations for duty performed on and subsequent to 8 May 1945. Terminal dates for eligibility periods and occupation territories in this area are as follows:

Italy	15 Dec 47
Trieste	25 Oct 54
Germany (except Berlin)	05 May 55
Austria	25 Oct 55
Berlin	02 Oct 90

(4) Occupation duty in the Asiatic-Pacific area may be credited to organizations for duty performed between 2 September 1945 and 27 April 1952. Occupation territory in the Asiatic-Pacific area includes Japan and such territories recognized as sovereign to Japan, and such parts of Korea and such adjacent islands as are recognized to be Korean, but exclusive of all the mandated territory formerly administered by Japan, as are under the governmental control of the United States or of an ally of the United States during World War II. Eligibility also includes ships operating in such home or territorial waters or contiguous ocean areas in direct support of occupation or aircraft based upon and operating from such

territories or ships.

(5) Units performing service in the Korean area
during the period 27 June 1950 to 27 April 1952, inclusive, and
eligible for the Korean Service Medal, will not be credited with
eligibility for the Navy Occupation Service Medal (NOSM) for the
same period.

c. Subsequent Awards and Clasps. An individual may
only be awarded one NOSM. Appropriate clasps marked "Europe"
and "Asia" are authorized to be attached to the suspension
ribbon of the large medal only to denote service in the
respective area. No distinctive device to denote these clasps
is authorized for wear on the ribbon bar. If earned, both
clasps may be worn.

d. Army of Occupation Service Medal. Individuals who
have been tendered the Army of Occupation Service Medal, and are
eligible for the NOSM, are not entitled to both, but may elect
which one to accept.

e. Eligible Units. Lists of eligible ships and units
are maintained by CNO and CMC. If a ship or unit is not on the
list prior to 1 January 1958, entitlement to the medal will be
denied.

6. Korean Service Medal

a. Authorization. E.O. 10179 of 8 November 1950.

b. Eligibility Requirements. Awarded to all members
of the U.S. Armed Forces who participated in operations in the
Korean area during the period between 27 June 1950 and 27 July
1954, under the following circumstances:

(1) Sea Duty. Service for one or more days in the
designated area, attached to and serving on board a naval
vessel.

(2) Shore Duty. Attached to and regularly serving
on shore in the designated area, for one or more days, with an
organization that participated in combat operations or in direct
support of combat missions.

(3) Temporary Additional Duty. Service of 30
consecutive or 60 nonconsecutive days in the prescribed area,
unless personnel participate in actual combat, in which case the
time limit is waived.

(4) Passengers. Individuals in a purely passenger status shall be ineligible unless the unit in which they are embarked engages in actual combat. Patients in a hospital ship are considered as attached to the ship.

c. Engagement Stars. The prerequisite for wearing a star on the Korean Service Medal shall be service in a ship, aircraft unit or shore-based force at the time it participated in actual combat with the enemy for which a star was authorized, or participation in duty considered equally hazardous.

(1) A 3/16-inch bronze star indicative of actual combat in an operation or an engagement, as authorized by SECNAV, will be worn two points down on the suspension ribbon of the medal and on the ribbon bar. A 3/16-inch silver star will be worn in lieu of five bronze stars. Participation in combat operations during the following operations establish eligibility for one bronze star for each operation listed:

North Korean Aggression	27 Jun 50 to 02 Nov 50
Communist China Aggression	03 Nov 50 to 24 Jan 51
Inchon Landing	13 Sep 50 to 17 Sep 50
1st U.N. Counteroffensive	25 Jan 51 to 21 Apr 51
Communist China Spring Offensive	22 Apr 51 to 08 Jul 51
U.N. Summer-Fall Offensive	09 Jul 51 to 27 Nov 51
2nd Korean Winter	28 Nov 51 to 30 Apr 52
Korean Defense, Summer-Fall 1952	01 May 52 to 30 Nov 52
3rd Korean Winter	01 Dec 52 to 30 Apr 53
Korea, Summer 1953	01 May 53 to 27 Jul 53

(2) Ships and units considered to have participated in combat operations are those which:

(a) Engaged the enemy.

(b) Participated in ground action.

(c) Engaged in aerial flights over enemy territory.

(d) Took part in shore bombardment, minesweeping, or amphibious assault.

(e) Engaged in or launched commando-type raids or other operations behind enemy lines.

(f) Engaged in redeployment under enemy fire.

(g) Engaged in blockade of Korean waters.

(h) Operated as part of carrier task groups from which offensive air strikes were launched.

(i) Were part of mobile logistics support forces in combat areas. Presence in a combat zone primarily for training or transit does not qualify.

7. Vietnam Service Medal

a. Authorization. E.O. 11231 of 8 July 1965.

b. Eligibility Requirements

(1) General

(a) Awarded to all members of the Armed Forces of the United States, serving at any time between 4 July 1965 and 28 March 1973, in the area defined under the Armed Forces Expeditionary Medal (AFEM) for Vietnam.

(b) Awarded to all members of the Armed Forces of the United States in Thailand, Laos, or Cambodia or the air space thereof, between 4 July 1965 and 28 March 1973, and serving in direct support of operations in Vietnam.

(c) Members qualified for the AFEM, by reason of service between 1 July 1958 and 3 July 1965, inclusive, in an area for which the Vietnam Service Medal (VSM) was subsequently authorized, shall remain qualified for the AFEM. Upon application, any such member may elect the VSM in lieu of the AFEM for such service. However, no person shall be entitled to both awards for service in an area for which the VSM has been authorized.

(d) Public Law 107-314 of 2 December 2002 stipulates that personnel who were awarded the AFEM for their participation in Operation FREQUENT WIND, during the period 29 to 30 April 1975, may elect the VSM in lieu of the AFEM for such service. However, no person shall be entitled to both awards for the same service.

(2) Personnel Eligible. Only personnel attached to ships or units, and who actually participated in the given operation, are eligible for the VSM. This includes personnel

attached to a squadron or unit embarked in a ship during the period for which that ship is eligible. Members of rear echelons, transients, observers, and personnel assigned for short periods or TAD and training duty are normally not eligible for the award; however, consideration will be given in those instances where the local commander certifies a particular and significant contribution by an individual. Such certification should be submitted to CNO/CMC, via the commander who exercised operational control in the area involved.

      (a) Shore Duty. Attached to or regularly serving, for one or more days, with an organization participating in or directly supporting military operations.

      (b) Sea Duty. Attached to or regularly serving, for one or more days, aboard a naval vessel directly supporting military operations.

      (c) Air Duty. Actual participation as a crew member in one or more aerial flights, directly supporting military operations.

      (d) Temporary Duty. Service for 30 consecutive or 60 nonconsecutive days, except that the time limit may be waived for personnel participating in actual combat operations.

      (3) Eligible Ships and Units. Ships and units present in the area merely for training purposes are not eligible for the award. Squadrons or units embarked in a ship, during the period for which that ship is listed as eligible, are eligible for the medal.

      (4) Limitations. The medal shall be awarded only for operations for which no other U.S. campaign medal is approved. No person may be issued both the VSM and the AFEM for service in Vietnam, and no person shall be entitled to more than one award of the VSM.

     c. Engagement Stars. A 3/16 inch bronze star is authorized for wear on the suspension ribbon and ribbon bar of the VSM for each of the following campaigns:

I.	Vietnam Advisory Campaign	15 Mar 62 to 07 Mar 65
II.	Vietnam Defense Campaign	08 Mar 65 to 24 Dec 65
III.	Vietnam Counter-offensive	25 Dec 65 to 30 Jun 66
IV.	Vietnam Counter-offensive II	01 Jul 66 to 31 May 67

V.	Vietnam Counter-offensive III	01 Jun 67 to 29 Jan 68
VI.	Tet Counter-offensive	30 Jan 68 to 01 Apr 68
VII.	Vietnam Counter-offensive IV	02 Apr 68 to 30 Jun 68
VIII.	Vietnam Counter-offensive V	01 Jul 68 to 01 Nov 68
IX.	Vietnam Counter-offensive VI	02 Nov 68 to 22 Feb 69
X.	Tet 69 Counter-offensive	23 Feb 69 to 08 Jun 69
XI.	Vietnam, Summer-Fall 1969	09 Jun 69 to 31 Oct 69
XII.	Vietnam, Winter-Spring 1970	01 Nov 69 to 30 Apr 70
XIII.	Sanctuary Counter-offensive	01 May 70 to 30 Jun 70
XIV.	Vietnam Counter-offensive VII	01 Jul 70 to 30 Jun 71
XV.	Consolidation I	01 Jul 71 to 30 Nov 71
XVI.	Consolidation II	01 Dec 71 to 29 Mar 72
XVII.	Vietnam Ceasefire Campaign	30 Mar 72 to 28 Jan 73
XVIII.	Operation FREQUENT WIND	29 Apr 75 to 30 Apr 75

8. Southwest Asia Service Medal

   a. Authorization. E.O. 12754 of 12 March 1991.

   b. Eligibility Requirements

      (1) Awarded to members of the Armed Forces of the United States, who participated in or directly supported military operations in Southwest Asia, or in the surrounding areas, between 2 August 1990 and 30 November 1995 (Operations DESERT SHIELD, DESERT STORM, and the Southwest Asia Ceasefire Campaign).

      (2) Individuals must have served in one or more of the following areas: the Persian Gulf, Red Sea, Gulf of Oman, Gulf of Aden, that portion of the Arabian Sea that lies north of 10 degrees north latitude, and west of 68 degrees east longitude, as well as the total land areas of Iraq, Kuwait, Saudi Arabia, Oman, Bahrain, Qatar and United Arab Emirates.

      (3) Individuals serving in Israel, Egypt, Turkey, Syria, and Jordan (including the airspace and territorial waters thereof), between 17 January 1991 and 28 February 1991, shall also be eligible for award of this medal. They must have directly supported combat operations.

      (4) Embassy security guard personnel are eligible for the period 2 August 1990 to 11 August 1991.

      (5) Specific eligibility criteria for award of the Southwest Asia Service Medal (SWASM) require that a service

member must be:

(a) Attached to or regularly serving, for one or more days, with an organization participating in ground/shore military operations.

(b) Attached to or regularly serving, for one or more days, aboard a naval vessel directly supporting military operations.

(c) Actually participate as a crewmember in one or more aerial flights, directly supporting military operations in the areas designated above.

(d) Serve on temporary duty for 30 consecutive or 60 nonconsecutive days. These time limitations may be waived by commanding officers for individuals participating in actual combat operations.

c. <u>Awarding Authority</u>. Commanding officers are authorized to award the SWASM.

d. <u>Engagement Stars</u>. Three service stars are the maximum authorized for the SWASM:

(1) Defense of Saudi Arabia: 2 Aug 90 to 16 Jan 91.

(2) Liberation and Defense of Kuwait: 17 Jan 91 to 11 Apr 91.

(3) Southwest Asia Ceasefire Campaign: 12 Apr 91 to 30 Nov 95.

SECTION 4 - MISCELLANEOUS

840. <u>Congressional Medal for Veterans of the Attack on Pearl Harbor</u>

1. Authorization. Section 1492 of Public Law 101-510 created the Congressional Medal for Veterans of the Attack on Pearl Harbor to commemorate the service and sacrifices of those veterans, and honor them on the fiftieth anniversary of the attack. All members of the Armed Forces of the United States who were present in Hawaii on 7 December 1941, and participated in combat operations when Japanese military forces attacked, are

eligible to receive the medal. Personnel who were injured or killed in the attack are eligible for the medal.

2. Application Procedures. The U.S. Navy is the Executive Agent for the Pearl Harbor Commemorative Medal. To request a medal, submit a letter containing the information listed in Article 820, paragraph 5 above, ensuring to specify unit assignment as of 7 December 1941. If available, also include any relevant supporting documentation, such as discharge papers or any official military document that confirms service in Hawaii on 7 December 1941. Submit the request to:

> Navy Personnel Command (PERS-312D2)
> Pearl Harbor Commemorative Medal
> 9700 Page Avenue, Room 5409
> St. Louis, MO 63132-5100

841. Cold War Recognition Certificate

1. Authorization. Section 1084 of the Fiscal Year 1998 National Defense Authorization Act authorized awarding Cold War Recognition Certificates to all members of the Armed Forces, and qualified federal government civilian personnel, who faithfully and honorably served the United States any time during the Cold War Era, from 2 September 1945 through 26 December 1991.

2. Application Procedures

a. The U.S. Army is the Executive Agent for the Cold War Recognition Program. To request a certificate, complete and print the application available online at https://www.perscomonline.army.mil/tagd/coldwar and submit it to the following address:

> CDR, HRC
> Cold War Recognition
> Hoffman II
> Attn: TAPC-CWRS, 3N45
> 200 Stovall Street
> Alexandria, VA 22332-0473

b. In addition to the form, supporting documentation providing proof of service must be submitted. This may include any official government or military document that contains the recipient's name, Social Security or Service Number, and a date showing at least one day of U.S. government service during the eligibility period. Examples of acceptable documents include a Leave and Earnings statement, DD214 or other discharge document, or an SF50, Civilian Personnel Action Form.

        c. The requestor must also certify his/her honorable service by signing and dating the application form. If the application cannot be printed, a signed and dated letter containing the same information contained in the application may be submitted. The letter must include the phrase, "I confirm my faithful and honorable service to the nation during the Cold War Era."

REQUIREMENTS FOR 10 U.S.C. §1130 RECOMMENDATIONS

Specific requirements for individual and unit awards are detailed in Chapters 2 and 3, respectively. Highlights of the requirements relevant for 10 U.S.C. §1130 award recommendations are listed below.

It is acknowledged that preparing an award recommendation years after an action occurred can be challenging. However, the requestor is solely responsible for assembling a complete award recommendation package. It is incumbent upon the requestor, not DON awards personnel, to conduct any historic research necessary to ensure the recommendation package is complete prior to submission. At a minimum, a recommendation package must include the following:

1. A completed and signed award recommendation form. The recommending officer must have been senior in grade, at the time of the action(s) or service, to the individual being recommended for an award. Additionally, the recommending officer must have knowledge of all of the action(s) or service cited; that is, the recommending officer must have either observed the actions or been provided information by an individual who observed the actions. Recommending officers who did not personally witness the action must have been associated, by virtue of their position in the command, with the incident and/or the individual being recommended for the award. If the recommending officer is not the Commanding Officer (CO), the CO, if available, must endorse the recommendation. If it is no longer possible to route the recommendation through the CO (e.g., the CO is deceased), a signed statement to that effect must be included. In this case, another officer who has knowledge of the action(s), and who was senior in the chain of command of the individual being recommended during the period for which recognition is desired, may endorse the recommendation.

2. If it is not possible to route the award recommendation through all levels of the original chain of command, official military documents such as unit logs, situation reports, investigations, after-action reports, fitness reports, and/or evaluations, must be included to aid in substantiating the actions delineated in the award recommendation. Since determinations regarding awards are based on verifiable facts, other forms of information such as letters, books, newspaper and

magazine articles, personal diaries, etc., will not be considered, as they are not official documents.

3. A Summary of Action that provides a detailed description of the actions or service performed by the individual or unit being considered for recognition.

4. A proposed citation.

5. For all individual combat awards, as well as non-combat awards for heroism (e.g., as the Navy and Marine Corps Medal), at least two notarized eyewitness statements, with contact information for the eyewitnesses, must be submitted. These statements must contain a complete description of the individual's actions and must be in the eyewitnesses' own words, not on a prepared form. Neither statement may be from the individual being recommended for the award. See Chapter 2, Article 213, for further information regarding eyewitness statements.

CHAPTER 9 - FOREIGN GIFTS TO U.S. PERSONNEL

SECTION 1 - GENERAL

910. PURPOSE. The purpose of this chapter is to provide policy
guidance governing the acceptance and retention of gifts from
foreign governments, and to establish procedures regarding the
receipt and disposition of such gifts, including decorations.
This guidance is based on DoD Directive 1005.13, the governing
instruction for acceptance of foreign gifts and decorations.

911. SCOPE. The provisions of this chapter apply to all
military and civilian personnel of the Navy and Marine Corps,
and the spouses (unless legally separated) and dependents of
such personnel.

912. POLICY

    1. Article I, Section 9, Clause 8, of the Constitution
provides that "no Person holding any Office of Profit or Trust
under [the United States] shall, without the Consent of the
Congress, accept of any present, Emolument, Office, or Title, of
any kind whatever, from any King, Prince or foreign State."
Congress, in 5 U.S.C. §7342, as amended, has sanctioned
acceptance of such gifts under limited circumstances, subject to
approval of the recipient's employing agency.

    2. The following guidelines apply:

        a. No individual shall request or otherwise encourage
the offer of a gift or decoration from a foreign government.

        b. Table favors, mementos, remembrances, or other
tokens bestowed at official functions, and other gifts of
minimal value received as souvenirs or marks of courtesy may be
accepted and retained by the recipient. The General Services
Administration (GSA) reassesses minimal value every three years;
it is set at $305.00 as of the publication of this Manual.
Regulations promulgated under 5 U.S.C. §7342 should be consulted
for current guidance on minimal value. The burden of proof is
on the recipient to establish that the gift is of minimal value.
Appendix A to this chapter provides the format for gift
recipients to request an appraisal of a gift to determine its
value.

c. Whenever possible, gifts of greater than minimal value shall be refused. When a gift of greater than minimal value is tendered, the donor shall be advised that statutory provisions and DoD policy prohibit DoD personnel from accepting such gifts, unless it appears that refusal may offend or embarrass the donor, or could adversely affect U.S. foreign relations. Under such circumstances, the gift may be accepted on behalf of the United States. The gift then becomes the property of the United States and shall be deposited with the DoD employing component within 60 days, for return to the donor, use within the employing component, or disposition by the General Services Administration (GSA). Appendix A to this chapter provides the format for reporting the acceptance of a foreign gift of greater than minimal value.

d. When more than one tangible gift is included in a single presentation from the same donor to an employee, or jointly to an employee and spouse, they shall be considered as a single gift for the purposes of determining the minimal value.

e. The approval authority shall take all necessary action regarding the acceptance and disposition of foreign gifts and decorations. The approval authority for Navy military personnel is CNO (DNS-35) and, for Navy civilian personnel, the Deputy Assistant Secretary of the Navy (Civilian Human Resources). CMC (JAR) is the approval authority for all Marine Corps personnel.

913. DEFINITIONS

1. Employee. An employee of a DoD component, as defined in 5 U.S.C. §2105; an expert or consultant under contract with a DoD component, including any individual performing services for a DoD component under 5 U.S.C. §3109 and members of the military Services, including retired and reserve members, regardless of duty status; the spouses of all such individuals (unless legally separated) and their dependents as defined in 26 U.S.C. §152; and non-appropriated fund employees under the awards policy in the Civilian Personnel Manual (DoD 1400.25M).

2. Employing Component. The DoD component in which the recipient is appointed, employed, or enlisted. If a recipient is a spouse or dependent of a serving individual, then the

employing component is that in which the serving individual is appointed, employed, or enlisted.

a. The Military Departments are considered the employing components for all military and civilian personnel assigned to them. The Military Departments also act as the employing component for all personnel, military and civilian, either directly employed or assigned to the headquarters of the Combatant Commands.

b. The Office of the Secretary of Defense (OSD) is considered the employing component for its military and civilian personnel, JCS, Defense Advance Research Projects Agency (DARPA), Defense Security Assistance Agency (DSAA), Ballistic Missile Defense Organization (BMDO), DoD Field Activities, and other DoD activities not specifically designated an employing agency.

c. The Defense Agencies (except DARPA, DSAA, and BMDO) are considered the employing components for their civilian employees and for military members assigned to duty with them.

d. For DON personnel, CNO or CMC, as appropriate, is the designated head of the employing component.

3. <u>Foreign Government</u>. Includes any unit of a foreign governmental authority, including any foreign national, state, local, and municipal government; any international or multinational organization whose membership is composed of any unit of foreign government; and any agent or representatives of any such unit or organization while acting as such.

4. <u>Gift</u>. Anything of tangible or intangible value that is tendered by or received from a foreign government, including decorations, except for educational scholarships or medical treatment.

5. <u>Minimal Value</u>. A retail value in the United States at the time of acceptance not in excess of the amount specified by the Administrator of General Services under 5 U.S.C. §7342.

6. <u>Travel Expenses</u>. Cost of transportation, food, lodging, and incidental expenses reimbursable under the Joint Travel Regulations/Joint Federal Travel Regulations incurred during the travel period.

SECTION 2 - FOREIGN GIFT PROCEDURES

920. RECEIPT AND DISPOSITION OF GIFTS AND DECORATIONS

1. Use or Disposal of Gifts and Decorations that Become the Property of the United States

a. Any gift or decoration that becomes the property of the United States under 5 U.S.C. §7342 may be retained for official use by the employing component. In such cases, the head of the employing component shall:

(1) Avoid, to the maximum extent possible, arbitrary action in approving or retaining gifts and decorations.

(2) Ensure gifts and decorations retained by the component are not used for the benefit or personal use of any individual employee, but that all employees are provided the opportunity to receive their indirect benefit.

(3) Report the gifts and decorations retained to the GSA under 41 CFR 101-49, subpart 2, within 30 calendar days after termination of the official use.

b. Gifts and decorations the employing component does not wish to retain or that are not approved for retention should be reported to the GSA within 30 days after depositing the gift with the head of the employing component. In this case, the head of the employing component shall:

(1) Complete Standard Form (SF) 120, Report of Excess Personal Property, and forward to GSA, Property Management Division, Washington, DC 20406.

(2) Exercise responsibility for the custody and security of gifts and decorations, and hold them until instructions are received from GSA regarding their disposition.

(3) Exercise responsibility for, and bear the cost of, the care and handling of gifts and decorations in its custody and for delivery of the items to the physical custody of GSA after the screening period.

c. Gifts or decorations for which there are no federal requirements, as determined by the GSA, may be offered for sale to the recipients before donation when so requested by recipients.

(1) If a recipient indicates an interest in purchasing a gift or decoration, the item is to be reported to GSA on SF 120 for utilization screening before sale to the recipient. The head of the employing component shall obtain a commercial appraisal and forward a copy of it, attached to a copy of the SF 120. The GSA shall notify the head of the employing component if the gift or decoration will be offered for negotiated sale to the recipient. The sales price, to be paid to GSA, shall be the appraised value of the gift or decoration.

(2) The GSA normally will not take custody of gifts or decorations for which recipients have expressed an interest in purchasing. Such gifts shall remain in the custody and be the responsibility of the head of the employing component until recipients either purchase or decline to purchase them. The GSA will accept physical custody of gifts and decorations that recipients decline to purchase and that are not retained for official use or returned to the donors.

2. Return of Gifts and Decorations to Donor. Before returning a gift or decoration to the original donor, the disposing component shall consult with appropriate officials in the Department of State to ensure its return will not adversely affect U.S. foreign relations.

3. Disposal of Firearms. Firearms received as foreign gifts may be offered for transfer to federal agencies, including law enforcement activities. Firearms not required for federal use may be sold to interested recipients, at the discretion of the GSA. A certification that the recipient shall comply with all state and local laws regarding purchase and possession of firearms must be received by the GSA prior to release of such firearms to the purchaser. Those firearms not transferred to a federal activity or sold to recipients shall be destroyed in accordance with Section 101-42.1102-10 of 41 CFR.

4. Recording of Gifts of More Than Minimal Value and Decorations

 a. Each head of an employing component, i.e., CNO and CMC, shall maintain records of gifts of more than minimal value and foreign decorations received by their employees from foreign governments. A compilation shall be made each year and transmitted to the Secretary of State no later than January 31. This compilation shall include the following information:

 (1) Name and title of recipient.

 (2) Brief description of the gift or decoration, date of acceptance, estimated value, and current disposition or location.

 (3) Identity of foreign donor and government.

 (4) Circumstances justifying acceptance.

 b. An employing component is not required to report travel or travel expenses of more than minimal value that were authorized by that component under conditions stipulated in paragraph 7 below.

5. Donation or Transfer of Gifts and Decorations. The recipient may recommend a gift or decoration for donation or transfer to an eligible public agency or non-profit, tax-exempt institution for public display, reference, or use.

 a. The employee recipient may indicate a recommendation for donation with a statement on the SF 120 citing the specific donee. Justification for the request must be supported by a letter from the recipient outlining any special significance of the gift or decoration to the proposed donee. The mailing address and telephone number of both the recipient and donee shall be included in the letter.

 b. The employee recipient may indicate a recommendation for transfer of a gift or decoration to an eligible public agency for public display or other authorized agency use. This request shall be indicated on the SF 120 citing the specific donee, and shall include a brief justification of the display or official use of the gift or decoration.

6. <u>Sale or Destruction of Tangible Gifts of Minimal Value or Less and Decorations</u>. Employing components are authorized to sell or destroy tangible gifts of less than minimal value and decorations not retained by the recipient.

7. <u>Gifts of Travel and Travel Expenses</u>

a. General. The policy against acceptance of gifts from foreign governments applies equally to travel and travel expenses tendered as gifts, but an employee may accept a gift of travel of more than minimal value if the following criteria are met:

(1) The travel begins and ends outside the United States, except when travel across the United States is the shortest, least costly, or only available route to the destination; e.g., Canada to Mexico.

(2) The travel is determined by appropriate authority to be in the best interests of DON and the U.S. Government, considering all the circumstances.

(3) The travel does not contravene other DoD or Navy regulations.

(4) Unless the above criteria are met, gifts of travel or travel expenses may not be accepted. The travel must be directly related to an official interest of the Navy or the U.S. Government. Travel may not be accepted for personal purposes, such as vacations.

b. Approval by an Order Issuing Authority. Acceptance of gifts of travel or travel expenses meeting the criteria set forth above may be approved by an order issuing authority instead of the usual approval authority listed in Article 912 above. Such approval may be granted:

(1) By issuing the employee official travel orders authorizing the acceptance of travel or travel expenses which are directly related to the authorized purpose of travel; or

(2) By issuing the employee travel orders which specifically anticipate the acceptance of additional travel or travel expenses incident to authorized travel.

(3) Issued orders must specifically certify that acceptance of the travel or travel expenses is in the best interests of the U.S. Government. A copy of issued orders, detailing all accepted travel and travel expenses, shall be forwarded to the appropriate approval authority by the order issuing authority.

c. Foreign Military Transportation. For the purpose of this regulation, travel on foreign military aircraft or other forms of military transportation, or travel expenses incurred at foreign military installations or facilities that meet the criteria listed in paragraph 7.a. above, are not considered gifts which are required to be reported.

d. Personnel Exchange Program (PEP). PEP personnel are authorized to accept travel, reimbursement for travel, and advance expenses for travel directly from the host Service, when such travel is necessary for the performance of their exchange duties, and is provided for in the Memorandum of Agreement (MOA) negotiated with the host Service to which they are assigned. Specific financial arrangements under the PEP may vary from country to country, as each MOA is individually negotiated. PEP personnel will comply with the particulars of the MOA negotiated with the host Service to which they are assigned. In no event may PEP personnel accept reimbursement for travel expenses directly from the host Service that exceeds the actual cost of the travel. When payment of advance travel expenses exceeds actual expenditures, the excess payment shall be promptly refunded to the host Service.

e. Reports. Acceptance of gifts of travel or travel expenses of more than minimal value, that are not exempted by the above paragraphs, shall be reported to the appropriate approval authority within 30 days of termination of travel. If several gifts of foreign travel are received from different foreign governments during one inclusive trip, a separate report shall be submitted for each donor country. Appendix A to this chapter provides the format for the report.

921. COMMAND RESPONSIBILITIES

1. Commanding officers shall ensure employees are aware of the provisions of this chapter and the penalties that may result from violations.

2. Commanding officers shall report to the appropriate approval authority any employee who is the recipient of a gift or decoration, or is the recipient of travel or travel expenses and who, through actions or circumstances within the employee's control, fails to comply with the procedures of this chapter.

3. The Attorney General may bring a civil action in any district court of the United States against any employee who knowingly violates 5 U.S.C. §7342. The court in which action is brought may assess a penalty against such employee in an amount not to exceed the retail value of the gift improperly solicited or received, plus $5,000.

FOR OFFICIAL USE ONLY
(WHEN FILLED IN)

1650
(Date)

From: Individual or Command
To: Approval Authority

Subj: REPORT OF FOREIGN GIFT OF MORE THAN MINIMAL VALUE

Ref: (a) SECNAVINST 1650.1H, Chapter 9

Encl: (1) Gift of _____

1. The following foreign gift(s) of more than minimal value is forwarded in accordance with reference (a):

    a. Name, rank/rate, social security number, and position of the recipient:

    b. Description of the gift (composition, size, type, brand, serial number, etc.):

    c. Circumstances justifying acceptance:

    d. Name and position of donor and identity of the foreign government:

    e. Date and place of gift acceptance:

    f. Estimated retail value of gift in U.S. dollars at the time of acceptance:

    g. Does the employee wish to participate in the sale of the gift if sold by the General Services Administration?

    h. Does the command desire permission to retain the gift for official use/display?

FOR OFFICIAL USE ONLY

FOR OFFICIAL USE ONLY
(WHEN FILLED IN)

1650
(Date)

From: Individual or Command
To: Approval Authority

Subj: REPORT OF AND REQUEST FOR APPRAISAL OF FOREIGN GIFT

Ref: (a) SECNAVINST 1650.1H, Chapter 9

Encl: (1) Gift of _____

1. The following foreign gift(s) is forwarded in accordance
with reference (a). It is requested that an appraisal be
performed to determine whether the gift is of more than minimal
value.

    a. Name, rank/rate, social security number, and position
of the recipient:

    b. Description of the gift (composition, size, type,
brand, serial number, etc.):

    c. Circumstances justifying acceptance:

    d. Name and position of donor and identity of the foreign
government:

    e. Date and place of gift acceptance:

    f. Does the employee wish to participate in the sale of
the gift if it is determined to be of more than minimal value
and is to be sold by the General Services Administration?

FOR OFFICIAL USE ONLY

1650
(Date)

From: Individual or Command
To: Approval Authority

Subj: REPORT OF FOREIGN GIFT OF TRAVEL OR TRAVEL EXPENSES

Ref: (a) SECNAVINST 1650.1H, Chapter 9

1. The following foreign gift of travel or travel expenses is reported in accordance with reference (a):

    a. Name, rank/rate, social security number, and position of the recipient:

    b. Description of travel or travel expenses, including dates and places:

    c. Circumstances justifying acceptance:

    d. Name and position of donor and identity of the foreign government:

    e. Date and place of gift acceptance:

    f. Estimated value of the travel or travel expense:

Appendix A to
Chapter 9

INDEX

E

F

G

N

O

S

T

U

V

W